FAMILY CENTRES AND THEIR INTERNATIONAL ROLE IN SOCIAL ACTION

Family Centres and their International Role in Social Action

Edited by
CHRIS WARREN-ADAMSON
Department of Social Work Studies, University of Southampton

Ashgate

Aldershot • Burlington USA • Singapore • Sydney

Published by
Ashgate Publishing Ltd
Gower House
Croft Road
Aldershot
Hampshire GU11 3HR
England

Ashgate Publishing Company
131 Main Street
Burlington, VT 05401-5600 USA

Ashgate website: http://www.ashgate.com

British Library Cataloguing in Publication Data
Family centres and their international role in social
    action : social work as informal education
    1.Family social work - Cross-cultural studies
    I. Warren-Adamson, Chris, 1946-
    362.8'28

Library of Congress Control Number: 2001095426

ISBN 0 7546 1424 7

Printed and bound in Great Britain by
Antony Rowe Ltd, Chippenham, Wiltshire

Contents

Acknowledgements   *vii*

List of Contributors   *viii*

Foreword   *xii*

1   Introduction: Family Centres, Integrating Practice, and   1
    Empowerment Journeys
    Chris Warren-Adamson

2   The Family Centre and the Consolidation of Integrated   15
    Practice
    Christine Stones

3   What's Happening in France? The Settlement and Social   29
    Action Centre: Exchange as Empowerment
    *Chris Warren-Adamson, with Anne-Marie David
    and Jean-Paul Ducandas*

4   Education and Empowerment in Family Centres   45
    Paul Montgomery and Claire Cook

5   Francophone Centres in Québec, Canada – Two Case   56
    Studies
    Irene Kyle and Maureen Kellerman, with Alla Ivask

6   The Referral Only Centre – Managing Changing   69
    Attitudes to Parenting
    Audrey Fessler

7   The Office as Centre: A 'Patch' Approach, Supporting   80
    and Protecting in two Massachusetts Communities
    John Zalenski and Carolyn Burns

8 Justice, Child Protection and Family Centres –   92
   Part 1 (Inside)
   Ellen Jones and Dave Ely

9 Justice, Child Protection and Family Centres –   105
   Part 2 (Outside)
   Terri Fletcher and Mo Romano

10 Aotearoa/New Zealand – Family Centred Practice from a   127
   Mental Health Perspective
   Lynne Briggs

11 Aotearoa/New Zealand – Working Differently with   146
   Communities and Families
   Robyn Munford and Jackie Sanders, with Ann Andrew,
   Peter Butler, Ripeka Kaipuke, Leland Ruwhiu

12 Contemporary Debates in Centre Practice in Youth   163
   Justice and Community Development
   Andy Lloyd and Nick Frost

13 User Participation in Family Centres in Greece   177
   Vasso Gabrilidou, Elpida Ioannidou and
   Evi Hatzivarnava

14 Make Your Experience Count: Social Work as Informal   189
   Education
   Di Holland

15 The Neighbourhood Centre as a Base for Social Action   201
   and Life-Long Learning
   Joy Adamson with Members of Togher Family Centre,
   Ireland

16 Conclusion – Lessons from Family Centres: the   225
   Authentic Site for Ecological Practice
   Chris Warren-Adamson

Acknowledgements

Thanks to all the contributors to this text, especially for your skills and patience; thanks to Anita Lightburn who's always there for me; thanks to those who contain, clarify, inspire, illuminate my route, including the background presence of Crescy Cannan, Hugh England, Tony Maluccio and June Thoburn, as well as Régis, Mireille and Jean-Louis, Patricia and Jean-Marie; thanks to *The Group* – Becca, Celia, Fatima, Karen, Kim, Lucy, Mandy, Mark, Miranda, for constancy and inspiration; and thanks to the *Family Centre Action Research Group* for what you teach and for what you do – Penny Coombes, Sheila Cullen, Ellen Jones, Mags Lewis, Mike Lloyd, Sue McKernan, Karen Southern, Jo Tulloch; thanks to Adam Dinham, Beveley Clifford and Tracy Jackson; and, of course, to JA, JW, RWA, R, B, and C.

List of Contributors

Joy Adamson is trained in social work, family therapy and play therapy and works in Sussex, England. She is developing two services, child and family therapy in primary care, from a doctor's surgery, and also a schools counselling service.

Ann Andrew is a community social worker and researcher in Aotearoa/New Zealand, providing intensive social work services to young people and their families and undertakes community-based research.

Lynne Briggs is the clinical Head of the Family Mental Health Service in Christchurch, New Zealand. She also is a Senior Lecturer for the University of Otago. Lynne teaches the Mental Health and Specialist Practice and Advanced Counselling papers on the MSW programme.

Carolyn Burns is Executive Director of the Berkshire Center for Children and Families, a substantial family resource centre in Massachusetts, USA. She also serves as a consultant to the Massachusetts Department of Social Services.

Peter Butler is a community-based youth worker in Aotearoa/New Zealand, working with high risk young males and participates in community-based research that focusses on the young people he works with on a day to day basis.

Claire Cook is the Early Years Development and Childcare Service Manager for Dorset County Council, England. She was Project Manager for NCH Action for Children at Abingdon and Didcot family centres in the 1990s.

Anne-Marie David trained as a conseillère en économie sociale and manages a centre socio-culturel in Lower Normandy, France.

Jean-Paul Ducandas trained as an animateur and manages a centre socio-culturel in Lower Normandy, France.

Dave Ely is Regional Social Work Manager for the South East Region, England, of the Children's Society, having worked previously in local authority social work. Dave Ely was manager of St Gabriel's Family Centre in the 1990s.

Audrey Fessler is formerly chair and committee member of the Elizabeth Fry Centre, in Nottingham, England, and is also the Centre's historian.

Terri Fletcher is project leader for the Children's Society's First Stop, Keeping Safe project which works from a housing estate in Brighton. Terri trained as a social worker and has previously worked in residential social work with children and adults who have learning disabilities. Her previous experience includes working as a rights advice worker, organising holiday playschemes for children with disabilities and teaching English as a foreign language.

Nick Frost is senior lecturer in Continuing Education at the University of Leeds, England. He has published in many areas of child welfare and lifelong learning and has particular interests in family support, residential care and the nature of professionalism.

Vasso Gabrilidou is a social worker in the National Organisation for Social Care (ex National Welfare Organisation). She is now Director of Oreokastro Children's Institution, Thessaloniki, Greece. She has worked for many years as social worker in various family centres of the National Welfare Organisation.

Evi Hatzivarnava is the Director of Research and Planning of the National Organisation for Social Care (ex National Welfare Organisation).

Di Holland, originally a teacher, is a part-time project worker at the NCH Action for Children Yeovil Family Centre, Somerset, England, with responsibility for groups run at the centre and at one of the infant schools. Previously she was an Education Welfare Officer with the Inner London Education Authority and also a Social Worker with the School Psychological Service on the Wirral.

Elpida Ioannidou is a social worker in Toumba Family Centre, Thessaloniki, Greece. The National Organisation for Social Care (ex National Welfare Organisation) is responsible for the centre.

Alla Ivask has been with the Canadian Association of Family Resource Programs for nine years. She has developed and managed million dollar projects in a career spanning immigrant/refugee settlement to social services.

Ellen Jones is Network Manager at St Gabriel's Family Centre, Brighton, England, and has worked for the Children's Society since 1983, having previously worked for a local authority as a residential social worker.

Ripeka Kaipuke is a school principal in Aotearoa/New Zealand, who in addition to managing a busy school, supports numerous initiatives that focus upon strengthening the capacity of families to care well for the children who attend her school.

Maureen Kellerman was program/project director at the Canadian Association of Family Resource Programs, in which capacity she both led and worked on numerous projects, and was also the author of several resources developed and published by the Association.

Irene Kyle is a leading researcher in family support in Canada and a founding member of the Canadian Association of Family Resource Programs. She has published many articles and research papers on family support and other related topics.

Andy Lloyd is the manager of West Leeds Family Service Unit, Leeds, England. His particular interest is in youth justice – especially in the implications of the early years.

Paul Montgomery was an MSc student at Barnett House, the Dept. of Applied Social Studies at the University of Oxford, England. He is currently a researcher in child sleep disorders at the University of Oxford, section of Child and Adolescent Psychiatry.

Robyn Munford is Head of School, Sociology, Social Policy and Social Work, Massey University, New Zealand. She has qualifications in both social work and sociology. Her current research interests include research on family well-being.

Mo Romano is the family support development worker for the First Stop Project in Brighton, seconded from the local Family Centre through Social Care and Health. Previously Mo has worked for 15 years as a Family Aide and Family Centre worker and is also a founder member of the Survivors Network for women who were sexually abused in childhood.

Leland Ruwhiu is a lecturer in social work, social policy and Maori development in the School of Social Work, Massey University in Aotearoa/New Zealand. He has written and researched on Maori development and indigenous models of practice.

Jackie Sanders is the Director of the Child and Family Research Centre, Barnardos, in Aotearoa/New Zealand. She and Robyn Munford were the research leaders for the action research carried out with the Whanau Centre and other groups in the area.

Christine Stones is the Manager of Barnardos New Fulford Family Centre in Bristol, England. She has written extensively on family centre development, of which her centre is at the forefront.

Chris Warren-Adamson is lecturer in Social Work Studies at the University of Southampton, England, and is substantially involved in the education and training of social workers at qualifying and post-qualifying levels. His interests include the educative, social action role of social work, and family centres.

John Zalenski is the Associate Director for Technical Assistance at the National Center for Family Centered Practice, a federally sponsored agency working across the US. His consultation and TA focus on family centered practice development in public child welfare.

Foreword

Our global interconnectedness shines through this exciting volume bringing into perspective shared challenges in meeting the needs of twenty-first century families. This is an important opportunity to think with practitioners and researchers on the front line about their experiences in building and maintaining family support and developing family centre practice. The authors bring to light a dynamic evolving resource for families, parents, children and communities that crosses political, cultural, and professional service boundaries. The international examples bring into focus differences that help us examine what is important in the way we help and support families everywhere. One of the considerable benefits that this particular collection of programme descriptions offers is an opportunity to see through the different lenses of culture, politics, tradition, and innovation to help us imagine how we can expand and renew our own policy and practice on behalf of families.

Family support programmes are expanding throughout the United States, sponsored by state and federal initiatives and increasingly are part of legislated mandates, as well as supported by foundations, such as the work of Casey Family Services that invests in grass-roots development in communities. These programmes are part of the services offered in faith-based and state funded social services, mental health agencies, community centres, early childhood programmes such as Head Start, and full service schools. As with many of the examples in this volume, there is wide variation in the structure and complexity of the programmes, as well as mix of the professional/lay service providers. Over the past thirty years there has been an increased involvement of professionals as a means for expanding preventive programmes, and integrating needed services for those in crisis. Significant directions that are defining family support programmes and practice include the continued emphasis on the importance of supporting early child development; the child welfare concerns for parents and children at risk; and the community based systems of care alternatives to meet the mental health needs of children and adolescents. Central concerns include: 1) funding, 2) programme development, 3) programme evaluation that supports programme development as well as provides the evidence to promote investment for broad based access, and 4) the support and development of practitioners who will provide the needed leadership, knowledge and skill in non-traditional approaches. Ideological tensions also exist between sponsors, service providers and parents.

Significant to this necessary dynamic responsive family support as ably demonstrated in this volume, is the centrality of shared goals and resources, flexibility of professional roles, attention to context based on ecological practice models, focus on capacity building, strength-based approaches, and, in addition, responsiveness to developmental needs of children, parents, and families, and to creating environments that offer opportunity and enable empowerment within the community. These different approaches to supporting families continue to chart a new/old approach that should be recognised as a vitally important investment in prevention as well as a normal way to intervene and offer intensive services. As case studies they are examples of grappling with all of these complexities. At their best they help us understand family support in practice. I will always remember the parents, in an early childhood family support programme I was evaluating, report that the family support staff and participants had become the family they had never known. This family did not go away or hurt them. The family support programme, full of diverse relationships, was their family.

The integrated model of family centre introduced in this volume presents a promising example of programmes that make services accessible in ways that transform traditional approaches to child welfare, mental health services, and education. Parents are engaged, their participation is sustained and they make significant progress toward their goals. This transformation of programme and practice depends on many factors. As recently identified by the Academy of Practice in the United States, inter professional practice in community based programmes (such as family centres) is one of the most important directions for practice to take. Systems of care are similar to the integrated model of family centres and require shared goals and resources, partnerships with parents, flexible roles, culturally responsive practice, wrap around services and innovative work with the community as the substantive resource for families. With increased demands on the family as care taker for family members who are mentally ill or have chronic health problems and disabilities, family support in community based programmes has the promise to help these families manage in the most difficult circumstances.

The scope of this volume should inspire us to find avenues for working collaboratively across professions, as well as within and across countries. As experience in the US has borne out, there is a long road to travel to support non-traditional practice that is needed in family support programmes. Training and support for professional development and investment in research and development of more inclusive practice approaches should include informal education, or education for life, as these are vital to the success of family support programmes and family centre practice. Interdisciplinary educational programmes are needed, and specialisation for family centre work, within professional degree programmes, such as social work, will be fundamental to the continued development of effective family centres. Social work in particular should become a leader in the development of this important area of practice.

It is to the credit of Chris Warren-Adamson, that his long-term investment and vision in furthering the development of family support programmes and practice has brought us so much to consider in this diverse group of contributions. His unflagging faith in the promise of these programmes is warranted. I heartily concur that our next challenge is to capture the attention of the social work profession to reorient social work practice curriculum and method to support the quality of practice evident in these innovative programmes. We also have an exceptional opportunity to learn from each other across the globe as we collaborate together for the development of this dynamic field of practice.

Anita Lightburn
Elizabeth Marting Truehaft Professor and formerly Dean
Smith College School of Social Work
Northampton
Massachusetts
USA

1 Introduction: Family Centres, Integrating Practice, and Empowerment Journeys

CHRIS WARREN-ADAMSON

This book identifies a rich vein of (family) centred practice which it is hoped will provide inspiration and ideas for those who work and participate in centres, and for those who are responsible for them. A crisis in British social work with children and families is also recognised and such centres are offered as an authentic alternative to such practice. A conclusion of the book is that the practice shown in the centres – social work as education – best fits the ecological paradigm for an understanding of human behaviour. The book concludes with a call for an international forum of (family) centres.

In this introduction the crisis will be explained, then the theory and potential of family centred practice is discussed, followed by a brief summary of the practice to look out for in the chapters of the book.

Chapters vary in simplicity and complexity and in structure; as do centres. This text will use the words family centre despite the difficulties it imposes. Family centres are resource centres and our concern is centre-based practice (as opposed to fieldwork); it is about parents and children and families broadly defined; and there are cross-overs with settlements, social action centres, community education centres, community mental health centres, and so on.

A Crisis for Practice

In the UK, the sigh of relief by public sector workers, and teachers and social workers in particular, at the arrival of New Labour in 1997, is short-lived. Ministers appear to mirror the attitude of their predecessors. In the struggle between ministries over the terrain of child welfare, the Home Office and the Department for Education and Employment appear to have taken off with universalism, development and prevention. The Department of Health (the traditional guardian of social work) is left with a preoccupation with targeting children who need protecting and looking after.

Social work with children and their families in many parts of Britain is greatly troubled, and there is much concern about its ability to balance intervention in protecting, supporting and promoting families (Parton, 1997, Parton & O'Byrne, 2001). What has happened is that social work in this context has become reduced to and equated with an administrative set of knowledge and skills concerned with policing abusive families. This has become the dominant discourse; practice appears to have become preoccupied with procedure and the achievement of assessment, not as a process, but as a short-term product. Moreover, many newly qualified social workers see qualification as escape from institutional practice and make case-management their first post-qualifying step.

Family Centres Endangered

In Britain, family centres – one of the major successful[1] developments in child care social work of the last twenty years – are endangered by a New Labour Government and its policy towards child protection and family support. The thrust of Government policy and its practical implications appear as follows. First, reduce the role of local authority social services departments in childcare to two main activities, a) policing families in matters of child protection and youth crime, b) looking after children under the Children Act, 1989. Second, transfer the exercise of the local authority's wider duties to support families under part 3 and schedule 2 of the same legislation to the plethora of partnership arrangements initiated by New Labour.

Family centres in England and Wales are endangered because – in the light of the above changes – the majority of family centres are paid for, directly or indirectly, by local authority social services departments. Departments, reduced in focus, are squeezed financially as monies are transferred to other preventive programmes. As social service departments define their 'core business' in the narrow sense of protection and the 'looked after child', family centres are in increasing danger of being

---

[1] So successful that the Children Act, 1989 makes it a duty for local authorities to 'provide such family centres as they consider appropriate…'

2

reduced themselves to a narrow assessment and policing role, or of being cut.

Managing the Paradox

There is a paradox here. Throughout the nineties, the Department of Health has expressed its concern about the reductionism of local authorities to a narrow protection role. It has urged concurrent thinking and practice in protection and support, culminating in a document published by the Department of Health, the Department for Education and Employment, and the Home Office, entitled 'Framework for the Assessment of Children in Need and their Families' (DH 2000). The document is underpinned by an ecological perspective of human behaviour and which implies a highly professional concurrent set of tasks for professional social work practitioners.

However, despite our ambitions for a positive local authority fieldwork practice, the conclusion is that such practice has been overcome by just too many difficulties: a) area team social workers are ham-strung by the case-management model, b) being beleaguered has become a key characteristic of the identity of the practitioner of the local state, c) 'splitting' is rife – good voluntary and private services, bad state services (on 'splitting', see Stewart, 1992: 258), d) there is a constant drain in capacity and experience, and staff take flight frequently, often to the temporary new Government initiatives, e) the practice world has little capacity to train its new practitioners; f) social work is tied to a dyadic, individulalised approach to practice.

Getting Beyond the Dyadic and Thinking Collectively

The individualised, private approach referred to above has had plenty of critics (Whittaker & Garbarino, 1983, Smale, 1995). How might a more collective approach take place? There are after all many examples:

- *Patch* – the organisation of services around a patch, locality, neighbourhood, retains an occasional profile in the UK national scene. (Hadley & McGrath, 1980; Smale, 1995), and in the US (Adams &

Nelson, 1995; Zalenski & Burns, this text), and in France (Freynet, 1995; Cannan, 1997).

- *Community Social Work* – Holman (1983) inspired us with his accounts of skill and stories of resourcefulness in this approach to neighbourhood social work.

- *Family Work/Therapy* – an early perspective was represented by Manor, (1984), Hoffman (1981), and many others, seeking to achieve 'first and second order change' (Watzlawick et al., 1979). More recent perspectives draw on Faucoult (White & Epstein, 1990).

- However, in the idea of *Network Therapy* (Carpenter & Treacher 1983), Treacher rebuked his family therapy colleagues for not pursuing the implication of their own enthusiastic adoption of a systems approach by reducing their practice to what Imber-Black called 'treating family therapy as an intra-family event'. Treacher recommended that, in the case of some families, there was a case to 'treat the whole street'. Imber-Black (1988) applied systems thinking to the world between agencies. Her *Families and Wider Systems* amounts to a handbook for those who need to unravel the messes between systems, often where several agencies, mis-communicating at every level, often mirror the chaos in the 'client system'.

- Connected to the above, Dimmock and Dungworth (1985) advocated the use of *Network Meetings,* using wider family therapy techniques in assessment and decision-making in 'statutory child care cases'.

- *Family Networking* – as early as the early seventies, Speck and Attneave (1973) in the USA were reporting on an approach to problem solving where meetings were held with large family and social support networks. The approach reads as a precursor to;

- The *Family Group Conference (FGC)* – The New Zealanders developed the FGC; there is now global interest and experimentation. Sensitive to the extended family networks and collective problem solving of the indigenous population and the plethora of island communities under New Zealand sovereignty, the New Zealand government enshrined a duty to employ the group conference in protection procedures (Connelly, 1994; Whiffen & Morris, 1997). Subsequently the group conference has been used internationally in general problem solving (not just high tariff abuse contexts) and the New Zealanders themselves are now extending its use to youth offending.

- *Neighbourhood Work* – Community work claimed a multi-layered terrain for itself in planning, inter-agency work, and the neighbourhood. In identifying the 'Skills of Neighbourhood Work', Henderson & Thomas (1987) made a claim for the neighbourhood as a distinctive site for action, and saw it as enduringly relevant despite a more mobile society (repeated in France – see Bourget-Daitch & Warren, 1997). Attempts have been made to add the protective agenda of social work to neighbourhood development (Baldwin & Carruthers, 1998; Annie E. Casey Foundation, 2000; Fletcher, this text). The challenge is to connect the above with other powerful ideas on neighbourhood development, for example, welfare modernising perspectives (Atkinson 2000) and eco-neighbourhoods (Barton 2000).

- *Social Group-Work* – is taught variously in British training courses but it is not underpinning.[2] Students find the world of largely individual work in practice placements to be a barren landscape when it comes to practising their group work skills. An exception is the local resource centre (family centre) where certain strands of group process are practised, from support and therapy to, for example, the informal or adult education model (Jeffs & Smith, 1990), feminist group-work (Howe, 1987: 121–133), and self-directed groupwork (Mullender & Ward, 1991).

- *Social Support Networks* – Whittaker (1983), drawing on the correlation between poor support networks and abusive behaviour, poor health and crime, made a powerful case for the development of informal support networks as a key feature of social work practice. This is now a part of the discourse of practice and particularly assessment (DH op. cit.) but despite available materials (Lovell, Reid, & Richey,

---

[2] Exceptionally and to its great credit, de Montfort University, UK, aims to place group care at the centre of the qualifying programme.

1992; Rickard, 1998) workers are still more inclined to report on the lack of networks than on their own success in constructing them.

Centres as Sites for a Collective Future

Few of these approaches have become identified as mainstream practice – the exception being (intra) family therapy although it tends to be associated with medical or quasi-medical settings. For most of the above, it is hard to see appropriate sites for their sustained development. Until, that is, the emergence of the family centre. Perhaps the most promising initiative for a creative and true social work practice is sited in family centres, especially those which have been termed 'integrated centres'. This is not a new concept (Gill, 1988; Stones, this text). In a six centre action research study (Warren-Adamson, 2000) the integrated centre was accounted for as follows: function, method, focus, and the empowerment journey.

Function and the Integrated Centre

The containment function – this explains the centre's capacity over time to parent, to contain, weather, absorb, and accept, and help to change troubling and challenging behaviour. This is a distinctive feature of social welfare. It is what social work should do. The concept of containment is taken from Bion and the idea of the parent as container of the projective force of the infant (see Shuttleworth, 1991, also Winnicott, 1990, for a similar concept of 'holding'). Connected to this is Howe and Hining's (1995) criticism of contemporary child and family work and legislation where, they argue, an assumption only of rational action in users – partnership, partnership – means that when users behave irrationally we appear not to have the tools and often we act with hostility, unjustly, and reject. Not so centres, which seem better placed to look both ways (see also Irvine, 1956, Menzies Lyth, 1989).

The casework decision-making function – this explains the centre's capacity to help families make decisions and participate in decision-making, and also it explains the centre's capacity to contribute data about families to help others make decisions (particularly the judicial and protection process). This also is distinctively the domain of social work.

The resource centre function – explains partly the centre's capacity to lay on a range of opportunities for families, accounting for diversity of need, and partly the capacity of centres to transform in the light of need. It is the development role of centres – spawning, nurturing, developing, moving on groups, moving from an emphasis on people's expressive needs to their instrumental needs and goals. This is a broader domain of social groupwork, informal education and community development. And it connects to:

The group autonomy function – this explains the world of self-help centres run by parents and provides another route to empowerment, through network, neighbourhood, and, for example, through the solidarity of women. Such centres are beacons in communities and have a particular role in engaging those families whose boundary between them and the outside – often because of male violence – is especially impermeable (see Liffman, 1978, for an Australian account, and chapters 5, 6, and 14, this text).

The Integrated Centre and Method

The integrated centre combines methods in individual work for families (counselling, play therapy, skills training), with work with whole families, with group work which concentrates on expressive needs. However, the integrated centre also encourages the separate development of groups, those which have grown from the centre and those which have different origins. Thus the centres can be seen to engage in a range of methods – social work, informal education, social action and community development.

The Integrated Centre and Focus

The integrated centre tries to combine a focus on a) the child as separate (need for care, play and education, and protection), b) the parent and child relationship, c) the separate needs of parents for containment and support, d) the separate needs of parents to participate, e) parents' needs to find education and training (Warren, 1997).

The Idea of the Empowerment Journey

Keiffer studied 40 successful community activists who had 'made it' from poverty and crime, and proposed that the 'journey' was on average 4 years

(Keiffer, 1984). Keiffer described specific phases of recovery. His research inspired Cochran (1985) and others to develop the idea of empowerment as a long process of containing and challenging experiences. See Warren (1997: 118-120) for stepping stones in this process and the connection to family centres and their range of interventions and opportunities. Chapter 15 demonstrates well such 'journeys'.

The Local Resource Centre

The key concept is that of *local resource centre. Local* means accessible. Many centres are accessible without being tied to a specific neighbourhood. Some are tied to the neighbourhood, and the variously constructed meanings of neighbourhood (Barton op cit). *Resource* means having a range of people and equipment flexibly available to empower users. It is something rather more than a service. And *centre* is an identifiable building, which is part of the architecture of the community, and contributes to what Wolfensberger calls the community's social glue. In that sense it is a universal structure, part of everybody's world. For some, it is a passing blur, for others it is somewhere to turn to, to return to one day, part of your development, somewhere deeply rooted in memory (Leichter 1978). Thus, *local resource centre* can include church, school, residential facility, even an office.[3] In this text, the *local resource centre* is applied to the world of children and their families.[4]

Jobs and Territory, Boundaries, Formality, Distance, Status, and the Invisibility of Good Parenthood

Another way of looking at the distinctiveness of centre practice is to examine some of the jobs in social intervention, their formality and informality, and their relationship to the family and the centre. In general, status and training go with formality, distance, secure territory and firm boundaries (Germain, 1991). Lesser status, closeness, negotiated roles, and informality are normally associated with semi and non-professional jobs.

---

[3] Remember the Essex Road social work office of the 1960s?
[4] The same principle can and does apply to centres for older people, and people with learning disabilities.

What is distinctive about the family centre is that, unlike most job territories, the boundary round the outside is relatively permeable. The family visits it and it visits the family over time. Most jobs in child and family social work, including doctor (except magistrate/judge/police),[5] have been undertaken in family centres, challenging staff to negotiate over distance, territory, boundary and status.

As a centre worker you represent your core professional self, without the trappings, the mythology, nothing else to rely on. Whereas closeness, negotiated roles, and informality are normally associated with the semi and non-professional, in the centre this is not the case. They are all part of a professional endeavour. Moreover, whatever the discipline, centre practices demonstrate an expression of parenthood, and, like good parenthood, it is often invisible.[6]

Themes of Practice Integration and Empowerment in the Chapters

So let us turn to the chapters where themes of collective practice, of social work as education, and the integration of approaches are much in evidence.

In chapter 2, Chris Stones (UK manager/practitioner) explains and brings alive the idea of the integrated centre. They say good ideas have many parents. Arguably Chris Stones and her colleagues at the Fulford family centre have been at the forefront, the first parents even, of the integrated centre, and over many years. Fittingly, it starts this text.

In chapter 3, Chris Warren-Adamson with Anne-Marie David and Jean-Paul Ducandas (UK academic and French practitioners) compare French and English centres and link two centre traditions – the settlement and social action centre on the one hand, and the family centre on the other. It also invites us to consider why the anglo-saxon tradition of social work in Britain has become so much more contested in Britain than its European counterpart. The chapter highlights the gains which can come from professional and user interchange.

In chapter 4, Claire Cook and Paul Montgomery (UK practitioner and student practitioner) introduce important practical lessons, a reminder that empowerment is not a glorious battleground but rather a painstaking task of putting together principles and good organisation. In the two case studies

---

[5] They visit, some often.
[6] See especially Chapter 14.

practitioners collaborate with another agency – the Community Education Department – and illustrate that empowerment practice is also about linking the formal and the informal. Curious to note that here the Community Education department is the formal component.

In chapter 5, two case studies,[7] assembled by Irene Kyle, Maureen Kellerman and Alla Ivask (Canadian researchers and National Organisation Manager), have been reproduced from the Canadian Association study of some fifteen different programs. Community education practice is central to these projects. Note the evolution of a feminist practice on the one hand and the headway which le Carrefour has made in developing a fathers-based practice on the other. The Report underlines the ecological approach to practice and its implication for the inner centre and its inter-connectedness with the neighbourhood and the wider community. The studies also show how conventional supportive and educative activities can accompany community and economic development.

Chapter 6, is by Audrey Fessler (UK, committee member of an independent, referral-only centre). Through interview and study of reports she traces its evolution and reflects the centre's and her struggle towards a new language, a new professionalism, and changing approaches to parenting education. A special problem for such centres is to keep their own self-help energy and self-direction whilst adapting to the world of external funders, the service level agreement, accountability, and the demands of evaluation and outcomes.

A feature of the United States has been the evolution of the large centre, combining all functions of child and family social work including child placement. In chapter 7, Carolyn Burns (manager of such a centre) and John Zalenski (US academic) show through their outreach and development roles, how the challenge of joining protection and support leads the United States into patch development. Courageously, like the French, and unlike the British, they assert and celebrate social work's distinctive occupation of the world of the *social*. Note, too, how the patch office shares the integrative features of the family centre.

In chapters 8 and 9, David Ely, Ellen Jones, Terri Fletcher and Mo Romano (UK practitioners from one centre) give us a double bill of practice examples. In chapter 8, case studies show how support and child protective practice is promoted within the centre. In chapter 9, there

---

[7] Regrettably, space precludes the inclusion of the Port au Port Community Education Initiative Inc (Stephenville, Newfoundland), a good example of the penumbral centre - a base and a range of satellite centres based in schools.

follows an account of child protective community work which has its roots in the same centre's inter-agency, development role. Both accounts – back-to-back – help us to enlarge our practical understanding of Margaret Boushel's (1994) important concept of the *child's protective environment*.

Chapters 10 and 11 give accounts of practice from a country which has provided creative inspiration to international child and family practice (for example, family group conferences enshrined in legislation). Moreover, a culturally sensitive practice is demonstrated from which we have much to learn. Chapter 10 is the 'grit in our vaseline',[8] a different practice culture. Lynne Briggs (New Zealand practitioner in a child and adolescent mental health service – CAMHS) gives an alternative view of a 'community-based service', which is assessment rather than intervention focused. It is full of diagnostic information, ecologically driven with a strong value-base. This chapter also holds a place here because the CAMHS comes out consistently as a regular companion to family centres, respected by users and professionals (Warren-Adamson, 2000). It reminds us too that studies are needed of inter-relationships between agencies (for example, assessment, case-management and centre), and that families' empowerment journey may take place *between* key agencies and the families' own private world. Complicated stuff.

In chapter 11, Robyn Munford and Jackie Sanders, with Ann Andrew, Peter Butler, Ripeka Kaipuke and Leland Ruwhiu (New Zealand academics with practitioners) provide us with new insights on several levels, including, a) the way youth offending, welfare and the liberation of sport are brought together, and b) the idea of *being available to parent*, an important concept rejecting the narrow idea of an accrued set of skills but rather ecologically based, part of a complex transaction or relationship.[9]

In chapter 12, Andy Lloyd and Nick Frost (UK practitioner and academic) combine messages from research on youth crime and family support as a basis for family centre intervention. Centres choose to ignore that these domains are inter-linked. Students of social work will find this an excellent example of the link between research evidence and practice, showing the match between prevention and good outcomes and a clear rationale for centre practice. And practitioners struggling with parenting orders will find helpful ways to proceed. Note, too, that in the scramble to claim first parenthood for the neighbourhood family resource centre, in the UK the Family Services Units have a strong claim.

---

[8] Expression credited to Jake Thackery, by Norman Tutt.
[9] See also Golding (2000).

11

In chapter 13, Vasso Gabrilidou, Elpida Ioannidou and Evi Hatzivarnava (Greek practitioners and a researcher) show how Greek family centres are so rooted historically in the political and social post-war context. We note how centres, principally engaged in rescuing children from a divided and traumatised post-war world, gradually engaged the local community in their endeavour. Development between systems in other words is a constant theme of centre evolution. As Greek centres have evolved they now reflect contemporary dilemmas, for example, how to combine targeted or universal services. Interesting to note that one response to changing needs and the rural context is the resource centre which supports a range of small scale outreach initiatives, what Villem Van der Eyken calls 'penumbral' development. Note the role of the quasi-Government organisation and its preventive role (like the French CAF in chapter 3).

In chapter 14, Di Holland (UK practitioner) shows how social work, a practice which seeks to contain vulnerable and sometimes challenging people, transforms itself in the family centre and eventually links with formal educational institutions. The detail provided here provides a workable model available to other centres.

Chapter 15 – when a paper was requested from Togher Family Centre in Ireland, they said – very respectfully and very modestly – that's not how we work. Come over and listen to some of the stories of the centre members. So we did, and heard many stories of social work as an educational endeavour. This chapter contains some examples – empowerment journeys, 'lifelong learning', the spectrum of formal and informal education, the importance of practical services, child care as the spine of the resource, time and generations, the centre as a beacon in the community, linking small and large institutions, social workers as facilitators and social educators, pre-school workers as social workers and community workers, managing private and the public stories, the power of exchange between centres and other countries, and so on. If you haven't read Freire (1985), or friends of Friere (Ledwith, 1997), or you haven't got your head round conscientisation, this chapter is a splendid testimony to Freire's ideas.

Inspired by the above chapters, the conclusion – Chapter 16 – wrestles with the notion of a different discourse for social work, as a distinctively ecological, educational and integrated activity, and argues that the formative and primary setting for child and family practice should be the family (resource) centre.

References

Adams P. & Nelson K. eds. (1995), *Reinventing Human Services*, Aldine de Gruyter, New York.

Annie E. Casey Foundation (2000), http://www.aecf.org/initiatives/ntfd/

Atkinson D. (2000), *Urban Renaissance – a Strategy for Urban Renewal and the Welfare Society*, Brewin Books, Studley.

Baldwin N. & Carruthers L. (1998), *Developing Neighbourhood Support and Child Protection Strategies*, Ashgate, Aldershot.

Barton H. ed (2000), *Sustainable Communities – the Potential for Eco-Neighbourhoods*, Earthscan Publications Ltd., London.

Bourget-Daitch M-R. & Warren C. (1997), 'Act local, think global', in Cannan C. & Warren C. eds. *Social Action with Children and their Families – a Community Development Approach*, Routledge, London.

Boushel M. (1994),'The protective environment of children: towards a framework for anti-oppressive, cross-cultural and cross-national understanding', in *British Journal of Social Work*, Vol. 24, pp. 173–190.

Brager G. & Specht H. (1973), *Community Organising*, Columbia University Press, New York.

Cannan C. (1997), 'Social development with children and families in France', in Cannan C. & Warren C. eds. *Social Action with Children and Families – a Community Development Approach,* Routledge, London, pp. 85–102.

Carpenter J. & Treacher A. (1983), 'On the neglected but related arts of convening and engaging families and their wider systems', in *Journal of Family Therapy* 5, pp.337–358.

Cochran M. (1985), 'The parental empowerment process: building upon family strengths', in Harris J. ed. *Psychology in Action: Linking Research and Practice*, Croom Helm, London.

Connelly M. (1994), 'An act of empowerment: the Children and Young Person's and their Families Act, 1989', in *British Journal of Social Work*, 24, pp. 87–100.

Dimmock B. & Dungworth D. (1985), 'Beyond the Family; using network meetings with statutory child care cases', in *Journal of Family Therapy*, 7, pp. 45–68.

Freire P. (1985), *The Politics of Education, Culture, Power and Liberation*, Macmillan, Basingstoke.

Freynet M-F. (1995), *Les Médiations du Travail Social*, Chroniques Sociales, Lyon.

Golding K. (2000), 'Parent management training as an intervention to promote adequate parenting', in *Clinical Child Psychiatry and Psychology*, Vol 5. (3) pp. 357–371.

Hadley R. & McGrath M. (1980), *Going Local – Neighbourhood Social Services,* Bedford Square Press, London.

Henderson P. & Thomas D.N. (1987), *Skills in Neighbourhood Work* (2nd ed.), Allen and Unwin, London.

Hoffman L. (1981), *Foundations of Family Therapy*, Basic Books, New York.

Holman R. (1983), *Resourceful Friends – Skills in Community Social Work*, The Children's Society, London.

Howe D. (1987), *An Introduction to Social Work Theory*, Ashgate, Aldershot.

Howe D. & Hinings D. (1995), 'Reason and emotion in social work practice: managing relationships with difficult clients,' *Journal of Social Work Practice*, Vol 9, No. 1, pp. 5–14.

Imber-Black E. (1998), *Families and Wider Systems – a Family Therapist's Guide Through The Labyrinth*, Guilford Press, New York.

Irvine E. (1956), Transference and reality in the casework relationship, in *British Journal of Psychiatric Social Work*, Vol 3, No 4.

Jeffs T. & Smith M. (1990), *Using Informal Education*, Open University Press, Milton Keynes.

Keiffer C. H. (1984), 'Citizen empowerment: a developmental perspective', in *Prevention in Human Services* 3 (Winter/Spring), pp. 9–36.

Ledwith M. (1997), *Participating in Transformation: Towards a Working Model of Community Development*, Venture Press, Birmingham.

Leichter H. (1978), *The Family and Community as Educator*, The Teacher's College Press, New York.

Liffman M. (for the Brotherhood of St Lawrence) (1978), *Power for the Poor; The Family Centre Project; An Experiment in Self-Help*, Allen & Unwin, Sydney.

Lovell M. L., Reid K. & Richey C. A. (1992), 'Social support training for abusive mothers', Garland J. A. ed. *Group Work Reaching Out: People, Places, and Power*, Howarth Press, Binghampton.

Manor O. (1984), *Family Work in Action,* Tavistock, London.

Menzies Lyth I. (1989), *The Dynamics of the Social*, Free Association Books, London.

Mullender A. & Ward D. (1991), *Self-Directed Group-Work*, Whiting & Birch, London.

Parton N. ed. (1997), *Child Protection and Family Support*, Routledge, London.

Parton N. & O'Byrne P. eds. (2001), *Constructive Social Work, Towards a New Practice*, Macmillan Press, Basingstoke.

Preston-Shoot M. & Agass D. (1990), *Making Sense of Social Work*, Macmillan, Basingstoke.

Rickard V. (1998), *Strategies for Working with Involuntary Clients*, Columbia University Press, New York.

Shuttleworth J. (1991), 'Psychoanalytic theory and infant development', in Miller L., Rustin Margaret, Rustin Michael, Shuttleworth J. eds. *Closely Observed Infants*, Duckworth, London.

Smale G. (1995), 'Integrating community and individual practice: a new paradigm for Practice', in Adams P. & Nelson K. eds. *Reinventing Human Services,* Aldine de Gruyter, New York.

Speck R. V. & Attneave C. L. (1973), *Family Networks*, Vintage, New York.

Stewart W. (1992), *The A-Z of Counselling Theory and Practice*, Chapman and Hall, London, New York.

Warren-Adamson C. (2000), 'Family Centres: their role in Fighting Social Exclusion,' Report of Action Research Project, Brunel University, Unpublished.

Watzlawick P., Weakland J. & Fisch R. (1974), *Change – Principles of Problem Formation and Problem Resolution*, Norton, New York and London.

Whiffen J. & Morris K. (1997), *Family Group Conferences: A Guide for Families*, Family Rights Group, London.

White M. & Epstein D. (1990), *Narrative Means to Therapeutic Ends*, W.W. Norton & Co., New York and London.

Whittaker J. (1986), 'Integrating formal and informal social care: a conceptual framework', in *British Journal Social Work*, 16, Supplement, pp. 39-62.

Winnicott D.W. (1990), *The Maturational Process in the Facilitating Environment*, Karnac Books, London.

2 The Family Centre and the Consolidation of Integrated Practice

CHRISTINE STONES

Introduction

This chapter describes the work of New Fulford Family Centre, illustrates the approaches used and explores some of the issues arising in integrated practice. In particular it explores the contribution of a combined or integrated approach to empowerment.

New Fulford Family Centre was established by Barnardo's in 1984 to serve two outer-city estates in South Bristol. The population of the estates is more than 20,000 but the area has few of the facilities which a small town of that size would enjoy. The area scores highly on indicators of poverty. There are significant numbers of lone parents and of young parents. Whilst a proportion of families have extended networks in the area, others are reluctant to be housed in that part of the city and lack support of family and friends.

The aim of the centre is, through partnership with parents, to facilitate opportunities for growth and development for children under five and their parents and, where appropriate, to prevent children needing to be looked after by the local authority. This aim leads to a number of detailed objectives that include:

- Challenging abuse and violence in families;
- Promoting children's rights;
- Aiding the functioning of families;
- Enhancing individual strengths;
- Promoting self help;
- Increasing community strength and development;
- Relieving isolation and stress.

As the list indicates the focus of the family centre's work encompasses the individual, the family and the community. The centre programme is based on an ecological perspective which views the opportunities and problems faced by children and families as multifactorial and interactive. Particularly such writers as Bronfenbrenner (1979) and Garbarino (1992) have expounded an ecological approach to children and families.

An integrated model for social work practice had exponents in the 1970s such as Pincus and Minahan (1973) and Goldstein (1973). Evans (1976) commented that an integrated approach, 'constitutes a shift from a predominantly "individualistic" model to an "interactionist" one'. Thus an integrated approach addresses more than one system and strives to ensure that the varied approaches work together to achieve the shared aim and that together they achieve more than the sum of the separate parts. So the family centre's activities reflect the belief that, to be effective in pursuing its aim, the centre needs to address the varied factors which arise in different systems impinging on children and their families.

> The need therefore is for an integrated approach, based on a perspective which sees individuals, families, groups and communities in dynamic interaction with economic, social, cultural and political systems characterised by mutual influence and feedback. (Preston-Shoot and Agass, 1990)

Programme

Empowerment is sometimes an explicit aim of a centre activity and on other occasions it is an implicit by-product of the work. The centre's programme is wide-ranging in its implementation of an ecological approach.

Services for Individuals and Families

Some of these can be classified as therapeutic, such as, individual counselling, couple counselling, play therapy and family play sessions. The latter medium can be seen as the equivalent to family therapy when working with families with very young children. Such services can empower individuals by building their confidence, increasing their self-esteem, transforming negative self-images and developing communication skills.

Her Health Visitor referred Tina to the centre. She was depressed, hardly ever went out and lacked confidence in caring for her children. It took some months to engage Tina in counselling at the centre. Several years later after involvement in many different activities and eventually becoming a volunteer at the centre, Tina emphasised how important it had been to her that the initial worker had persevered at engaging her. This had demonstrated the worker's and centre's commitment to her and a belief that things could change for her. It had enabled her to take the first step in her journey.

There can be subtle empowerment issues when working with families. Power is not distributed equally between family members; age and gender often determine power and children are usually the most powerless. Thought needs to be given to how children can be empowered. We have found it helpful when engaging in play therapy with a child to clarify with the child if there are things that they want shared with their family and if so how they can be enabled to do so.

Regular review sessions were built into the work with Kayley and the review would take place with Kayley and her parents. Before each review the worker would spend part of Kayley's session talking about the review and what she might want to say to her parents about the work. Kayley had used some of her sessions to re-enact fierce rows that took place between her parents and which she could hear from her bedroom at night. She told her worker that she wanted to ask her parents not to shout at each other because it frightened her. Until then, Kayley's parents had convinced themselves that she was quite unaware of their frequent arguments.

Other individual and family-focused services involve advice and advocacy. The centre regularly provides welfare rights advice which, most commonly, addresses benefits and housing issues. Advice and advocacy is also offered to families experiencing racial harassment. Efforts are made to undertake advice and advocacy work in a way which seeks to share knowledge and skills so that the advice seeker can develop their confidence and ability to become their own (and sometimes another's) advocate.

Work with Groups

Groups have considerable potential for empowering their members and examples of groups at New Fulford include closed therapeutic groups, mutual support groups, and carer and toddler groups. Therapeutic groups share similar outcomes to work with individuals and families. Empowerment may not be the primary or explicit aim of the group but may be a significant effect.

> Therapeutic intervention combined with the support of group members empowered Mary to leave a violent relationship that had been putting both her and her children at risk.

> Encouragement from other parents in a mutual support group enabled Tracy, in her mid-twenties, to sign up for a training course. The same mother truanted from school during the final years of her compulsory education and vowed never to have any further contact with formal education.

Group members facing similar pressures can share skills and experience in combating difficulties. A group for black and multi-racial families enables members to support each other in coping with racial harassment. Parents in this group were keen to develop knowledge and understanding about issues specific to caring for a black or mixed parentage child. The group worker together with a student worked with the group in clarifying needs and designing a programme that would meet those needs.

An identity group was run for mixed parentage children living with a white parent. Many of the children attending the group had low self-esteem and some expressed the desire to be white. The group workers used a variety of exercises and educative processes to extend the children's understanding of their black heritage. At the end of the year-long group the members demonstrated improved self-esteem and a more positive sense of their identity.

Community Development

Over a number of years the focus of community development at the family centre has varied. It has depended on the issues facing families in the neighbourhood and in the wider context. For an extended period one concern was the needs of families bringing up children in high-rise flats. This need was identified through examination of census data to identify the location of higher percentages of young children. The family centre both provided a service by running parent and toddler groups and also worked with families to influence housing policy and the provision for families in flats. This eventually led to reductions in numbers of families living in multi-storey flats and to improvements within the blocks.

In recent times the centre has focused on training and education related to childcare. This achieves two separate objectives as it both increases community resources by expanding the pool of people available to provide quality childcare and it develops individual strengths. A playcare course run at the centre now carries OCN credits and a BTEC award. Our experience suggests that many mothers have left formal education early taking with them dissatisfaction with learning and a sense of failure. Other parents who may have studied or worked in the past may, during their period of full time parenting, lose confidence in their abilities and skills. As a result many mothers are hesitant and reluctant to sign up for college courses even when serious attempts are made by colleges to reach them.

A familiar environment such as the family centre can provide the vital first step onto a ladder of training opportunities. This has been demonstrated by a number of participants in these courses who have gone on to undertake further education and training or obtained employment. The course builds on and develops the knowledge and skills that parents have gained through parenting. Staff running the course promote a supportive learning group environment whilst also offering considerable individual encouragement.

> Helen had no family support in the area in which she lived and, after much encouragement, a neighbour brought her along to a centre drop-in. Helen described the centre as a 'lifeline, it's brought me out of myself'. When her youngest child started school she said she 'wanted to give something back' and quickly mad arrangements to volunteer as a playworker. She enjoyed the volunteer course which accompanied the role of volunteer playworker. Centre staff responded to her enthusiasm and growing ability and Helen was encouraged to enrol for the playcare course. When that was successfully completed, she gained admission to the local college to undertake qualification training in Childhood Studies. Helen identifies the support and encouragement from staff as a key element in each step on her road to qualification. The college BTEC diploma course was extremely demanding and a high proportion of students dropped out. Helen felt like giving up on many occasions and at such times talked things through with staff at the family centre. She has gained her qualification and is now hoping to obtain employment in the neighbourhood and make further contribution to the local community.

Processes

The processes involved in any part of the programme can either contribute to empowerment or hinder it. Thus for any of the services provided, it is important that referral, engagement, review, completion and evaluation processes express shared responsibility and control.

A statement on the Family Centre's referral form requests joint completion by the referrer and the appropriate members of the family being referred. This small detail provides some indication to families before they cross the centre threshold that they are viewed as competent and rightful definers of their needs and aspirations. Of course, this is not invariably a straightforward process. As indicated earlier, the family centre is partly funded by the local authority and undertakes some work focussing on issues of child protection. In these circumstances there are obvious power inequalities between workers and families that must be acknowledged. Parents and the referring social worker may have very different perspectives on the needs of the family and the areas for change. Such differences have to be clarified and the details of proposed work with the family carefully negotiated and expressed in a contract.

Efforts are made to implement the principles of empowerment in each stage following referral. Thus the way in which work is reviewed seeks to ensure that users views are central to the review process.

From its earliest days New Fulford Family Centre has sought to facilitate collective influence by users as well as empowerment of individuals. It has been important to establish appropriate structures through which this could be achieved. A consultative process involving as many users as possible led to the establishment of a Parents' Council which comprises representatives from each centre group. The Council is therefore the formal body through which users can contribute to the management of the centre. It meets fortnightly and once a month meets with the staff group in a Joint Meeting.

Evaluation of the centre's effectiveness includes an annual review in which users play a key role. To provide a degree of objectivity, someone other than a permanent member of staff usually undertakes a survey of views of participants and of other agencies. On some occasions the task has been completed as part of a student placement and at other times a sessional worker has been employed.

Through the Parents' Council, centre participants both influence the process of evaluation and provide much of the content. Parent representatives have worked with a sessional worker in designing the feedback questions. In addition they have joined the worker in running structured interviews to obtain feedback from other agencies. Parents' Council representatives have also accompanied the worker in undertaking review sessions in centre groups.

One of the aspects always examined in the annual review is the participants' views of the opportunities for them to have a say in the running of the centre. Involvement in aspects of the management of the centre has been identified as an empowering experience for individuals.

> Sue had worked as a Health Care Assistant before having her children. She found the loss of her work identity removed her confidence. She felt restricted to a single role of mother and rarely went anywhere. Sue came to a drop-in and to a parent support group. Sue was appointed as a representative to the Parents' Council. Eventually she became chair of the Council. She also undertook the Playcare course and an Equal Opportunities Training course. Her confidence in her abilities increased greatly and she enrolled on a local Access to higher education course. Sue is now studying Psychology at a local University. Sue identifies her experience on the Parents' Council as of key significance in her journey. She gained from being in a forum where she learnt to disagree but respect others' views and through a role which required her to help other parents to participate.

Policies and Procedures

As indicated in the previous section, from the centre's inception, staff have been committed to users sharing some responsibility and control over resources. Thus empowerment has not only been an individual journey for many centre participants, it has also been a journey for staff and users together.

Staff may unintentionally convey a message that the influence of parents is of less value than that of staff or other agencies. Independent research at the project looking at partnership with parents reported an interesting parental comment; 'our items are always last on the agenda' (Daines et al., 1989). Although this was not strictly accurate it was important to register the perception of some members of the Council. Since then items from 'Parents' Council' immediately follows matters arising from the previous minutes on the Joint Meeting agenda.

Empowering users to influence policy and practice at the centre requires that opportunities be provided for parents to develop the necessary skills and knowledge to participate. It is easy to forget the considerable experiences workers have of contributing to decision making processes and as a result their familiarity and ease at meetings. Workshops on meetings and other topics such as assertiveness are run each year for Parents' Council representatives and any other interested centre participants. An external consultant is always employed to run the workshops.

Attention also has to be given to approaches in meetings that encourage participation, particularly as the membership of the Joint meeting is large. Each year when the newly constituted Joint Meeting convenes for the first time, an exercise is undertaken in small groups and then in the full meeting to establish agreed ground-rules for the year. Efforts are also made to ensure that for part of each Joint Meeting some time is spent in small sub-groups to facilitate contributions by all the members.

The Parents' Council has been involved in different aspects of policy making. The degree of influence is prescribed by the amount of influence the wider organisation delegates to the project leader and staff. Thus some policies are national or regional and parents may be consulted or make representation but cannot directly determine the policy. In others there may be a requirement to produce a local policy, an example of this is the Equal Opportunities Policy. This took some years to produce jointly between the parents and staff but the final policy was the result of a genuine partnership. The process involved two staff working with the Parents' Council to produce a draft policy statement. This was then widely consulted on with the centre's constituent groups. Once agreed, the implementation and maintenance of the policy was assisted by training sessions at special Joint meetings, which were open to other users. Thus every two months or so one aspect of the policy would be examined and its implications for staff, users and activities explored. The discussions were assisted by the use of external facilitators.

Members of the Parents' Council participate in various management and practice tasks. They share in decisions about priorities in the use of resources. They contribute to decisions about staff recruitment. A representative of the Council, usually the chairperson, serves on the selection panels when a new member of staff is appointed. Members of the Council have contributed to the Project Leader's annual appraisal.

Parents share in service provision, for example by running a Nearly New Shop. They have also extended provision by suggesting the solution to the gap between the need for an additional activity and the lack of resources to provide it. When the weekly Drop-in became oversubscribed there were no staff available to set up a second session. Members of the Parents' Council proposed that with appropriate training, combined with some support from staff, volunteer parents should run a second Drop-in.

As a Barnardo's project, which receives local authority funding, there are a number of parties with a legitimate expectation of power and influence over the centre. These different interests are brought together in an Advisory Group which is made up of representatives from Barnardo's, the Parents Council, the Local Authority Social Services, local councillors, and other local agencies. It was recognised that for parents to have a genuine voice, they needed to have sufficient representation. There are, as a result, six seats on the Advisory Group for Parents' Council representatives and the Group has an Independent Chair.

Patterns of Use

A fundamental feature of an integrated approach is the scope for participating families to engage in a package of activities. At any time there is a varied pattern of use of the centre by families. Many parents may use the centre to meet a particular need and so participate in a single service that might be individual counselling, welfare rights advice, play therapy for their child or attendance at a group. Alternatively some parents may attend a number of different activities. The varied activities may be taken-up simultaneously, leading to an intensive pattern of involvement, or may be developed over a period of time. The journeys of family centre users are diverse although many share similar patterns.

> Diane and her two children were very isolated. They moved to the area after Diane's partner left her. Diane's lack of confidence and low self-esteem were compounded by the loss of the relationship and rehousing in an unfamiliar part of the city. After considerable encouragement from her health visitor, Diane began to attend a Drop-in. She tended to sit on the edge of the group whilst her two children joined in the activities in the playroom. After a few weeks Diane asked one of the workers at Drop-in if she could see someone for counselling. Counselling was arranged and Diane gradually worked through some of the issues underlying her low self-esteem. She also identified anxieties resulting from considerable financial problems. Some Welfare Rights sessions were arranged which

enabled Diane to begin to tackle her financial difficulties. When Diane started a new relationship with Pete, her children's behaviour towards Pete was rejecting and Diane and Pete had increasing arguments about how to handle this. They requested joint counselling sessions to help them look at the issues together. Diane's growing confidence was demonstrated by her increased participation in Drop-in and her offering to become one of the Drop-in representatives on the Parents Council.

Cherry was referred by Social Services as a result of a child protection case conference and an unexplained injury to her son. Two members of staff carried out a risk assessment. At the end of the assessment Cherry was offered individual counselling and family play sessions. The former enabled her to work on her confusion and anger surrounding her own childhood. The play sessions encouraged the development of her relationship towards her son and her skills in parenting. Over time, Cherry's enjoyment of relating to her own son through play was such that she volunteered to become a playworker at the centre.

Issues

Race and Gender

There are a number of issues arising from an integrated approach in a family centre, which are pertinent to a consideration of empowerment. One question is whether or not all users benefit from an integrated programme. Most writing on family centres acknowledges that the predominant users are white women. A recent study of the use of family centres by black families, reported by Butt and Box (1998), warns, 'Family centres are not intrinsically providers of accessible and appropriate services to black families'.

Our experience at Fulford has been that black and multi-racial families access services that target their needs but much more rarely use other activities at the centre. This means that an integrated service may be harder to provide for black users. Examination of some of the issues took place through a survey by a black student obtaining the views of black users and subsequent discussion of the findings within a Joint Parents' Council and staff meeting and also at a meeting of the Advisory Group. The survey highlighted issues of how welcoming to black and multi-racial families are groups which were currently all white. Each group at the centre was also asked to look at the findings of the survey and think about its implications for them.

A further way in which we seek to address issues about sensitivity and accessibility of services to black users is through a race equality action plan. This plan is reviewed within the team meeting at least every year and every three months part of the team meeting is set aside to focus on one aspect of the plan.

Gender and family centres have received some attention in recent years. The question of why fathers are in a small minority of centre users has challenged most centres and New Fulford is no exception. Examination of the pattern of use of services and its relationship to gender has revealed that we are quite successful in engaging fathers in the range of therapeutic work including individual counselling, couple and family work. Fathers also attend outings and social events. But only a small number of fathers attend mutual support or parent and child groups. In the past year the Parents Council has had a father representing a group for the first time for some years.

Family Centres are, of course, not alone in experiencing this gender imbalance. The issue cannot be separated from implications of social policy and attitudes towards gender and child care. Agencies often unwittingly perpetuate an expectation that involvement in welfare provision will be the responsibility of mothers. New Fulford is currently involved in the development of a Sure Start programme for children under four and their families. As part of this, a small task group has been looking at developing work with fathers from before the birth of their child. Fathers involved in the group indicated that they often feel excluded from services and disempowered by the attitudes and approach of professionals.

A further dynamic is the ambivalence of mothers concerning the involvement of men in family centres. There are varied reasons for these feelings; two prominent ones will be mentioned. Women users of centres are often victims of abuse and violence from men. In addition, child care and family centres are some of the few arenas where women hold power and understandably they may be reluctant to risk forfeiting this by encouraging fathers to attend more activities at the centre. This is a complex area that needs further attention if both mothers and fathers are to be empowered through family centres.

Role Strain

The range of different activities encompassed by an integrated approach requires the fulfilment of different roles. This provides significant opportunities for gaining experience and confidence in undertaking varied roles and moving between roles. But it can also lead to role strain for both parents and workers. For example, moving from counsellor/client to joint committee members involves subtle changes of relationship. It can be important to acknowledge and work with some of the transitional difficulties within the counselling. Attention to details of timing and location of different activities can be important. Moving rapidly between very different roles or using exactly the same space for the contrasting activities can make transitions more difficult.

Conflict and Competition

An integrated approach risks polarisation and conflict. There can be a danger of polarising competent and vulnerable parents. Families struggling with particular difficulties do not always induce empathy in less vulnerable parents, who may resent their non-participation in user led events or their demands on staff time and other resources. At the same time the parents with least confidence may not feel encouraged to develop participatory skills by the more assertive parents. However a key element of an integrated approach should include the acknowledgement of the presence of both strengths and weaknesses within individuals and a community. Mutual support between families can be built on common needs but different strengths and vulnerabilities.

Tensions can develop between different approaches. Inevitably limited resources can lead to competition not only for funds but also for space and time between the needs of different approaches. The needs of groups can be experienced as competing with individual needs or community development work might be viewed as crowding out therapeutic work. Where different perspectives and foci operate alongside each other there can be the risks of one or another dominating or of barriers developing which prevent effective communication and movement between the varied parts of the centre and its programme. Respect between proponents of different approaches is essential and time spent exploring connections and conflicts between perspectives reaps numerous benefits.

There is always a question of whether participation and empowerment is reality or rhetoric. Research suggests that the extent of user participation and influence in family centres may not be as great as users desire or workers intend. The study of the use of family centres by black families by Butt and Box (1998) comments, 'the interview material demonstrated that for the majority of service users, partnership and participation at family centres goes no further than an increased level of openness with staff and occasional evaluation forms'.

This echoes a survey undertaken of models of Family Centres. A self administered questionnaire included questions about the role of users offering a scale with the three categories of recipient of a service, participant in the centre, and controller of the centre. In addition questions addressed the opportunities for users to be volunteers and the existence of a user committee. It was surprising to discover that out of a sample of 76 centres, 26 described users as participants yet had no user volunteers and 16 of those 26 centres never featured a user committee (Stones, 1994).

Centrality of the Staff Team

Staff attitudes and skill are central in either assisting or impeding an empowering culture within the centre. The wider context of societal attitudes and status hierarchies can be an unhelpful influence. Some family centre workers have comparatively low status reflecting the value society places on work with children and they may find it difficult to relinquish the little they have without support and training. But an empowering culture relies on the willingness of professionals to give up a status of expert, through the sharing of their expertise and knowledge. This requires a level of confidence and maturity.

The culture of the wider organisation has significant influence on empowerment practice within a family centre. An agency which is bureaucratic and strictly hierarchical and which fails to consult staff on key issues neither models nor encourages empowerment. On the other hand a democratic style of management and leadership which respects staff and expects them to actively influence the direction of the organisation supports the pursuit of empowerment.

It is not easy to maintain an integrated approach. Addressing different systems and using varied methods can lead to multiplicity and confusion rather than integration. Staff are key in developing effective pathways between the parts of the centre and in ensuring that there is a sense of wholeness rather than fragmentation. The degree to which staff can work together across some of the distinct parts of a centre's programme and processes influences the extent of an integrated approach. An effectively integrated approach does require a lot of time working at issues in the staff team. Closed Days are essential for maintaining integrated practice through planning and reviewing work. Relationships within the staff team and between staff and users are paramount both for integration and empowerment. Parents identify the staff as the key factor facilitating their development and maintaining the centre's culture.

> Sue, a past chair of the Parents Council, viewa the approach of the staff as central to her growth. She felt staff treated her as an equal and recognised the potential within her which she had lost sight of. Christina, the current chair of the Parents Council, writes, 'I came up with...a long list of words that describe the staff, such as professional hard-working, supportive, informative, non-judgemental, understanding helpful, warm, friendly, welcoming and approachable...Staff are determined to ensure that parents are involved in policy and decision making and mutual respect which makes the Joint Parents Council/Staff meetings so successful'.

References

Bronfenbrenner U. (1979), *The Ecology of Human Development*, Harvard University Press, Cambridge.

Butt J. & Box L. (1998), *Family Centred: a Study of the Use of Family Centres by Black Families*, REU, London.

Daines R., Lyons K. & Parsloe P. (1990), *Aiming for Partnership*, Barnardos, Ilford.

Evans R. (1976), 'Some Implications of an Integrated Model of Social Work for Theory and Practice', in *British Journal of Social Work*, 6, 2, pp. 178-200.

Garbarino J. (1992), *Children and Families in the Social Environment*, Aldine de Gruyter, New York.

Goldstein H. (1973), *Social Work Practice: A Unitary Approach*, University of South Carolina Press, Columbia.

Pincus A. & Minahan A. (1973), *Social Work Practice: Model and Method*, F. E. Peacock Pub. Inc., Itasca, Illinois.

Preston-Shoot M. & Agass D. (1990), *Making Sense of Social Work, Psychodynamics, Systems and Practice*, Macmillan Press Ltd., Basingstoke.

Stones C. (1994), *Family Centres: Patterns, Profiles and Pressures*, M.Phil thesis, University of Bristol, unpublished.

3 What's Happening in France? The Settlement and Social Action Centre: Exchange as Empowerment

CHRIS WARREN-ADAMSON, with ANNE-MARIE DAVID and JEAN-PAUL DUCANDAS

Introduction

This chapter compares aspects of family centres in England (the integrated centre) and France (the centre socio-culturel). The material derives from a pilot study undertaken by the main author in order to establish a beginning framework for a more detailed study of French 'family centres'. Jean Paul Ducandas and Anne-Marie David are managers of centres in France. Programmes and priorities are discussed, as well as the directions set by the different centre movements in both countries. Judicial and protection frameworks for children are considered. Professional traditions are reviewed and we revisit the settlement and social action centre and consider practitioner and user exchange as empowerment.

The Family Centre and the Centre Socio-Culturel

British Family Centres of a certain kind appear to have an equivalent in the French Centre Socio-Culturel. This is a complex proposition we face when making generalisations about family centres. Typologies about family centres abound (Phelan, 1983; De'Ath, 1988; Holman, 1992; Warren, 1993), describing a range of centres, from those rooted in social work and a function in child protection procedures, to the community development centre, uneasily connected to social welfare. Nevertheless, a common model of family centre development is the Integrated Model (see the

Introduction to this text) and it is this which resembles the French Centre Socio-Culturel.

Six Family Centres in a south coast urban area (five local authority and one voluntary organisation) and ten centres across the channel, run by a quasi-governmental organisation (the Caisse d'Allocations Familiale – la CAF), have many similarities. Both are concerned with supporting 'the family' and are multi-purpose. They are concerned with community, employ social workers, community workers, educationalists, especially pre-school. In short, both sorts of centre embrace social welfare, adult education and community development.

This chapter begins to consider what influences the direction of the centres, how looking at other countries might help us towards an understanding of some of these questions? The two models of centre will be examined according to the following headings.

- Mix of activities – the range of services?
- History?
- The centre's relationship to family law and the judicial framework?
- Location in the local organisation of services?
- Auspices – who runs the centre?
- Professional tradition?

Mix of Activities – The Range of Services?

We turn to a more detailed look at two centres, one English, and the other French, which resemble each other in their range of social action. The technique for examining similarities and difference in the two centres draws on Bronfenbrenner's ecological framework (Bronfenbrenner 1979). He proposes the idea of a set of nested systems where a) the micro-system is the inner system – the location of child/parents, b) the exosystem – is the next outer system, the location of the tangible world which has a direct influence on the child and her/his inner system (school, work, church, neighbourhood, town council institutions and so on, c) the macro – system is the wide outer system connoting the broad ideological, historical framework in which the other systems are located. The link between two or more systems is called the meso-system (for example, the child and the school). In the following adaptation of the idea:

a) the centre is represented as the micro-system, the site for the centre's individual and groupwork with users;

b) the outside community – neighbourhood and beyond – is represented by the exo-system and;

c) the link between the inside system – the centre – and the outside world is represented by the terrain which is the link between systems, in Bronfenbrenner's language, the meso-system.

This framework was shared with centre managers and together a rich picture (Checkland 1981) of the centre was constructed, which prompted questions from a number of perspectives. The following is an account of two rich pictures (see figures 1 & 2).

The Family Centre

Let us focus on a) first. Here there is a series of groups represented by the ellipses and individual practice – play therapy, counselling, information, and informal advice. Some of the groups reflect squarely the social work agenda – teenage mothers group, parent and child game, day programme. Here direct goals include assessment and behavioural change and direct outcomes claimed include 'better parenting'. Individual practices share the same agenda, for example, counselling, play therapy, and you can add couples work, family therapy, and the occasional, specific behavioural programme. This could be termed secondary and tertiary prevention. Users are most likely to be referred to the centre in some way. The fathers' group may be for men who do not directly care for their children and are looking for direction in their role as 'absent fathers'. The crèche supports the work, makes it possible for parents to take time out both informally, and formally to participate in programmes of work. The crèche also provides work for some parents and supports other centres and initiatives. The drama group and the painting groups are directly recreational, and indirectly they are expressive – they support their members, develop social skills, and create friendships.

Groups in the exosystem have different relationships to the centre. The centre, by virtue of its early preventive stance and flexible and effective practice, may be asked to manage Surestart. And Playlink, a universal, early intervention project, which has independently earned its credentials,

31

may be based in the centre or may work collaboratively with the centre. Independent groups describe, firstly, the range of separate organisations which use the premises of the centre on which the centre has indirect influence. It is argued that they ensure full use of the space, represent in their constitution a broad front to the world of early intervention, and offer the possibility of connections, a network.

Drop-in and Community Mornings occupy a position between systems. They are a link between the inner and the outer. They are not just about a link with the neighbourhood but represent stepping over the threshold informally. Here also, they are seen as low priority by the social work agenda but score highly amongst users (Cigno, 1988). Lowest in priority might be the gardening group, albeit represented as a link between inner and outer. Goals might be expressive, offering support, or might include educational goals e.g. knowledge of soil technology, eating proper greens.

The direct role of centres in setting up independent organisations is hard to measure. First Stop is an example of a project, which combines the direct connection with the social work agenda (risk, keeping safe), with the method of primary preventive work. Other initiatives are hard to measure having been the outcome of professional networks of which centres are a part.

Le Centre Socio-Culturel

Centre 2 (see Figure 2) is run by the Caisse d'Allocations Familiales, a quasi Governmental Organisation which principally administers benefits to families but also runs a small social action programme in many areas of France.

Community work team – engaging in much external activity, this involves participation in a weekend city-wide arts festival, neighbourhood based on Saturday and meeting up with the other centres and neighbourhoods on the Sunday in the city centre. Other programmes include spare time activities for local families targeted at young and new families, with an emphasis on knowledge of other cultures and across the generations. A young people's video project engages in 7 video commentaries of the local neighbourhood. Such activity is the responsibility of the *animateur*, which we translate as social education community worker – one who promotes many skills in the *vie associative*, the participative world of large and small non-state organisations.

A team develops and promotes vocational activities for families, usually within-centre activity. This includes the nursery run by qualified day care workers. They call it the 'gang-plank to school'. Tied to this is the parent support group, a 'music for parents' initiative and 'vendredidoux' a Friday drop in for parents and their toddlers. Participants in these activities are also drawn into small community development activities, neighbourhood festivals, at Christmas and on Pancake Day.

A (global) social education day, which include spare time activities for all in the neighbourhood including holidays and what are called cultural and educative activities – art workshops most prominently. Under 'the child and the family', the programme comprises case work for marginalised families including the administration of the French RMI programme, the promotion of work and education to those on minimum benefits. There is also a 'training programme' for the equivalent of children in need, and those in need of protection. A children's clinic run by a children's nurse is part of basic health provision. Welfare rights including housing advice is a regular service.

Under the heading of social intervention, the centre has four programmes a) l'acceuil – more than reception, this is elevated in such centres to a programme of its own, recognising the importance of the first point of contact and therefore the knowledge and interpersonal skills which need to be demonstrated at this point, b) action against literacy, c) an inter-agency school inclusion project, d) a drop-in service for local young people.

Historical Perspective

Both centres come from different traditions of social intervention; the centre socio-culturel is rooted in the settlement movement, the family centre from its own more recent tradition. Cannan and Warren (2000) have compared the two traditions, highlighting the very different roots of both movements as well as the many and sometimes unexpected similarities.

The more recent Family Centre tradition in Britain, emerging in the late nineteen seventies, was a response to a changing welfare state and specifically the impact of change upon voluntary child care organisations which had invested in institutional care, for example, residential nurseries and homes. Such establishments were closed and re-opened (or sold and reinvested) as family centres (Birchall, 1982). Like the settlements, the word family was important. As well as a moral selling point, the family also had professional, psychological implication, meaning the acceptance of inter-connectedness between child, parents, wider family and community. Family work, family therapy, as well as community work, could be developed in such settings. The Church of England Children's Society (now Children's Society) was at the forefront of these developments (Phelan, 1983) and by appointing social workers and community workers it was soon managing, in the context of the parent and child, a mix of intervention methods, from the individual to the collective. By the time of Warren's survey of centres in 1990 (some 352 centres in England and Wales), the 1980s was shown to be the major period of growth of family centres, many now being run directly by local authorities (Warren, 1991). By the early nineties the name 'family centre' had become troublesome. For some, welfare had intruded upon the pre-school agenda and it could be rightly argued that numbers of previously straightforward day care centres had been transformed into family centres, thus diminishing the pot of day care provision. Cannan contributed to this debate, describing family centre development as 'the regulation of motherhood' (Cannan 1986a). She also identified a consistent dilemma for the centres ever since. Could the claim of the centres to be a sanctuary for women in particular be undermined by the stigma of welfare (Cannan 1986b)?

On the other hand, the French centre socio-culturel claims to have different roots. Pimlott's account of Toynbee Hall gives us a good picture of the Settlement tradition, which has its roots in the late nineteenth, early twentieth century (Pimlott 1935). The French centre social and centre socio-culturel have their roots in this same Anglo-Saxon tradition, in Britain and the United States (Bassot & Diémier, 1927). The French national organisation, the Fédération de Centres Sociaux, is closely allied to the British Association of Settlements and Social Action Centres (BASSAC), rather than the Family Centre Network (FCN), to which many English and Welsh family centres have at least a mailing link.

What is striking about a reading of Bassot and Diémier is its similarity with the language of contemporary accounts of family centres – multi-disciplinarity, flat hierarchies or collective organisation, range of methods from the individual to the collective, the idea of a range of services and activities undertaken under one roof, the struggle between targeted work and universal services, participation, commitment to the neighbourhood, and so on.

So, What is a Settlement?

The first settlements of the early nineteen hundreds owe their establishment to the early educationalists, often Christian Socialists, who combined a moral position about family life with a genuine concern for the exploitation and harm visited on the working class by an industrial Britain. The settlement was a bridgehead into poor neighbourhoods from which the reforming middle classes undertook their particular brand of anti-poverty social action.

> It captures a central tension in the movement: on the one hand seeking social progress by providing centres through which local people can widen their participation. On the other, fearing the spiritual vacuum into which industrialism seemed to have cast the urban working class, the settlers introduced 'higher' culture and ideals. It is not then about self-activity in the fullest sense though it has often gone some way towards this, in, for instance, support of the trade union movement in industrial disputes and in promoting co-operatives. Barnett and Addams did not seek to overturn the social order of the late nineteenth century but they certainly sought to change it and to do so in ways which would improve the material and spiritual life of the poor. Their Christian socialism (called social Christianity in the USA) and pacifism deplored violent confrontation and sought mediation and evolution instead (Carson, 1990). It is the socialism of Ruskin, the early William Morris, Fabianism and Tolstoy, not Marx. (Cannan and Warren, 2000)

In Britain in the post-war period, settlements had to redefine themselves in the modern welfare state and reflected a social action concerned with information, rights, benefits, social groupwork, adult education, community development, and community arts, with some of the passion of the sixties social action (for example, Collins et al., 1974). Some of the settlements, for example, Blackfriars and the Albany, were at the forefront of sixties and seventies community action, partners in critical thinking with other major community work projects, for example, the twelve British Community Development Projects (The CDPs) which ran from the late sixties into the early seventies (Corkey & Craig, 1978: 36–66). Nineties/millennial settlements whilst having still the flavour of their post war tradition now reflect a more measured, wider partnership based community development, along with service development, innovations in welfare, jobs, adult learning.

The Legal Framework and Centres' Relationship to the Judiciary

Unlike its French counterpart the English centre is specifically named in family legislation. Part 3 schedule 2 para 9 of the Children Act 1989 imposes a duty on local authorities as follows:

> 9.-(1) Every local authority shall provide such family centres as they consider appropriate in relation to children in their area.
>
> (2) 'Family centre' means a centre at which any of the persons mentioned in sub-paragraph (3) may –
> (a) attend for occupational, social, cultural or recreational activities;
> (b) attend for advice, guidance or counselling; or
> (c) be provided with accommodation while he is receiving advice, guidance or counselling.
>
> The persons are –
> (a) the child;
> (b) his parents;
> (c) any person who is not a parent of his but who has parental responsibility for him;
> (d) any other person who is looking after him.

It means that in theory local authorities may provide centres for the generality of children in their area (and their 'families'). However, UK centres have historically been run by or largely paid for by local authority social services departments (including service agreements with voluntary organisations). Paradoxically the family centre movement owes its flowering and its potential demise to the evolution of such departments. The requirements of such departments has always reflected a tension between their specific duties to 'regulate' families and their prevention brief. Nevertheless, to a degree, the liberalism of the social work culture has allowed experimentation, preventive practice.

In the late nineties, however, the duty to safeguard and protect children is leading to a narrow interpretation of centre practice (Warren-Adamson, 2000) and English centres are increasingly constrained to be a part of the protective, investigative arm of social services departments.[1]

---

[1] In contrast, video proceedings of the 1992 National Conference of French Social Centres show a French senior minister underlining the role of the centre in France in contributing directly to solidarity, social inclusion, and the local development of the neighbourhood.

So, ironically, schedule 2, paragraph 9 of the Children Act, 1989, describes French centre practice rather more closely than it does English centre practice. In France, safeguarding and protecting children has been observed to be a less contested, more collaborative process (Cooper et al., 1995). Helping a child and his or her family, when in danger or facing grave difficulty, brings into play two possible procedures, one administrative and one judicial. These two procedures, in the spirit of the legislation, are not conceived of as punishments or sanctions but as help. The administrative procedure seeks the written agreement of parents; the judicial procedure also seeks the agreement of parents but is imposed by the children's judge, the single magistrate who, in the French judicial system, operates under the framework of a non-criminal system for children. In France the children's judge is a juge d'instruction, in a broad sense a case manager (Cooper et al., op. cit. Wilford & Hetherington, 2000). For example, a juge des enfants in Normandy confirmed a typical caseload of 800 where perhaps less than a quarter of the caseload is similar in complexity to English and Welsh counterparts. The need for assessment and action in relation to serious matters before the court will be referred to a specific service for the court run by a voluntary organisation with a service contract.[2]

The French social worker in the centre will not be a stranger to work with the children's judge and may accompany a parent to the Tribunal. But she will have no concept of the consistent demand and pressure to assess families. Nor will she be conscious like her English counterpart of the general low regard society has for her profession (or professional class). Nor will she feel that the mistakes and transgressions of her profession are a special target for media. She may feel she is on the threshold but, unlike her English counterpart, she will not see herself quite yet as a paid-up member of the audit/blame culture.

Organisation of Services

English family centres operate within a local authority social services department constituency. Social services departments were set up in 1970, combining local authority departments for children, mental health, and older people. This was an age of genericism in practice and a focus on

---

[2] For example, in Rouen, l'Association Les Nids undertakes to run a 'Service d'Education et de Prévention'.

community. It was expected that social workers would work with, and be at home with all needs. In the new millennium, a similar structure remains, but specialism predominates and a new and highly contested welfare politics has taken the place of the old (Parton, 1994).

Some centres serve the whole social services constituency. In major urban areas particularly, centres offering a specialism – for example, family assessment in child protection – may serve the whole social services constituency. Most will serve a sub-division of a social services constituency – for example, an area of a town, and often a specific neighbourhood. Inter-agency partnership is a firm feature of protection procedures and is a requirement of the managerial structures of development and prevention initiatives.

French family centres operate within a social action district – a *circonscription d'action sociale.* Such districts were established in principle by the French Government as early as 1966. They were to be based on a territory of social work activity which demonstrated a degree of social homogeneity in the local economy and in lines of communication and which cut across the normal bureaucratic, vertical département structure. Within a *département* there would be several *circonscriptions*. A circular of 15.11.75 required:

- a concrete knowledge of local needs;
- the allocation of personnel and institutions necessary to respond to those needs;
- the concerted action of all of the practitioners of the social action district including a dialogue with the local population, elected representatives, and the local voluntary organisations.

Most *départements* have signed agreements to put the policy in place. A published critique of *circonscription* practice (Freynet 1995) is based on a circonscription in Western France, where there are six districts. The first agreement was signed here as late as 1980 and re-affirmed in 1986 during local authority de-centralisation. The signatories were the health and social work section of the *département* (DDAS), the national non-governmental organisation which supports the family through finance and a small social work/social action programme (CAF), and the agricultural insurance society (MAS), with the following statement:

...to promote in a concerted manner a social action programme whose aim is to help people and groups in difficulty, and to re-discover and develop their autonomy. Social workers...amongst others...will intervene at the individual and collective levels. Their objective is to enable each person to gain control of their life, to feel useful and recognised, as well as to think beyond their own situation and to become conscious of the need to act in solidarity with others. Social workers participate at the local level with the local population, members, partners in local organisations to promote social developments, according to the policy of their employers. (cited in Freynet, op. cit.)

Auspices

Of the six English centres in this small comparative study, five are run by the local social services department and one is run by a national voluntary organisation. The latter receives something under 50% of its funding from the same local authority and is therefore subject to much of the policy which influences the other five. This is not an unfamiliar pattern in England. Sometimes local authorities will require voluntary organisations only to run their centres.

A minority of centres, which emerge as a grass-roots initiative, may establish themselves as a separate voluntary organisation. Rarely, centres are run by a school[3] or by a combined education department and social services department.

The ten centres in our study are employed by the Caisse d'Allocations Familiales (CAF), the national quasi-governmental organisation in France responsible for financial support to families. The CAF has a small social action arm which varies in its budget and commitments nationally. In this *département* the *action sociale* of the CAF has decided to commit itself to ten centres. Centres may be run by the *département* direct, the *canton* direct, or by an *association* (voluntary organisation). Each centre has a different service agreement, but each receives proportions of money from la CAF, the *département*, and, for some, the *canton*.[4]

---

[3] A significant movement in the USA.

[4] In France, the *commune* is the smallest administrative unit (a village, small town), thereafter the *canton*, then the *arrondissement* (a grouping of cantons), *the département*, and *région* (a grouping of *départements*).

Professional Tradition

The managers of English centres may be social workers, less frequently teachers, nursery nurses, nurses, and community workers. A range of practitioners in social intervention may manage French centres, particularly trained social workers of different kinds. In both countries, a variety of professional roles are played in the centres, as well as lay or volunteer roles.

British social work training has been based on a two-year professional curriculum delivered at undergraduate or postgraduate levels in Universities. It produces social workers. French social work training – located in local non-governmental organisations in higher education institutes – provides three year training for four social work roles. They are the *assistant social* (the social worker – occupying a variety of settings but not associated in the public's mind as in the UK with the particular role of case manager); the *éducateur spécialisé* (a role rooted in education, working individually and collectively in specialist settings – group settings and often running the assessment service for the *juge des enfants*), *conseillière en économie sociale* (a role also rooted in education, individually and more collectively, located in the domestic space); and the *moniteur éducateur* (also rooted in education and particularly located in the group setting). Another key role in the centre is the *animateur/trice*, an educational role associated with community education, community arts, play, cultural animation, and, sometimes, what the French call *développment local* – community or neighbourhood work.

Conclusion

This albeit superficial consideration of some similarities and differences between two apparently similar types of practice encourages a heightened curiosity about the European, educational tradition of social work and specifically the potential role of the social action centre or settlement. It also highlights an enduring concern about public social work in the Anglo-Saxon tradition (especially Britain and the United States) where it seems to be in a major predicament, having become associated with a narrow and much contested, protection-based *welfare* tradition. In contrast, the *European* tradition has educational roots, in adult and informal education, and cultural and community development. It appears to enjoy greater national consensus and appears to be a more productive domain for practice.

An action research study is to take place to compare practices in both traditions. This area appears to be undeveloped. There are reviews of the difficulties of such research (Connelly & Stubbs, 1997), some descriptive material comparing services and welfare institutions (Colton, Hellinikx & Williams, 1997), documentary analysis of practice and policy material (Cannan, 1992), but language and cultural hurdles mean that there has been little close analysis of the way day to day practice is negotiated in a European tradition.

An exception is work by Brunel University colleagues in their study of child protection in France (Cooper et al., 1995). Their methodology of practitioners shadowing their French counter-parts and analysis of their reports and experience showed a much more collaborative, less contested approach to the judicial, protective context of work with children and their families. Such a methodology will be adopted in this study but extended to the world of supporting families and community development. Comparisons between French and English family resource centres are proposed, using partnership or shadowing techniques – practitioners closely accompany counter-parts in day to day practice and are then debriefed.

The study also aims to explore and alert practitioners to one practical method for user empowerment in family resource centres, namely national and international exchanges for users. User national and international exchange as an empowerment measure is reported in Bourget-Daitch and Warren (1997) about French local practice – and is also evident in accounts by Togher Family Centre users in Ireland (Adamson, this text).

Dipping our toes into the French cultural world of family support and social and community development has powerful consequences. We come to France and we revisit settlements and social action centres. An initial comparison of centres leads us on to another step, to find ways for practitioners and users alike to experience and learn from the day to day detail of each other's worlds, and to hope, as it has for others, that it will be empowering.

References

Bassot M-J. & Diémer M. (1927), Les Centres Sociaux, first published in *Cahiers du Redressement Français*, and re-published in *Ouvertures: La Revue des Centres Sociaux*, 1991-1992, No. 6–7.

Bourget-Daitch M-R. & Warren C. (1997), 'Act local, think global', in Cannan C. & Warren C. eds, *Social Action with Children and Families – a Community Development Approach to Child and Family Welfare*, Routledge, London.

Bronfenbrenner U. (1979), *The Ecology of Human Development*, Harvard University Press, Cambridge.

Cannan C. (1992), *Changing Families, Changing Welfare*, Harverster Wheatsheaf, Hemel Hempstead.

Cannan C. & Warren C. (eds), (1997), *Social Action with Children and Families – a Community Development Approach to Child and Family Welfare*, Routledge, London.

Cannan C. & Warren C. (2001), 'Family centres in the settlement tradition', in Jeffs T. & Gilchrist R. eds. *Settlements, Social Change and Community Action – Good Neighbours*, Jessica Kingsley, London.

Checkland, P. (1981), *Systems Thinking, Systems Practice*, John Wiley & Sons, Chichester.

Collins S., Curno P., Harris J. & Turner J. (1974), *Community Arts*, RKP, London.

Colton M., Hellinikx W. & Williams M. eds (1997), *International Perspectives on Family Support*, Arena, Aldershot.

Connelly N. & Stubbs P. (1997), *Trends in Social Work and Social Work Education Across Europe*, NISW, London.

Cooper A., Hetherington R., Baistow K., Pitts J. & Spriggs A. (1995), *Positive Child Protection – a View from Abroad*, Russell House, Lyme Regis.

Corkey D. & Craig G. (1978), 'CDP: Community work or class politics', in Curno P. ed *Political Issues and Community Work*, RKP, London.

De'Ath E. (1988), The Family Centre Approach, Briefing Paper, Focus on Families No. 2, The Children's Society, London.

Freynet M-F. (1995), *Les Médiations du Travail Social*, Chronique Sociale, Lyon.

Holman R. (1992), *Research Highlights,* National Children's Bureau, London.

Parton N. (1992), 'Problematics of government, (post) modernity and social work', *British Journal of Social Work*, 24: pp. 9–32.

Phelan J. (1983), *Family Centres – a Study*, The Children's Society, London.

Pimlott, J. A. R. (1935), *Toynbee Hall: Fifty Years of Social Progress 1884–1934*, Dent, London.

Warren C. (1993), *Family Centres and the Children Act 1989 – a Training and Development Handbook*, Tarrant Publications, Arundel.

Warren-Adamson C. (2000) 'We must not bypass family centres', in *Community Care* 5.10.2000, p.15.

Wilford G. & Hetherington R. (2000), 'Experiences of child care services in Europe', in *Context*, 5.8.2000.

Figure 1: Family Centre (England)

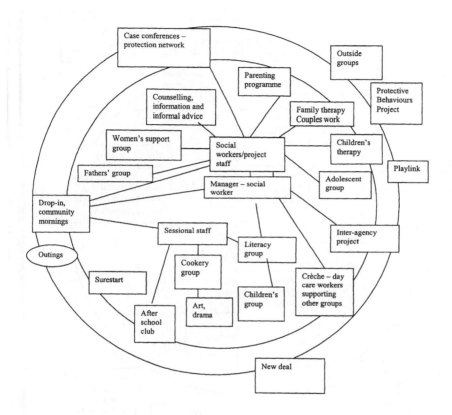

Case conferences –
protection network

Outside
groups

Parenting
programme

Protective
Behaviours
Project

Counselling,
information and
informal advice

Family therapy
Couples work

Women's support
group

Social
workers/project
staff

Children's
therapy

Playlink

Fathers' group

Manager – social
worker

Adolescent
group

Drop-in,
community
mornings

Inter-agency
project

Outings

Sessional staff

Literacy
group

Surestart

Cookery
group

Crèche – day
care workers
supporting
other groups

After
school
club

Art,
drama

Children's
group

New deal

Figure 2: Centre Socio-Culturel (France)

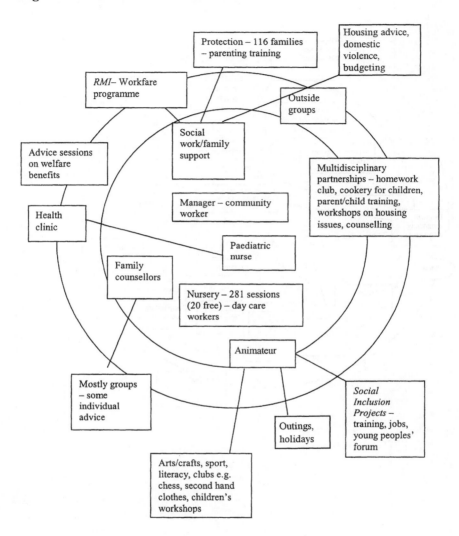

Protection – 116 families – parenting training

Housing advice, domestic violence, budgeting

RMI– Workfare programme

Outside groups

Social work/family support

Advice sessions on welfare benefits

Multidisciplinary partnerships – homework club, cookery for children, parent/child training, workshops on housing issues, counselling

Health clinic

Manager – community worker

Paediatric nurse

Family counsellors

Nursery – 281 sessions (20 free) – day care workers

Animateur

Mostly groups – some individual advice

Social Inclusion Projects – training, jobs, young peoples' forum

Outings, holidays

Arts/crafts, sport, literacy, clubs e.g. chess, second hand clothes, children's workshops

4 Education and Empowerment in Family Centres

PAUL MONTGOMERY and CLAIRE COOK

In this chapter two different approaches to empowerment will be considered. The first case study will examine a family centre parenting programme run for women who had identified that most of these sorts of courses did not fit their needs. The example shows how empowerment can be achieved by due consultation. The second example, known as the Birthday Book, shows how community education can be made relevant to users' needs and wishes. In both cases it can be seen that whilst the workers were important and had many useful skills to offer, these skills needed to be shaped by the users if they were to be of practical benefit.

Abingdon and Didcot Family Centres

The examples in question are both NCH-Action for Children projects jointly funded with Oxfordshire Social Services. These centres are open-access facilities aiming to promote the personal development of parents/carers as well as supporting their involvement with their children, based on the concepts of partnership, parental responsibility and empowerment. The atmosphere is easy-going and there is a positive culture, which is highly inclusive. The centres broadly follow the neighbourhood model where staff have very flexible roles. There is a wide range of activities, and local participation is high. There are also some referrals from social services, where some children are deemed to be at risk.

To put this material into context it is important to know something of the areas around each centre. The Independent Needs Survey (1987) showed that Abingdon has had to deal with both a rise in population and a reduction in the amount of day care available, and this situation has not changed in recent years. Ethnic minorities make up only 1.4% of the population of 30,000 people in the town. More than half of their respondents had taken up residence in the town during the last five years, and a third of the total said that they had no other family links locally. This figure is significant in helping to explain the number of isolated, anxious and depressed mothers with young children in this area. 20% of households with young children had only one-parent and workers currently report that they have fewer than five families using the centre in which both parents are living together. Unemployment is currently estimated at 4.9% in the ward in which the Abingdon centre is located; this is one of the few wards to show an increase. The social services department has reported that this area has one third of all the town's childcare referrals but only one sixth of the population. Data from the probation department and child guidance service was not available, but workers from these agencies reported subjectively that many of their cases were centred on South Abingdon, and certainly at a rate out of proportion with its population.

This situation is not greatly different at Didcot. This town's needs survey piloted in the family centre's catchment area of Didcot showed an influx of new families to the area, a lack of play resources for children and insufficient public transport. The expected growth of young families is demonstrated by the county structure plan to build another 5000 new homes by 2004. This is reflected in the usage of the family centre where the predominant child user is under two years old.

The Parenting Course

Users had identified through the drop-in sessions that one of their problems was in managing the behaviour of their children and their inability to use groups in the past to help rectify this. To consider this, two users were taken on an observational visit to a course at a local college of further education. This helped to explain some of the difficulties that such courses present. Many of the mothers complained that previous groups had been patronising and used unrealistic examples which they found difficult to apply to their situation. Some users said that they saw the facilitators of these groups as 'middle class white married women with a husband and that the examples usually showed well-off couples with one small child whose behaviour they wanted to change'. This group had one member who was a lone parent with three children aged eight, seven and three, one of whom was disabled and thus it was important to ensure that this group would address her needs. Many parents felt that they were not really able to explain to workers how they saw their problems and situation, because they feared that the result might be that they 'had their children taken away'. They wanted a course that would focus more equally on the children as well as on themselves and that would work with both adults and children. This would, they said, reduce their feelings of guilt and blame over their children's poor behaviour and allow them to receive the practical support they needed as well as the skills. Many of the mothers were highly motivated and keen that their lives take a turn for the better as soon as possible, and that one way in which this could be done would be to modify their children's behaviour.

The users established that they wanted to regain more control over their children and that the course would focus on the more serious issues, the children's challenges to their authority. The parents wanted the workers to support this by reinforcing specific behavioural objectives on a week-to-week basis through the crèche, drop-ins and after-school clubs, but in such a way that the children were not be stigmatised. The users agreed that they would attend all the sessions and bring their children into the centre as often as was practicable to enable this support work to happen.

It was agreed that a series of groups would be run over five weeks which would have child care available to allow them to focus properly on the work to be done. There would be formal sessions with mothers on Wednesday mornings for two hours and then this work would be followed up throughout their children's contact with the centre. Each formal session was discussed with other workers from the centre to ensure that consistency could be maintained. All participants were offered one-to-one support as necessary and take-up of this was high. Each session was to have a small number of behavioural goals attached to learning objectives and these would be client-driven.

A strictly behavioural approach seemed to be the most appropriate way to help users achieve their goals, given the well defined needs which the users reported. NCH Action for Children have a behavioural programme known as 'Handling Children's Behaviour' and in consultation with other workers, it was decided that this would provide a good basis from which to work. There is also a handbook which the users liked, particularly its cartoon and list-based format. However, the programme is almost entirely centred on the parents, and the users had felt that they were being blamed for the behavioural problems their children were presenting. They recognised that while they have to accept some responsibility for their children's behaviours, they could not accept all of it. To help remove some of this element, it was felt that a better partnership was to combine work with all parties. Clearly this would involve some sessions with parents on their own, but it seemed important that the parents, who were largely lone mothers, needed to get some practical help in implementing the modifications they wanted. The family centre is, of course, well placed to give this assistance, primarily by modelling appropriate strategies and reminding them of the goals they had set themselves. This more integrated approach also involved all the workers at the centre, which would give long-term continuity to the work.

In the first session, a fifteen-minute segment of a video from 'Network First' showed a concentrated behaviour modification course run by Marlborough House in Swindon. This was chosen because it has many lone parents demonstrating many of the difficulties the group also has to deal with, and that the behavioural management methods used are very similar to those used on this programme. For example, an early scene shows a lone mother dealing with two children fighting in an old car. It was also important that the tape was not seen to contain only middle class examples. The users previously taken to a course on modifying children's behaviour at a local college of further education had been shown a case from a QED documentary about work at the Maudsley Hospital. The users complained that this example was extreme and that their children were not 'nutters'. The therapist on the QED video, a psychiatrist who was exhibiting a very controlling relationship with the parents, did not help matters.

In the second session, the group was asked to generate a list of tasks that parents do, in the form of a job description, and we considered whether, if such a job were to be advertised, any applicants would emerge. This proved useful in terms of building self-esteem, and if the clients were to be properly empowered, this was going to be a real issue. We went on to get individual members of the group to generate lists of their household rules, bearing in mind that rules needed to be realistic and enforceable. We also discussed the importance of the fact that all the carers of the children needed to be in agreement with the programme if the children were to receive a consistent approach. This was clearly an issue for the one member who had a partner, but also for another whose parents looked after one of her children most weekends, lest others undermine their newly enhanced feelings of control. In the first two weeks, a great deal had already been accomplished. The mothers were happy that the sessions were going as they had wanted and were pleased that their wishes and feelings were being confirmed. Attendance remained at 100% and already reports of improved behaviour were coming from the mothers and from workers at the centre.

All group members spoke highly of the programme and reported significant improvements in the behaviour of their children and in their relationships with them. Comments included:

> The children have calmed down, seem more reasonable, but that has a lot to do with me changing my attitude and views on behaviour, (expectations).

One mother said:

> I have been watching the kids and keeping a diary of their misbehaviour and its funny how I now don't see them as being as naughty as I used to.

All mothers described the programme as 'very helpful'. The intention to set up a better partnership with the mothers by basing the work around the family centre seemed to have worked as one mother pointed out that she felt comfortable in the group 'because I knew the people involved and that they would support me...'.

The family centre workers said they thought that all the children had improved, some more than others, but that all had made significant improvements, most obviously at mealtimes and in the incidence of tantrums. Feedback from the children was less easy to gain. One said that her mother had got stricter but that it was easier to go to sleep because her brother did not play up at bedtime. Another said that he had to clear up his toys before going to bed now, but that his mum helped him.

This example seemed to show some of the main principles of practical empowerment. The users were listened to, having been given some concrete information on which to base their views. The process of taking users on a course with a view to hearing how it might be improved is not a new idea. However, developing the idea into the day-to-day world of the family centre is not necessarily easy.

It may have been significant that a social work student, rather than one of the centre's full-time staff ran the programme. The users were in no doubt that the student would be gone on a given date. It may be that as a student the clients felt that they could be more open about what was actually going on in their households and that perhaps they felt a greater degree of control over the proceedings. Students are a commonplace feature in many social work agencies including settings such as family centres and this sort of imaginative use of them benefits all. In any event moving the intervention style to a position where the clients were empowered allowed this programme of behaviour modification to succeed in a way in which many previous ones had not.

The Birthday Book

Didcot Family Centre is committed to helping parents develop their strengths, self-esteem and confidence. Promoting literacy is seen as a way not only to meet these aims but also to provide educational opportunities and the chance for parents to gain practice and knowledge. Previous experience of adult literacy groups showed that whilst many parents wished to become involved, they did not continue to attend. Maintaining commitment and making the group accessible both in content and practicality was deemed crucial in attracting participants.

The Family Centre was due to reach a milestone – its two year anniversary. The project manager thought it was important to mark the occasion and the two ideas of community education and marking the anniversary started to intermingle. Discussions with parents and the Community Education Department were held and the idea emerged that parents could develop their literacy skills whilst writing about their views on the activities that went on at the family centre. The Birthday Book became a programme which was set up in conjunction with the parents so that they could develop and experience all aspects of literacy. This was seen as a stepping stone towards other educational opportunities. The programme would also take into account adult learning theories such as building on parents' existing skills and experiences. The tasks incorporated interviewing people, writing up by hand, developing questionnaires and typing using computers. It also involved learning life skills such as photography, learning about deadlines and expectations of others, doing what you said you would, displaying items, and involving their children.

The idea was that the children's work would be incorporated into the book as well. This gave the parents a great sense of personal achievement as well as empowering them to say what they felt was good about Didcot Family Centre. Most of the work that was produced was in no way censored and the things that were oncluded were the views, ideas and words from the actual consumers who were interviewed or who wrote the book. The community education worker, Catherine de Lord, was to facilitate the group and encourage user involvement and develop their literacy skills through giving their ideas and views and helping them find different ways of overcoming their problems.

The user group was self selected; they were the consumers who had shown an interest in adult education at various times when the topic was discussed at the family centre. We found that they were all people who had not completed school for one reason or another. For example, one had been in trouble with the police in her teenage years and had not finished school because of her criminal activities, and other people had babies as teenagers and had not finished school. One participant had been abused in many ways as a child and felt she had not benefited from her education because of this disadvantage.

Setting up the group was difficult logistically. It was very hard to meet a varying number of needs in terms of time when there was space free and when there were workers available. In the end other activities happening at the Family Centre did dictate to a certain degree the day on which we could hold the course. The timing was crucial as many of the users not only had under five-year-old children but also had school age children. So, to make the group accessible we had to fit into their lifestyles – it was no good saying 'well we've got to run this group at this time because this is when we've got the workers'. We really had to think about what it is like to be a single parent, dropping children off, picking them up, and often we provided food, either breakfast or lunch. There were a couple of occasions when independently parents brought snacks for each other. This not only helped people reach deadlines but also added to the cohesiveness of the group. The money to run this project came from the basic skills budget which meant the deadline for completion of the group was flexible, although we did have to take into account the end of the financial year, so we gave ourselves a whole year to complete the task of producing the book.

The problem in setting up the group always revolved around the care of the children of the participants. If a crèche had not been provided, parents would not have participated. Childcare needs have to be addressed appropriately when attempting to empower parents, particularly women. There were various other levels of support, an important one being the Community Education department; the head of the Community Education department in Didcot was extremely supportive in setting up this course. This was not something they normally did. We required them to adapt a regional literacy course to meet not only the parents' individual needs but also the needs of the project and the Family Centre. All those involved had their own agenda and the Community Education department needed to show that the money, which we had applied for, had been used appropriately. The family centre wanted their book to show other family centres what had happened in setting up a brand new project, including parents' views and the views of the children. The parents themselves had set their own agendas with their own aims and objectives about what they hoped to achieve by the end of the course. Once the group was up and running, the workers at the family centre gave a lot of ongoing and regular support during each week before the next session, helping to deal with any specific problems.

A major problem was that the programme took a long time to get off the ground. Initially everyone was very keen and well motivated but the application for funding took a long time to be processed. As the Birthday Book project aimed to meet the individual needs of the users involved, so the community education tutor held meetings with each of the women who were interested to ask them what they hoped to achieve at the end of the sessions as well as completing the set task. It was quite complex working out what the outcome measures might be as the group had a three-fold brief. We could have ended with a book which everyone could say had been a success, but individual parents would not have reached their set goals.

Participants in the Birthday Book set up the rules of the group. They met at the beginning of January 1998 to look at what tasks they wanted to achieve, what they wanted to go in the book and what their ideas were, and how they felt they could achieve them. See appendix for tasks and topics which were incorporated in the book.

Different people brought different skills. One person was very computer literate who was extremely useful in encouraging the others to have a go and showing what she could produce. This gave everybody much encouragement to have a go themselves. Another asset was commitment; parents were very keen to produce this book. They seemed to want to have something collective and tangible at the end of the course and not to have people leave with their individual pieces of work. As they were all, to some extent, beholden to each other, it encouraged them to work together and become absorbed into this piece of work.

There was a lot of peer pressure from each participant to finish tasks and quite often people said to others that they were disappointed that someone had not completed their particular task by a set time. This self-regulation seemed far more effective in getting the desired result than pressure from the tutor.

However, there had to be a degree of flexibility. If someone's child was ill and they could not come when they had a key task which needed doing, before something else could be completed, we had to be able to wait for a week and do something else. For instance, someone was interviewing and their response sheets were needed but they could not come in for two weeks because their child had chicken pox. This meant that some parts of the work were temporarily delayed.

Discussion

Empowerment practice is not just about how we get consumers involved. They must also feel able to make suggestions and have them taken up. As neighbourhood-based centres which also do specific pieces of work, each has a broad-based knowledge of the local community. The Centres reflect the local culture and ethnicity in their staffing as well as providing a broad variety of services, some in conjunction with other voluntary and statutory agencies. The places are seen by the people who them us as family resource centres. People see them as maybe not necessarily being able to provide what individuals want all the time but as a place where they can find someone else who can help. As well as knowing our locality, parents and staff together are involved in many local and countywide groups, including Under Five's Liaison Group, and the Family Centre Forum.

At an individual level, the empowerment ethos is now part of integrated practice within the work being addressed at the Family Centre. It is a way of life, part of the value system. We believe it is crucial to be open and honest about staff and consumer relationships and where the power lies. We try to clarify both ways – what is negotiable and what is not, where we can make a difference and where we cannot. We are aware that some of the parents have low incomes, and could be classed as being on the poverty level, but as individual people in a small project there is little we can do about it apart from dealing with it on a one-to-one level, supporting people dealing with debt issues.

This does not mean that we are not attempting to address difficult issues. Some of the concerns that parents have complained about include favouritism, parental responsibilities and access to services. However, we try to find a way that we can work together to improve things. We offer a 'Time to Talk' service for anyone who wishes to use it which was very popular throughout, helping individuals to have their own time to be able to work through some of the tasks and problems they had taken on board.

Staff in general act as catalysts or enablers, encouraging and nurturing both parents and children as they become involved. The crèche that ran alongside this project produced some artwork by the children which was incorporated into the book. Parents learnt individual skills such as taking photographs by having a photographer coming to teach them. We feel that these are skills for life and that users will have learnt things they can use in the future.

The evidence of success is seen in people who achieved the goals they set themselves. In some people we saw overt changes, in their characters, their appearance, how they behaved towards their children, how they responded to adults, the language they were using. In many cases their writing improved, they felt more confident, their self esteem was raised, their participation increased. Many people volunteered to do things that they had not done before. Participants also talked about improved health. Some said they were considering their use of anti-depressants or they had gone to the doctor to talk about what else they might take which did not make them feel quite so controlled by the medication. Another thing which made us feel people were being successful was that they were full of ideas and expressing them. They felt empowered to say what they thought.

The Birthday Book has been displayed around Didcot, in the library, the civic hall, the family centre, and at NCH-Action for Children. There was a tremendous sense of achievement, loss and relief on its completion. Now the group has finally come to an end, the highs and lows of the whole process are talked about in wistful, sentimental terms and there is an ongoing and, hopefully, permanent change in many of the participants. Included in the feedback materials were many constructive comments:

> Friday mornings will never be the same again.
> What can we do next?
> I'm meeting with a careers tutor to look at doing GCSE Psychology. I've always wanted to do it.
> If there's ever any typing or help you need at the family centre just let me know.
> I'd never done anything like this before. I didn't realise how much I would enjoy it.
> It was great. The women in the group had a good chat about this and that and really helped each other.

Conclusion

In their different ways these two case studies reveal a great deal of the practicalities of empowerment. Many commentators seem to say that it is difficult to truly empower users. In some settings this is undoubtedly true, as there are legal and other constraints which prevent full empowerment. However these obstacles are not universal and there are a great many circumstances where it is necessary and appropriate for users of family centres to shape the way in which their needs are met. If workers take the time actively to listen to consumers and ensure that conditions are in place to make it possible, good outcomes can be achieved.

Acknowledgements

All users and workers at Abingdon and Didcot family centres;
Ann Buchanan and Teresa Smith at the Department of Social Policy and Social Work, University of Oxford;
NCH – Action for Children.

5 Francophone Centres in Québec, Canada –Two Case Studies

IRENE KYLE and MAUREEN KELLERMAN, with ALLA IVASK

This chapter profiles two *centres de ressources familiales* – family resource centres – which feature in a major study of Canadian family support programmes (Kyle & Kellerman 1998).[1] The two projects chosen – amongst many profiled in the report – are smaller and similar in scope to UK centres. *Centres de ressources familiales* appear to be generic words for a range of projects. For example, in Québec, unless specified in the name, centres are normally called *Maisons de la Famille*. In British Columbia, they are called *Family Places*.

Le Carrefour Familial Hochelaga (Montreal, Québec)

Introduction

This is a centre for popular education and a family resource program situated in south-east Montreal. Its goals are to develop self-reliance among participants, to foster a sense of personal and collective empowerment, to reinforce participants' self-esteem, and to support parents and stimulate children. Services include a drop-in reception area, parent education, personal growth and support groups, recreational activities, a *halte-garderie* (a part-time child care program to provide parent relief) and a sewing workshop to provide support to young mothers. Le Carrefour has also developed a number of programs for fathers and men, including support groups and short-term emergency housing.

---

[1] The Report is representative in its selection of the full regional diversity of Canada - Atlantic (Newfoundland, Nova Scotia, Prince Edward Island and New Brunswick); Québec; Ontario; Western (Manitoba, Saskatchewan, Alberta and the Territories); Pacific (British Columbia and the Yukon). In choosing case studies for the study, evaluators had to ensure that each centre had an employment support program.

Le Carrefour has a Board of Directors of eight members, including program participants directly involved in the activities of le Carrefour, one employee representative, and various community resource people. Le Carrefour works as a collective with five full-time and 3 part-time staff and about fifty volunteers. Staff experience and training represents adult and popular education, early childhood education, community development, social work, business, theology and accounting.

Community Context

Hochelaga-Maisonneuve is a long-established, inner city neighbourhood near the Olympic Stadium, inhabited by a low-income, mostly French-speaking population. There are very few immigrants. Over time, the neighbourhood has been significantly affected by the decline in Montreal's manufacturing sector and the associated loss of blue collar jobs. The unemployment rate in the neighbourhood is very high and residents have little formal education; many receive social assistance. The growing poverty has contributed to a variety of social problems, including isolation and high mobility within the neighbourhood, as young people leave home early and new families move into the neighbourhood, attracted by low cost housing. Unemployment has created stresses on family life as families struggle with poverty. In particular, many men have become discouraged with the lack of employment opportunities and may experience a lack of direction.

Almost half the families participating in le Carrefour's programs are single-parent families; about 15% are headed by single parent fathers. Many families include step-parents or temporary partner of the parent. Members of extended families, often including two adult generations of the same families, take part in activities at le Carrefour.

The main location is in a three storey, 4 unit apartment building – the basement apartment is used for meetings and group activities, the ground floor apartment is used for meetings and a drop-in reception area. La Maison Oxygène (short-term housing) is on the second floor, and le Carrefour's offices are on the third floor. The *Halte-Garderie* is in a seven-room, ground floor apartment round the corner, and the sewing workshop is a block away.

History

At a meeting convened by several Roman Catholic parishes in the Hochelaga-Maisoneuve neighbourhood in 1976, three women set up a booth to collect information about the needs of local families. The results were unanimous; families wished to overcome their feelings of isolation. So a committee of volunteers was formed that included the women and a parish priest. They applied for and received a small Local Initiatives grant from the federal government to form a neighbourhood family support program and rented an apartment which became the meeting place that families had requested.

As the years passed, le Carrefour developed various programs in response to the needs of local families. The *Halte Garderie* established in 1985 was expanded and is now located in a seven roomed apartment. During the past decade, men have become much more involved in le Carrefour, so that some services have been created specifically to suit their needs.[2] La Maison Oxygène was set up in 1988 and the sewing workshop started in 1991.

Program Components

Many participants become involved with le Carrefour through a drop-in reception service, which offers an informal place for neighbourhood residents to meet together with volunteers. As staff and volunteers become familiar with participants and get to know their needs, they refer them to other activities. Over time, participants are encouraged to become volunteers and take on responsibility for various aspects of the program; ongoing training and support are provided to assist them in their developing leadership skills.

Parent Education and Support

- *Parent education*: Nobody's Perfect program is offered to parents of children 0-5 years old;
- *Parents' mutual aid group*: for parents of children 6-18 years old;

---

[2] Le Prix Persillier-Lachapelle was awarded by the provincial government to le Carrefour familial Hochelaga in 1996 in recognition of excellence in working with fathers and men.

- *Fathers'/men's mutual aid group*: discussion topics include men's relationships with their own fathers, communication within the family, and their relationships with their partners and children;
- *Personal follow-ups*: staff provide individualised support to participants;
- *Sewing program for young mothers*: includes two groups; each group meets one day a week while children attend the *Halte Garderie*. Participants make items for themselves and for the annual bazarre. Materials and supplies are donated by local business and manufacturers. The objectives of the program are: to reduce the isolation of the mothers (about 80% are single-mothers), to raise their self-esteem and confidence, to encourage them to take personal responsibility, work as a team member and develop partnerships;
- *Family outings and celebrations*: activities for families and children include a Christmas party, sugaring off, and apple picking;
- *Family camps*: provide vacations for low income participants; forty families attend two week sessions at a camp operated by another organisation, accompanied by two workers from le Carrefour.

Child Care Program

- *Halte garderie*: is a respite child care program which provides low-cost, part-time child care for up to thirty children at a time, aged birth to five years. The service is open two and a half days per week. The primary goal of the program is to offer respite to parents and to enable them to participate in le Carrefour's activities. The specific objectives are: to offer an educational service for children, to familiarise children with a group program, to provide a safe and warm atmosphere, to promote each child's physical, emotional, social, and cognitive development, depending on his/her age and individual pace, to respect the specific needs of children experiencing psychological and socio-emotional difficulties. The facility includes separate rooms for infants, toddlers and pre-schoolers, and a room for naps. Hot meals are provided on the two full days the program operates. The program is co-ordinated by two staff members with training in child development. They in turn train and supervise a team of twenty volunteers including grandparents, mothers of older children and other long term participants at le Carrefour. The program provides an opportunity for a number of volunteers to provide parenting skills that they are able to use at home with their own families.

Housing

- *La Maison Oxygène* ('oxygen house'): This program provides temporary housing for fathers (with or without children) who are experiencing marital or family problems; their average stay is three months. Its name refers to the need for residents to get 'a breath of fresh air', or a respite from stress. It is located in a three bedroom apartment in le Carrefour's main building. Residents are responsible for meal preparation and housekeeping and must attend school, work, or some kind of day program while in residence. While staff are not directly involved in running the apartment, they provide advice, help to integrate the residents into le Carrefour's other programs, and link residents to other neighbourhood resources. Additional peer support is provided by former residents who also offer advice on the program's ongoing operations. *La Maison Oxygène* was first subsidised as a pilot project by Centraide (United Way); it now receives regular grants from Centraide and various charitable donations of about $30,000 annually.

Other Adult Education and Recreation Programs

- *Reception meeting place*: is located in the kitchen on the first floor of the building, a drop-in service which offers participants a sympathetic ear, information and referral, as well as opportunities to share experiences and provide mutual aid. It often serves as an entry point to other activities in le Carrefour. The reception service also provides volunteers with a place to become involved and learn new skills;
- *Personal growth groups*: for women and for men and women together. These groups involve discussion, relaxation and other activities designed to facilitate personal exploration;
- *Informal monthly dinners for men*: food is prepared by participants with funding from le Carrefour;
- *Weekly vacations*: facilitated by staff for separate groups of up to fifty women to enable participants to have fun, take a break and develop friendships in an informal atmosphere. The women gather at an outdoor recreation centre on an island in the Montreal area; the men rent a cottage;

- *Annual bazaar*: involves many participants who assist in planning and carrying out the event; the proceeds are to finance the family camps and other activities at le Carrefour.

Community Development: Education, Leadership Development and Advocacy

- *Community education sessions*: are open to everyone and include lunch presentations on various issues (for example, drugs, children), sessions on current events (for example, politics, referenda, the public dept, elections), and presentations by community groups (according to participants' interests);
- *Volunteer training development*: the involvement of participant volunteers is an essential component of all le Carrefour's activities. One of the organisation's main goals is to offer training and support to encourage participants to become involved in le Carrefour and the neighbourhood and to take greater responsibility for their personal lives and their lives as citizens. To accomplish this, le Carrefour offers volunteers training in reception and child care work, and offers information and support to volunteers who are involved in internal and community committees;
- *Public awareness and advocacy*: le Carrefour is involved in a number of neighbourhood events and community initiatives on various social issues, such as a public awareness campaign to promote sensitive images of fathering and the *Forum Pour l'Emploi,* a one day community forum on employment issues. Le Carrefour involves participants in these initiatives to demonstrate the importance of taking part in socio-economic issues that have an impact on their lives, such as social assistance reform, in order to better understand their circumstances and to develop their ability to take action on their own behalf and to protect their rights.

Community Linkages

Le Carrefour refers participants to other community agencies according to their needs, for example, in areas related to food, family violence and substance abuse. Representatives of le Carrefour are involved at the neighbourhood level:

- On the board of the Conseil de Développement Local (local development council) which brings together 37 neighbourhood agencies;
- With Table Enfance-Famille (forum of organisations concerned with child and family issues) and its inter-sectorial committee which analyses neighbourhood needs;
- With le Collectif du 8 Mars (March 8 collective) to plan International Women's Day events.

At the city level, representatives of le Carrefour are involved with:

- The board of the Regroupement des Haltes-Garderies (Network of Respite Child Care Services);
- Cencertation Hommes Montréal (Montreal Men Together);
- Le Front d'Action Populaire en Réaménagement Urbain (FRAPRU; public action front for urban development);
- La Table de Regroupement des Organismes Voluntaires en Education Populaire (TROVEP) group of voluntary agencies involved in popular education;
- le Regroupement Intersectoriel des Organismes Communautaires de Montréal (RIOCM; intersectoral network of community agencies in Montreal.

At the provincial level le Carrefour is a member of:

- le Fédération des Femmes du Québec (Federation of Québec Women);
- l'Association des Resources Intervenant Auprès des Hommes Violents (ARIHV; Association of resources for violent men);
- la Fédération des Unions de Familles (Federation of family unions);
- le Mouvement d'Education Populaire et d'Action Communautiaire du Québec (MEPAQ; Québec movement for popular education and community action);
- la Fédération des Associations des Familles Monoparentales et Recomposées du Québec (FAFMRQ; Québec federation of associations supporting single and step-parent families);
- le Mouvement Québecois des Camps Familiaux Inc (MQCF; Québec movement for family camps).

Staff from other organisations occasionally work out of le Carrefour on specific projects; examples include the CLSC (Centre Local des Services Communautaires), local community service centre; la Corporation de Développement Economique de l'Est et son Guichet Multi-Services (emploi) (CEDEST; economic development corporation of East [Montreal] and its multi-service employment centre); and the Centre St Pierre, which provides training for people active in community organisations.

Re-Nou-Vie (Châteauguay, Québec)

Introduction

Re-Nou-Vie is a women's centre that provides services and support primarily to single mothers, women in blended families or women in the process of separation. Services include information and referral, individual counselling, parent education and support groups, and a home visiting service for so-called at-risk families with young children. The organisation has an explicitly feminist philosophy and is very active in advocating about issues relating to single mothers. Re-Nou-Vie's name refers to the centre's goal of offering women opportunities for personal renewal and help in starting a new life.

There are 4 full-time and 2 part-time staff, experienced and training in home child care, sexual assault counselling, working with unions and working in shelters for battered women. The Board of Directors of Re-Nou-Vie is made up of seven directors (five activists who are single mothers or women in blended families, and two designated members who are resource persons).

Community Context

Re-Nou-Vie is located in Châteauguay, a city about 25 kilometers from Montreal on the south shore of the St Lawrence River. The Châteauguay area is experiencing major changes as people in a precarious social and economic position arrive from Montreal in search of low-rent housing. Pockets of poverty are appearing, and the immigrant and anglophone population is increasing.

About 80% of women participating in Re-Nou-Vie programs are on welfare or have low-paying jobs; many participants have experienced spousal violence. Because the Mères-Amies (mother-friends) home-visiting program is intended to reach high-risk families, almost all participating families are impoverished and experience isolation.

All activities are offered at one location, with the exception of the Mères-Amies program, which takes place through home-visits. Re-Nou-Vie was located in a single-family house in a suburban residential neighbourhood of Châteauguay from 1995 until it moved to new facilities in Rue Principal.

History

In 1980, several women facing problems related to divorce or separation approached the Châteauguay CLSC (local community service centre) to discuss their need for a self-help group and a place where they could come for help. In response, a social worker from the CLSC developed a series of workshops. Following these meeting, six single mothers decided to continue to meet on a regular basis in order to help each other out.

In 1981, the CLSC applied for a grant to the *Oganismes volontaires en éducation populaire* (OVEP; voluntary popular education organisations) to train volunteers to lead groups and to provide counselling. The successful outcome led to the birth of Re-Nou-Vie, a self-help and support organisation for single mothers, which was initially organised as a collective. In 1985 Re-Nou-Vie became incorporated and developed a more formal organisational structure. A grant from *Centraide* (United Way) made it possible to hire a full-time co-ordinator. In 1985, a legal clinic was added to the other services provided by the organisation.

In 1992, as a result of organisational conflicts, two workers (including the co-ordinator) and the members of the Board of Directors resigned and their were cuts in subsidies from Centraide. One worker continued to maintain basic services on a voluntary basis for seven months. In 1993, the women involved in the organisation developed an action plan that addressed a number of outstanding issues and extended the mission of the group to include offering support to women in blended families. The organisation started up again on a firmer foundation, and a new board was elected.

In 1995, with federal government funding from the Community Action Program for Children (CAPC) and the support of several organisations (including the CLSC, the local hospital and La Leche League) Re-Nou-Vie developed Mères-Amies, a home visiting program designed to prevent neglect and abuse of young children by offering non-professional peer support to their mothers.

Program Components

Program in action – the first contact many women make with Re-Nou-Vie is by telephone. New participants may receive short-term individual counselling, but are encouraged to make contact with other participants or join a group activity because the organisation believes strongly in the value of mutual aid. Consistent with the feminist philosophy, participants are encouraged to view their personal struggles in the context of broader social and economic contexts, and to develop the confidence and skills to take action on behalf of themselves and others. To ensure that the centre remains responsive to the needs of participants, the organisation's programs and activities are formally reviewed twice a year by the staff and Board and revised as necessary. All services at Re-Nou-Vie are free of charge.

Parent Education and Support

- *Self-help groups for single mothers*: meets weekly in the evening for twelve weeks;
- *Mère-ados (mothers-teens)*: is a self-help group for single mothers of adolescents; meeting weekly for 10 weeks;
- *Y'a personne de parfait (YAPP;* nobody's perfect): a six to eight week educational program designed to strengthen parenting skills for parents of children up to five years old. This is the only service offered by Re-Nou-Vie that is open to men as well as women;
- *Family Summer Camp*: Re-Nou-Vie offers financial help to low-income families to attend a one week session at a family summer camp near Valleyfield run by another organisation;
- *Social Activities*: organised to celebrate holidays and special events such as Christmas and International Women's Day on March 8.

Family Preservation

- *Mères-amies (mothers-friends) program:* is designed to prevent child abuse and neglect in families of children up to five years old. The mères-amies are mothers without professional training who visit the homes of families experiencing difficulties to offer information and

65

support and to work on an action plan developed with each family. The mères-amies discuss various topics such as health, safety and nutrition and seek to help parents and children bond through parent-child activities. The personal link formed with these peer home visitors makes it easier for the participating mothers to join in Re-Nou-Vie's other activities, including Nobody's Perfect courses. Families are referred to the program by the local hospital, the CLSC, and the *Centre Jeunesse* (Youth Centre) or refer themselves;

- *Telephone service and individual counselling*: provides women with advice, information and referrals concerning issues related to family and marital violence, separation and divorce, and legal rights;
- *Accompaniment*: Staff or volunteers may accompany women to court, to the employment insurance offices, etc.

Child Care Program

- *Child minding*: on site child-care is available to women who are participating in group activities.

Material Support

- Donated clothing is available for distribution.

Other Adult Education and Recreation Programs

- *Connaître ses droits, c'est payant* (knowing your rights pays off): is a ten-week course, offered twice a year, that deals with issues related to family responsibilities, housework, housing, welfare rights, debt, budgets, survival techniques, child care, the labour market, educational programs, unemployment support and social programs. After completing the course, participants identify a project and work together on it. For example, one group studies the possibility of opening a drop-in day care centre that would be open 24 hours a day, seven days a week;
- *Réseau soleil* (sun network): is a self-help network organised by separated or divorced women whose children are teenagers or adults. The women meet every two weeks for social activities, to break their isolation;

- *Cafés-rencontres* (get togethers over coffee): informal discussion groups are held on an occasional basis. Discussion groups include mother-child relationships and helping with homework;
- *Monthly newsletter RE'NOUVELLE*: includes information about the organisation's activities;
- *Respite weekend*: in an annual weekend for women only, held at the Botte de Foin (a large old house); no formal activities are scheduled;
- *Self-defence classes*: are offered annually to members.

Community Development: Education, Leadership Development and Advocacy

- *Volunteer training*: an annual three day training session is offered to twelve to fifteen women (not necessarily single mothers) who are members of Re-Nu-Vie. This training is an opportunity for consciousness-raising about the condition of women and prepares women who want to become activists (*militantes)* on behalf of the organisation. During these sessions, the organisation's philosophy and feminist intervention approach are explained, and participants are encouraged to reflect on their own values and attitudes. A few follow-up training sessions are also offered throughout the year, depending on the needs of the activists, staff and board members. For example *Inform'elle* (a non-profit organisation that provides legal information to women) provides Re-Nou-Vie's staff and activists with training about various legal topics, such as family law. For some women who have been out of the job market for a long time, the experience acquired as an activist for Re-Nou-Vie is valuable employment preparation;
- *Public education and advocacy*: issues relating to poverty and the concerns of single mothers are an important aspect of Re-Nou-Vie's work. Various collective actions are undertaken to raise public awareness, improve living conditions, and develop local and provincial alliances. For example staff and participants formed a local coalition to fight the introduction of fees charged to supervise children's lunch hours at school; they also joined in the 200-kilometre Québec Women's March against poverty in 1995 and are actively involved in issues related to child support.
- *Legal clinic*: is offered twice a year by a lawyer who works with the *Inform'elle* group; this service is open to all women in the community.

Community Linkages

Re-Nou-Vie works with a number of women's organisations such as shelters and the *Centre d'aide et de prévention d'assauts sexuels* (CAPAS; centre for help and prevention of sexual assault) making referrals as needed. Re-Nou-Vie participates in several community committees at the local level, including:

- *Table des organismes communautaires de la sous région de Châteauguay* (Committee of community organisations of the Chateauguay sub-region);
- *Table des regroupements des organismes volontaires en éducation populaire de la Montérégie* (TROVEP: committee of associations of voluntary popular education organisations of the Montérégie;
- *Table de concertation violence de la sous région de Châteauguay* (Consultation committee on violence in the Châteauguay sub-region;
- *Table Négligence Châteauguay* (Châteauguay committee on neglect).

References

Kyle I. & Kellerman M. (1998), *Case Studies of Canadian Family Resource Programs Supporting Families, Children and Communities,* Canadian Association of Family Resource Programs. Suite 101, 30 Rosemount Avenue, Ottawa, Ontario K1Y 1P4. Tel: (613) 728-3307 Fax: (613) 729-5421 Email: info@frp.ca

Ce livre est aussi disponible en français sous le titre: Études de cas des programmes de ressources pour la famille au Canada: Soutenir les familles, les enfants et les collectivités.

6 The Referral Only Centre – Managing Changing Attitudes to Parenting

AUDREY FESSLER

The Elizabeth Fry Centre

This account of the Elizabeth Fry Centre covers development from its establishment in 1975 until 1999, more detailed consideration being given to its work since 1990. Families attend by referral, two days a week normally, for up to two years. A nursery is provided for children under 5 years old. The Centre is run by the Executive Committee, is financed in part by Statutory Authorities and in part by fundraising activities and is staffed by professional and volunteer workers.

Introduction

The Elizabeth Fry project has, from the beginning, involved a variety of relationships between voluntary, statutory organisations, professional and volunteer workers, parents and children, the centre and the wider community. It has also had to respond to changes in social theory and practice over 25 years and to ensure that the idealism which brought it into being is sustained.

The Elizabeth Fry Day Centre (Registered Charity) was set up in 1975 as an integral component of a collaborative project involving Nottingham Probation Department and the Elizabeth Fry Executive Committee. It was a multi-functional project devised to cater for hitherto unmet social needs within Nottingham and included provision for women and children of families of men with whom the Probation Service was involved. It aimed to help women achieve greater understanding of relationships, home management and childcare. A nursery for children under 5 years old was included in the provision.

However, over a period of time, thinking on social issues changed and the Probation Department no longer regarded preventive family centered work as a priority at a time of increasing financial constraints. Therefore, in 1990 the project became independent of the Probation Department, was re-located and in 1994 re-named The Elizabeth Fry Family Centre managed exclusively by the Elizabeth Fry Committee. Funding was obtained from Nottingham Social Services (on an annual application basis), joint funding from Nottingham Area Health Authority and funds raised by the Elizabeth Fry Committee.

A development group is charged with monitoring policies, setting targets and producing a development plan based on the constitutional objectives. Families attend the Centre by referral, by the Probation Service (until 1990), the Health Authority, Social Services and other organisations such as Home Start. Attendance is voluntary but a contract with the client is agreed to establish commitment. The most common cause for referral has been 'inadequate parenting skills'. Other reasons have included isolation, depression, ill health, poor hygiene, lack of domestic skills, budgeting and literacy skills.

Over the past 20 years the age range of clients has changed slightly. Fewer are under 20 and most are between 20-35. Marital status is largely unchanged, with slightly more co-habitees. Ethnic origin remains predominantly white, with slightly more of African-Caribbean than Asian origin. There are some dual heritage children.

The centre is staffed by remunerated professional staff and volunteers with limited expenses. The work of the Centre is organised by the family centre manager, who is responsible for the parents' programme, nursery provision, family transport, establishing a welcoming atmosphere, managing the staff team, overseeing referrals, liaising with other organisations, keeping records, managing a budget, attending case conferences and undertaking training as appropriate. The professional staff in the nursery are a senior family worker and two family workers, one specialising in the care of babies, the other with special skills relating to activities with older children.

Volunteers provide help and support in the nursery, working as part of a team. They are drawn from all walks of life, including students and grandmas. Although the centre has an equal opportunities policy, men have not often chosen to work in the nursery.

A few volunteers assist tutors in the parent group. Another important role for volunteers is to provide transport for families to and from the

Centre. Not only does this encourage families to attend but it is an opportunity for the volunteer to offer support and a 'listening ear' and to alert staff to possible problems. All volunteers have a probationary period and training sessions are offered. Management is carried out by Trustees (members of the Executive Committee) and on-going work is undertaken by working groups for development, finance, fundraising, personnel and volunteers. Two client representatives now attend Executive Committee meetings.

The Nursery

The Children

The Elizabeth Fry project has always catered for small numbers only, which has facilitated the creation of a family atmosphere. The number of children averages 13–14. The age ranges have changed over the years; there are now few aged 4–5 and an increase in those 0–1 years. Reasons for referral include failure to thrive, isolation, child protection requirements, poor health/hygiene, lack of parental interaction. A home visit form is completed by the family centre manager on referral and subsequent visits. Problems, such as feeding/eating/sleeping difficulties, over/under activity, are identified initially. A child development form, completed termly by the staff and parent, is used to monitor development. Visits to the Health Centre are noted. The senior family worker finds that most of the children follow normal developmental stages but slowly. The centre follows procedures expected by Nottinghamshire Area Child Protection Committee relating to injuries to children or suspected physical, sexual or emotional abuse or serious neglect.

Theoretical Approach

Through their professional training, staff are familiar with psychological studies of child development. The Centre does not follow any formally stated theory but has agreed policies which exemplify its beliefs about conditions conducive to optimum development. These give an important baseline to all our work.

- A secure and relaxed environment is needed;

71

- There are community rules – children are not allowed to hurt themselves, each other or damage the environment, equipment;
- Freedom of choice is important. Children themselves are best able to determine the type and duration of activities to follow (they do not need adults to do this for them);
- Group activities can begin to contribute to social development but at this stage should not predominate;
- Children learn from role models;
- Play is an important experience in itself and also contributes to learning concepts;
- Play materials can contribute to positive concepts of people and should therefore include images of both male and female from a range of ethnic and cultural groups with and without disabilities;
- Children's concepts follow developmental stages. Therefore, behaviour, acceptable and unacceptable, must be handled in a developmentally appropriate fashion, respecting individual children's level of understanding and maturity;
- Play should include a chance to relax and have fun;
- From the earliest age, reasons should be given why things should or should not be done.

Provision

The aim of the nursery is to empower and liberate so that development can take place rather than to follow a programme of pre-school training. The Centre is open 2 days a week 9.30am to 2.30pm for 36 weeks of the year during Nottingham City School terms. From the start of the Project there has been concern that families are not supported during the long summer holiday. The feasibility of a drop-in centre was considered (Nottingham Business School Project 1999). However, the preferred option was to extend the service to longer terms. For the children this present arrangement means that going to the Centre is not a daily but a fairly special event. Time is sufficient for them to get to know the people and routines and feel at home. The hours allow for 'settling in' when mothers can be with them, for choosing from a range of possible activities in the Centre, for short excursions, for a shared meal, some group activities and a 'going-home' time when mothers can hear about or see what their children have been doing.

The present nursery is held in a large hall within a hired church-owned property. The children have a large space but because the needs of all ages must be met, the area for babies has to be fenced off in an ad hoc way. Activities in the nursery are facilitated by professional and volunteer staff. A keyworker scheme allows a supportive, but non-directive, adult to be with each child, to talk with them and prevent them from harming themselves, others or equipment. Perseverance or concentration on an activity for a period of time is encouraged but activities are child-led not adult directed.

Volunteers in the nursery attend training sessions on such topics as child protection and coping with challenging behaviour. They also meet regularly with the worker. It is important to discuss challenging behaviour as ways of responding must be consistent with the policies of the Centre and followed in a similar way by all those working with an individual child. When confronting difficult behaviour it is important to separate the 'action' from the 'person' and to give reasons, at an appropriate level, why certain behaviour is/not acceptable.

The Parent/Child Process

When the centre opened in 1975 there was a clear continuation of the original approach of Elizabeth Fry herself that 'inadequate'[1] mothers could be helped by training in some of the basic home management skills they lacked. By the 1980s it was recognised that the programme offered needed to be broadened and courses on handling relationships and assertiveness were included.

> They are learning a great deal about child care (eg. from formal sessions and from being with others at meal times) and are becoming more sensitive to the way they care for their children and handle them, but this is reached in indirect ways not by working directly with the children and staff in the nursery.

More direct involvement of mothers with their children was planned through the introduction of a Toy Library (1985) and more formal structuring of joint mother/child activities (1986). These sessions were not easy to run as mothers sometimes wanted to 'play', for example, make Christmas decorations on their own and resented their children 'spoiling'

---

[1] In the language of the time.

what they were doing. They also found the idea of taking their child's play seriously quite foreign to them and felt such activities were just for nursery staff and volunteers. Mothers found the fortnightly visit to the mobile bus library easier to understand. They were keen for their children to learn to read, though some of them were embarrassed that they themselves found reading so difficult that they could not read to their children. In the 1989 Annual Report the organiser writes:

> We have made a point of including, in the day's routine, a short shared singing session which children can enjoy on their parent's lap.

In this way the children are able to associate the happy times they have in the nursery with their parents as well as with the staff, and the parents become less self conscious about spending time like this with their children. Parents also had the chance to stay in the nursery one at a time to play with their child alongside one of the workers and to talk through any anxieties or difficulties related to their child. The parents learn a great deal by seeing how the staff relate to the children and the way in which they can use firm discipline without recourse to physical punishment. Parent-child sessions were also seen as valuable, helping staff and volunteers to see how mothers relate to their children so that they understand better how to help with child management problems. Staff could also use these insights when involved in case conferences.

Over the past 10 years the initiatives begun in the mid 80s have been consolidated. In the words of a staff member:

> Parents are involved in the nursery from the moment that they walk through the door and whenever they are present in the area. They are involved with us with all aspects of childcare and our aim is to help them gain more confidence and responsibility.

The programmes for the parents facilitate this. Included in the parents' programme (January–April 1998) were 6 tutor led session on positive parenting, a talk on writing a book for children and 2 sessions devoted to activities for parents with their children in the nursery. On these occasions the nursery staff discuss with the mothers how they want them to be with their children, what to do and what not to do. After discussion the mothers 'shadow' their child/ren, which they find quite difficult to persevere in (they want to chat amongst themselves or 'interfere' with what the child is doing). The children mostly continue to play as usual but some find it difficult having their mum around. The Senior Family Worker feels it would be helpful to spend more time with mothers discussing child development and why play is important.

When asked about their involvement in the nursery all the mothers said they spent time there, some would like to spend more. All said they talk to the staff about their worries and like to hear about their children's progress and interests.

A few mothers would like more pre-school activities, such as literacy work. Observations by staff and use of development records suggest that children do benefit from attending the Centre, particularly in social development. Many mothers said that their child was less shy, got on better with other children and was learning to talk more.

From the start of the project, the focus of the centre has been the family. However, it has never been possible for male partners to be fully included until quite recently. A few fathers have been in the nursery, where they were encouraged and helped to play with their children, but they have not been able to maintain the involvement. Time seemed to hang heavily and integration proved difficult. Then, in 1999, a men's group was set up following requests from some of the fathers whose families attend the centre. The basis of the group is to provide a safe and supportive framework for the men to raise issues that concern them and to work through difficulties and challenges they may face at home with partners and children. A staff facilitator organises weekly sessions and makes visits or phone contact with men unable to attend. Whatever is said at sessions is treated in a confidential way within the boundaries of child protection. However, there is no collusion by the facilitator with oppressive attitudes and comments. Men meeting together to discuss parenting and relationships is a fairly new and challenging idea. Fathers are an isolated group in our society and breaking through long established attitudes will take time, patience and commitment.

Provision for Parents

Over the period 1975-99 there have been changes in the programmes offered to parents in both content and approach. Course content changed from basic home management skills to include social and personal development. Since 1996, due to changes in the wider community as well as user interests, more time is spent on communication skills, confidence building, art and craft, numeracy and whole day activity outings. Sessions initially were formal and tutor-led. This gave way to a group work approach. Users valued this:

> ...we can help one another sort out our problems. We now know how to listen to each other and give advice and support.

The approach is now to offer fairly structured topic-based courses led by a tutor who integrates group discussion. Volunteers sometimes assist in activities. The manager liaises with tutors and also has feedback from clients. When the users at present attending were asked which of the things they have done at the Centre they enjoyed most, the most frequently mentioned were art and craft.

> I like doing creative things.
> I love doing things with my hands.
> I never did craft till I came to Elizabeth Fry.
> Drawing faces was good. It enabled me to sit and draw which I enjoy but don't seem to get the time to do this at home.

In terms of usefulness the most frequently mentioned was the assertiveness course: 'I've learnt to say 'no'. Moreover, communication skills and number work were mentioned as helping to make up for things not achieved at school:

> I didn't do well at school.
> My spelling and punctuation has (sic) improved.
> It's given me confidence to speak out.
> Gives me a chance to make my brain active.
> Maths is very helpful because I cannot add up as quick as I would like.
> English is very helpful because I had a lot of desrocktion [distraction] when I was at school.

Transitions and the World Outside the Centre

The Elizabeth Fry Family Centre has always had as one of its aims helping users to integrate with their local community and has tried to address problems they may face on leaving the Centre. The Centre organiser has always discussed with the women what new possibilities there might be for them. Various follow-on groups were set up either by working with an existing group (for example with a local Residents' Association) or offering an informal drop-in group (open 2 hours 1 morning a week). Volunteers also accompanied women leaving the centre on visits to other local mother and toddler groups to support them in the transition. However, none of the schemes were successful during the period 1980–90. Clients were usually looking for an exact replica of the Centre they knew, with the same people attending. Since they had been provided with transport to the centres hitherto, they found it difficult to make travel arrangements themselves.

The problems of transition are not caused solely by the users' emotional attachment to the Centre and their lack of self-confidence in unfamiliar surroundings but also by the inadequacy of suitable provision in the community. For example, mother and toddler groups cannot help parents when children are 5+. In recent years there have been some improvements in the provision and the Centre has tried to devote more attention to facilitating transition. Users now may realistically hope to join adult education courses which will give them additional skills, as more of them have achieved sufficient levels of literacy and numeracy skills and increased their self-confidence through the courses they have followed at the Centre.

Users are asked about their plans on leaving the centre. If interested they are helped to find out more about courses they could attend. The Centre itself does not offer details about local employment or voluntary work but will help the client to find sources of information herself. Issues such as the balancing of family responsibilities, personal development and employment are discussed in group sessions. When asked (in 1998) whether they had any plans for the future, 3 mentioned possible college courses, 3 possible work (responses from 9 group members available). However, as it has not been possible to keep in touch in a systematic way with users after they have left the Centre. There are no records to show how many have taken employment, followed educational courses, done voluntary work or joined other groups. The Centre is in contact with a number of other organisations which may be able to help users, such as Relate, Home Start, Samaritans, Agenda (male domestic violence), the Radford Shared Care Projects. Some of these give talks at the Centre.

Evaluation

It must be stated that, in terms of allocation of resources, the work of the centre to support families has had priority over evaluation procedures which can be very time-consuming. It is also true that there can never be any cut and dried conclusions about something which seeks to effect subtle changes in human nature. For the purpose of the review of the Elizabeth Fry Centre by the Nottinghamshire Probation Service in 1985, relevant areas of work are identified:

- issues of nutrition, hygiene, cookery and budgeting;
- issues of health care for women and their children, including child development issues;
- social skills work including literacy, communication skills and assertiveness training;
- direct child care training;
- the provision of constructive nursery facilities, which enable women to learn skills and develop relationships with their children.

Since that time, attitudes to evaluation have changed considerably. It has become increasingly important in the work of the Elizabeth Fry Centre, both as part of an educative process for individual clients and to monitor the effectiveness of the management of the Centre for its own benefit and to justify its work to those giving financial support.

It has been extremely difficult to look back over past records and compare progress and change. By reading through pages of notes kept by past project leaders it is possible to find that a record of, for example, an 'increase in self-confidence' has been made. However, it is extremely time consuming to abstract this information when faced with pages and pages of notes on each parent, most of which provides very little factual content (Vanstone 1996).

A formal evaluation procedure was therefore devised using forms designed in line with the database in standardised record keeping. This procedure was intended to supplement, not to replace managers' notes. It involved a self-evaluation form, to be used termly, and an evaluation form was also prepared for use by the manager to note progress. Users' needs on entry are indicated. These include parenting skills, isolated, depressed, health and hygiene, confidence building, home skills, basic skills, budgeting skills. Progress is indicated by using the categories: improved, no change, slipped back, and the date of the evaluation.

These ways of record keeping and evaluation are now being reviewed as they have proved difficult to administer. Ideas currently being explored include the modification of the forms, the use of diaries kept by mothers, systematic recording of observations of children's behaviour by keyworkers and the use of a modified version of the Graded Care Profile Scale (Srivastava & Polnay 1997).

Conclusion

An independent Family Centre faces major challenges in terms of organisation, finance and in its relationships to the formal and informal agencies it needs to work with. Above all, and especially reflected in these pages, there have been major changes in assumptions and theories of intervention about the subject of parenting. Since the Centre's beginnings in the mid-seventies the evolution has been startling. Our understanding and practice has evolved from the training approach and the 'inadequate parent', to the contemporary holistic perspective which tries to account for both the separate and shared needs of child and parent. It increasingly involves a broad educational approach to parents, and an ever growing appreciation of the context in which families live. Moreover, all family centres have to assimilate an attitude to evaluation in which it can no longer be acceptable to rely on professional subjectivity. The user perspective, evidence, outcome-based evaluation and an ecological view of human behaviour means that centres must strive continually to keep connected.

References

Beale L., Beeby H., Brahmbhatt S., Redmond D., & Whatley S. (1999), 'To examine the feasibility of a drop-in centre during the summer holiday at the Elizabeth Fry Centre', Nottingham Business School, The Nottingham Trent University, Postgraduate Diploma in Management Studies, Team Consultancy Project. March.

Fessler A. M. (1989), The Elizabeth Fry Day Centres 1975-1989, Elizabeth Fry Centre, Nottingham, unpublished.

Srivastava C. P. & Polnay L (1997), 'Field trial of graded care profile (GCP) scale: a new measure of care', in Archives of Disease in Childhood, Vol 76, No 4, pp. 337-340, April.

Vanstone, L. (1996), A review of the work of the Elizabeth Fry Family Centre from 1990 to 1995/6. Elizabeth Fry Centre, Nottingham, unpublished.

7 The Office as Centre: A 'Patch' Approach, Supporting and Protecting in two Massachusetts Communities

JOHN ZALENSKI and CAROLYN BURNS

For Gerald Smale, who worked so hard to humanize the systems intended to serve families.

Introduction

Indications that a Patch approach is taking root is that unhelpful barriers begin to fall. A mother walks into a Patch office with a question. Her worker is off on a home visit, but she doesn't leave, or spend hours waiting for her worker to return. Instead, another member of the Patch team sits down with her and resolves a problem about an upcoming court appearance. A mother who had her children removed when she was a young and inexperienced parent stands up at a state wide meeting and says that she is willing to try to trust The Department of Social Services (DSS, the state public child welfare agency) case workers once again and she welcomes them into her community. A family, and a DSS 'family worker' (a new designation to signal a new way of working with families) attend a community barbecue as a part of a family reunification plan. A father suggests holding a visitation in the common room of the Patch office. A family worker smooths a placement, making it local, with a known family and with much less trauma to the child. A school system withdraws it's objection to 'more foster kids' as a result of involvement on the Patch Council and closer relationships with the Patch team. Patch council members start something involving local pediatricians in the discussion of sensitive issues of abuse and neglect in the community in order to improve professional involvement and working relationships with the child welfare agency.

The Patch Approach

The Patch approach has been a growing part of the social service vernacular in the US since the early 1990s. At that time it was introduced as an innovation from Great Britain. An early Patch experiment in the US took place in Cedar Rapids, Iowa. Here the Patch approach was tied to the State's project for devolving funding and service development authority to local jurisdictions under the 'decategorization' framework. Patch in Cedar Rapids became a service innovation linking public child welfare caseworkers, and later income maintenance workers, together with teams from family service organizations and local community based resources to begin to rethink community based child protection. Patch later evolved, in a dynamic reform environment in Cedar Rapids, into one of four sites sponsored by large philanthropic foundations to develop a 'community partnership for child protection'.

Through a core group of 'product champions' scattered about the country, in conferences and workshops, word of the Patch approach began to spread. Since the mid-1990s principles of the Patch approach have been used to move forward community based social services reform agendas in Denver and Philadelphia, in Vermont and in Duluth Minnesota and elsewhere. Perhaps most notably, the Patch approach is currently being implemented in the Commonwealth of Massachusetts.

Traced to its origins in Great Britain, 'Patch' means neighborhood. While there remain connections to these roots, Patch has taken on new meaning. In Massachusetts, Patch is a problem solving approach focused on creating constructive child welfare reform in community settings by renegotiating roles and relationships between public child welfare agencies and the people that they serve. This approach, a way of 'seeing with new eyes' the strengths and challenges faced by families and communities, initiates a powerful process of renewal with, potentially, far reaching consequences.

Patch was first introduced in Massachusetts as a DSS 'systems integration' strategy. This starting point can be traced to the federal Family Preservation and Support Services Program (FPSSP, US federal legislation which provided funds for family support services for the first time). Having developed a strong system of family based services in child welfare throughout the 1980s, Massachusetts invested the federal funds in the development of family support services through the Community Connections coalitions. Community Connections organized stakeholders outside public child welfare to better support families in diverse ways. A strength of this approach was to increase capacity in the underdeveloped service area of family support where a challenge was to defer strategies for linking family support to child welfare. In many cases the Community Connections Coalitions worked with only loose ties to public child welfare providers. In this context, Patch became a strategy to link the protection and safety work of public child welfare with the prevention work of family support in a neighborhood based setting. Within the framework of an evolving partnership, two DSS Area Offices, one in Greenfield (in rural Massachusetts) and one in Boston, joined with two Community Connections coalitions, Dorchester Cares, (a family services collaborative), and Valuing Our Children, (a family support and parenting education organization) to initiate Patch in two sites.

Principles are the Foundation of Accountability

Because Patch is an approach responsive to local conditions, principles that are negotiated and endorsed by key constituencies become critical to successful implementation. In the two Massachusetts sites, principles like the ones which follow helped to provide a frame work to guide the work of Patch development.

- Public social services must be accessible;
- 'Us-them' boundaries between families and the service system, and between human service organizations public and private, perpetuate problems and limit solutions;
- Prevent problems in neighborhoods and communities by creating opportunities for individuals and families to grow in healthy and constructive ways;
- Strengthen local resources and the everyday ways people care successfully for each other;
- Use teamwork to model a way of working, of problem solving, with the community;
- Encourage participation of residents of the Patch in the initiative;
- Respect the diversity of individuals, families, and neighborhoods.

(Smale, 1996)

The Different Levels of the Patch approach

Strategies complementary to these principles emerged from negotiations with key people and constituencies and created the Massachusetts Patch initiative. To work on the complex agenda described by the principles, Patch has to operate on a number of levels simultaneously: the neighborhood team, the Patch community council, the administrative team.

Neighborhood Teams

Neighborhood teams were deployed in the two pilot sites. These teams are made up of DSS case workers and supervisors, other state agency representatives such as Department of Youth Services and domestic violence specialists, staff from community based family support agencies, a Patch team coordinator, and others. There is no set definition for the make-up of the team; it is a group of people with a mix of skills working to get the work done. Final make up of the team is determined by local opportunity and neighborhood need.

These teams are assigned a geographically defined caseload, and they work from offices located in the communities they serve. The offices are comfortable, welcoming places. Families and residents come in with any and all kinds of questions and concerns related to DSS services or other matters. The office becomes a setting equally appropriate to holding a family visitation or an open house and pot luck supper to introduce Patch team members to local families. The office can become whatever the team and the residents want it to be. It becomes a center in a network of open communication and equal exchange within which the work of DSS becomes embedded in the life of the community. This is demanding, and it raises challenges of all sorts, but it offers to a community an opportunity to promote the safety and well-being of its children and families.

The team's growing effectiveness is tied to being allowed to evolve their own local practice approach while working within the mandates of DSS. There are many dimensions to team practice. Although it takes time and effort and ongoing outreach, strengthening relationships with families and cultivating greater familiarity and understanding of neighborhoods works to improve all outcomes. Having a respectful relationship with a family makes necessary removals more constructive. This avoids certain kinds of trauma that generate problem behaviors in children, problems that can, over time become indistinguishable from those contributing to certain removals in the first place, complicating assessment and service planning ahead. Knowing families and children better makes placements more successful, closer to home. Knowing families and children better facilitates the possibility of timely reunification. Or it makes the identification of best permanency options a process focused on maintaining as many successful relationships for a child as possible.

Team work refocuses good intentions within a fuller context. We seldom see beyond the confines of our intentions. If our intentions for families are good, how can we go wrong? The truth, up close, is different. Well-intended interventions, even good ones, do not necessarily produce positive effects for a family. What counts is not the specific integrity of an individual intervention. What counts is the entire context within which the intervention rests. For example, an excellent substance abuse program that requires a mother to separate from her responsibilities to her children and family in order to enroll, may undermine the necessary conditions of success for her. Interrupting those primary relationships can affect her motivation to finish the treatment program, and it may ignore the patterns of daily life that are key to long term success. Patch team practice is based on understanding the networks of social relationships within which families are embedded as a way of knowing how best to assist them to help themselves. This 'decenters' professional knowledge and intentions, and 'recenters' the strengthening of families' networks as the overriding purpose of our efforts. This focus on the successful practice of everyday life for families can turn attention to 'family strengths' from rhetoric into reality.

Further, working in neighborhood settings in a team allows greater knowledge and familiarity with families' circumstances. One participant to the process describes how conventional practice is like 'looking at a family through a pinhole.' You just can't know them well enough to have a constructive relationship. And you end up relying on second hand information that predefines family problems, the layers of pejorative language that describes their history with the system. Up close, the team can sort through problems more differentially. In a conventional setting, a family that is 'resistant' and 'non-compliant' can cause workers to shift the focus of their efforts to the family's attitude towards caseworkers. Up close however, the family may be independent and resourceful. Reframed, the problem becomes a quality to work with.

Child welfare involved families lead very complex lives with multiple system involvements. This releases a range of 'system effects.' For example, a family may have 'problems with the school'. However, through working closely with families in the community, it may become clear that the problem may be about misunderstood expectations and competing agendas between agencies, with the family caught in the middle. System effects can sometimes become family problems. Often solving a problem is not something a family can do without changing relationships in the involved systems. Professional treatment orientations, expectations professionals have of one another, past relationships between agencies, the adversarial nature of court processes, a family's history at school, all can produce 'system effects' that need to be addressed in ways other than direct family work.

Patch team members need to develop a variety of practice skills as a result of this wide variety of work. *Direct work* with families to understand the patterns that maintain problems, *linking families* with concrete supports or specialized services, *systemic reform interventions* to sort out and minimize unintended 'system effects', *building community resources*, *advocating* within their own agencies for changes in official policy or procedure to get a better job done – all of this becomes the work of the 'family workers' on the Patch team (Smale, 2000).

The core skill of team members is 'change mapping.' Change mapping is rooted in identifying and defining with a family the social networks within which their daily life takes place. It is in this network, this fabric of relationships, that problems crop up, and resources for their solutions can often be found. 'Patch change mapping' draws on the tradition of solution focused techniques, as well as familiar family centered practice techniques such as the genogram and the ecomap. However, rather than having a diagnostic slant, change mapping emphasizes attention to often unrecognized resources in a family's network, resources with the potential to encourage, facilitate and sustain the changes needed to help a family meet its necessary goals.

The Patch Council

The widening of the circle of accountability for children and families at the sites extends to the Patch council. Patch councils in Dorchester and North Quabbin are diverse bodies. They comprise community leaders, elders or 'guardian angels'. They include service users and service providers, residents who want to play a role, and concerned professionals who want to give something back to their communities. That is in fact the key. The councils must be made up of people who want to make a contribution to their communities. Sustainable partnerships are rooted not in what participants gain, but in what they contribute.

The Patch council plays an important role. As a Patch approach begins to take hold, participants learn that family and community problems have solutions that must be pursued at different levels. Team members may work with individual families on solutions, but in the process they will encounter larger issues requiring collective solutions. A child missing an important vaccination may simply require a referral to a health clinic. A child missing a vaccination also may indicate an isolated family requiring outreach or coaching.

But a pattern of families with children missing vaccinations indicates larger issues. Defining the problem, and constructing a local solution involves the council. Working the issue may reveal the need to find residents to help translate health care needs and requirements across cultures, or it may indicate to create a new clinic to make access possible. In its work to create a community level response to emerging issues, the Patch Council helps to perform an indispensable community development function. As the team works the community, creating in the process an ongoing assessment of resources and needs, the Patch council works to meet the ongoing assessment with appropriate service and resource development strategies. The council provides a broad base of opportunities for resident participation in the activities of the Patch.

The Administrative Team

The 'Admin Team' is composed of Area Office Directors, Area Program Managers, Family Support Specialists (Community Connections technical assistance providers), Dorchester Cares Director (in the Boston site) and Valuing Our Children Director (in the North Quabbin site). The 'Admin Team' addresses problems at a policy level.

In addition to the ongoing complexities of managing 'matrix teams' composed of representatives from a variety of organizations, the 'Admin Team' faces other tasks. What changes in personnel, policy and procedure need to happen to allow teams to practice more flexibly? Can the teams work be more tightly integrated, allowing teams to do family assessments, and even investigations, to extend the range of Patch practice (currently most Patch cases come to the team through the DSS assessment unit)? Can caseloads be weighted in some way to allow the Patch teams to balance the work of prevention and protection necessary to remain accountable to the shared principles of the initiative? As you can imagine, there are no easy solutions here. But these are the kinds of questions the 'Admin Teams' wrestle with, and it is in wrestling with the right issues that Patch generates long term reform.

People and their Social Networks Make Patch Work

Patch developers in Massachusetts have discovered that the complexities of implementing Patch require a 'staged' development process. The primary focus to date has been on the work of the teams. This work has taken place in a 'practice development forum' within which leaders from both teams have been meeting periodically to work on practice issues. The focus of this effort has been on understanding the 'social nature of social problems'. Many of the problems faced by families and communities are created by breakdowns in social relationships (for example between teachers and parents), weakened or insufficient social relationships (in cases of neglect, for example), or inappropriate relationships (the role of peer groups in substance abuse). Understanding the complicated social networks which make a community work is critical to understanding how to promote the safety, stability, and well being of families and children.

Practice Development: Partners in the Path of Change

The Patch Teams in Athol and Dorchester practice with families and children in their distinct areas. While this initiates definitive changes in practice, in the beginning, all team members bring an established approach to their work with families. This approach is founded in their 'home agency' culture.

The transformation from a 'business as usual' approach to family work into Patch practice evolves over months and years. The transformation grows out of a team-based process of 'practice exchange' in which emerging issues with families and in the neighborhood provide opportunities to apply innovative, strength-based services and activities to identified problems. Examples of this process exist in negotiations with neighborhood service users over 'case transitions' in the Patch neighborhoods. Over time, and with appropriate support, this approach releases opportunities and opens up an unlimited fund of service innovations and creative problem solving strategies for families and neighborhoods. The real goal of Patch is to promote family and neighborhood development and resiliency rather than 'plugging in' services.

Leadership, and the tools to sustain innovative thinking are critical to making Patch work. Areas for staff and organizational development include:

- Sustaining the Vision for Patch;
- Team Building;
- Knowledge Building;
- Practice Skills and Technique Building.[1]

In the beginning, team members need to spend time getting to know each other, each other's agencies, and the people they serve. If people on the team already know each other, that fact facilitates helping each other begin to think outside of their normal patterns of practice. Learning more about each others agencies serves to clarify boundaries in each agency's work, and how boundaries may be shifted to remove barriers to better coordination. Initiating a discussion about the people served by the variety of programs involved on the Patch team creates a collective understanding of the ways in which providers are addressing neighborhood needs.

Once the Patch team has developed some of the communication patterns characteristic of a functioning team, the other issues emerge. In addition to statistical data on the provision of social services in the neighborhood, the population served, and whatever outcomes data may be available, the need for greater consultation with services users becomes apparent. The main goal of the team is to initiate community centered practice, using the resources of the team to work collectively with families. Team members need to experience the value of drawing on the team's growing knowledge of neighborhood resources in order for the Patch process to take hold.

---

[1] This includes the patch network map – 'a picture of practice opportunities' for both the family and the Patch worker/team. It is the primary practice tool to understand the 'social' aspect of the work which can be done with a parent's participation.

The Meaning of Practice

As Patch has developed over time, it has become clear that, in the sustained work to implement a Patch approach, we have begun to discuss practice in ways that are new to everyone involved. In this regard, it is helpful to see 'practice' from a variety of vantage points in order to clarify what we mean when we talk about practice. Typically, when we talk about practice, we are thinking about 'professional practice'. Practice, in this sense, refers to a body of specialized knowledge, which is applied in specific ways with individuals who fit into certain categories. The physician's practice is the application of medical knowledge to people who are sick. In child welfare this kind of professional practice would include conducting investigations and/or assessments, planning and brokering services, monitoring service plans, testifying in court on behalf of children, and so on.

The meaning of professional practice has implications for Patch practice, and for the ways in which we create and sustain changes that make Patch a reality. Professional practice confers identity within a peer group and status with those outside the group. In addition, it is important to recognize that this type of professional practice is fundamental to maintaining child welfare institutions. In many ways, as we analyze and develop practice, it becomes important to recognize that child welfare institutions are not 'things' made of mandates and regulations. Institutions are the sum total of professional practices needed to recreate them everyday. This has implications for organizational change and how we go about understanding what changes and what stays the same as a result of our efforts. At the same time professional practice also carries with it the weight of the status quo. What we do as professionals conveys a whole culture, as well as the standards of that culture for how we see things, what we believe, what actions we ought to take at what time, and how we judge our efforts. So, when we talk about changing practice, we talk about taking on a major task: individual, institutional, and culture change. But each of us has substantial power to make it happen.

If anything, the foregoing should make clear what a different conception of practice we are discussing when we talk about Patch practice. First of all, when we talk about practice we are talking about how everyday practice can create systems change. Second, when we talk about Patch practice we are shifting 'paradigms'. We are moving from a psychological perspective to a social one. We are beginning to test the idea that social problems require a social analysis and social solutions. When an infant experiences the risk and deprivation of neglect, we are, first and foremost, testing the possibility that the problem is at its root insufficient nurturing, attendance, care from a primary caregiver, generally a parent. Any number of other appropriate people from extended family members to close friends, to paid child care can help resolve the absence of relationships that appear as 'neglect'. When we seek to redress the neglect, we do so by creating more and better relationships around the infant and parents, and between the network of people who make up what we might name the child's 'primary, extended network' – the collection of individuals, less and more professional in nature, less or more informal, less or more embedded within one another's lives in multiple ways, potentially, as co-workers, neighbors, kin, friends, or paid service professionals.

This is hard because it requires a new way of working. It requires the need for and support of a team with whom to share the work of a community, and a variety of people dedicated to developing this same new way of working at other levels inside and outside of the system. It requires the participation and assistance of many people involved in the day to day lives of individuals and families who experience difficulties at some times and are able to become a supportive part of a social network at others. It requires working against the grain of what you might normally, automatically, do because you are undertaking a problem solving approach with people rather than accessing a diagnosis, or interpreting the results of an assessment, or plugging in services which seem like they might help. In this way Patch practice becomes *social* work: not professional activity based on dispensing specialized knowledge, privileged information, and resources to which you are the gatekeeper, but practice that works to make social solutions to social problems.

Conclusion

The question then becomes: if Patch teams are supposed to maintain their normal ways of working, their professional practice while developing Patch practice, what is the relationship between Patch and conventional practice? The answer is that Patch represents a simpler mode of practice, but it carries strong implications for the way we pursue professional practice. Again, patch practice is *social* in the most fundamental sense. It requires working with the basic weave of relationships that comprise everyday life in neighborhoods. How do residents as individuals and as members of families successfully negotiate everyday life? The foundation of this kind of practice is the 'exchange'.

This becomes so basic to practice because it builds from the primary principle that Patch is about human and humane qualities of dignity, equality, and respect. This is clear from each and every one of the practice principles documented above. This introduces a major change in relationship between the worker and family members. Not expertise and absence of expertise, but dialogue and exchange.

The Patch approach is a vision of change, and a problem solving approach. As the cycles of reform turn, we are becoming seasoned beyond the kind of 'policy optimism' that has us looking to the 'next big thing' as the solution to the woes of child welfare. It is increasingly clear that really there are no final solutions to the problems we face in child welfare. There are, however, viable, long-lived reforms rooted in humanistic practice and a sound working knowledge of ways to promote and manage change successfully. There may be many paths to improvement, but as we get to a viable social service system we will recognize it....whatever we call it, it will look and act like the Patch approach.

References

Adams P. (1994), *Strengthening Families and Neighborhoods: A Community Centered Approach*, University of Iowa School of Social Work, Iowa City.

Smale G. (1996), *Mapping Change and Innovation*, HMSO, London.

Smale G. (2000), *Social Work and Social Problems*, Macmillan, London.

8 Justice, Child Protection and Family Centres – Part 1(Inside)

ELLEN JONES and DAVE ELY

St. Gabriel's is a Children's Society project that opened in 1979. The project offers a range of family support and child protection services alongside use by the local community. The Children's Society is committed to social justice for children and young people. The project aims to provide integrated child centred and holistic support and protection services to enable children and young people to live safely in families and communities.

Introduction

Boushel's 'Protective Environment' model provides a framework which family centres can use in providing integrated child protection practice and family support which empowers and promotes change for families and children (Boushel 1994). Also, Boushel's model fits with the holistic model of child protection practice outlined in the 'Framework for the Assessment of Children In Need and their Families' (DH 2000). A case study illustrates holistic empowerment practice, in a matter of serious child abuse.

Family Centres and Child Protection

Family centres are commonly recognised to synthesise a range of different themes and concerns in the issues they address (Roberts, 1992). These include partnership with parents, importance of community and informal networks, self help, need to avoid children becoming looked after by the local authority, flexibility of welfare services, child centredness, seeing the user as more than just a client, and the issue of child abuse/protection (De'Ath, 1988; Hester, 1985; Warren, 1986; 1993; Roberts, 1992). The wisdom and viability of this mix has been much debated (Warren, 1986;

Cannan, 1992; De'Ath, 1988) yet it seems clear that it implies a commitment to an holistic and integrated view of families, children and the issues in their lives.

In the current climate there is a risk of social services departments being reduced to undertaking only child protection work and work with looked after children and young people. Wider support to families then becomes confined to other Government regeneration initiatives. It is of key importance to reiterate the successful way family centres synthesize support and protection, in a way that is both effective and valued by users (Warren-Adamson, 2000).

It is suggested that child protection came to be ever more dominant in the family centre world through the 1980s (Warren, 1981). Although some commentators argued for the viability of making child protection work part of a family centre mix (Gill, 1988) there has been considerable pessimism to the effect that child protection work draws family centres to narrow, individualised, pathological views of families. This detracts from a wider set of family centre principles and ethics (Cannan, 1992; Holman, 1992, 1999). This concern has been reinforced by the view that the concept of child protection has been primarily individualistic and paternalistic. (Parton 1985, 1991, 1997; Thorpe, 1991; Farmer and Boushel, 1999).

The Ecological Perspective

However, concepts of child protection exist that are more holistic. Tzeng et al. (1991) proposed ecological views of all forms of harm. Following the influential work of Bronfenbrenner (1979) and Belsky (1980), there has been the development of ecological models of child abuse. These models recognize the multi-factorial nature of abuse and examine the impact of a range of factors at different levels, including the individual, the family, the community, and wider social and cultural influences. Feminist and systemic perspectives also urge consideration of structural social and cultural issues within child abuse (Macleod & Saraga, 1988).

These perspectives have probably not informed family centre views of child protection sufficiently. The risk remains that family centres too readily accept that child protection work inevitably means a narrow individualistic focus. However, practice based on an ecological model has to be linked to partnership and empowerment. To achieve change substantially for a child or young person who has been harmed or is at risk, child protection interventions need to be located within, and take account of, the wider social world in which children and their carers exist. Change needs to be at the social and systemic level, not just at the individual or family level, in order to achieve social justice for children and young people.

Work at St Gabriel's has been influenced by the concept of the 'Child's Protective Environment' (Boushel, op. cit.). This model provides an ecological and holistic framework for assessment and intervention. Boushel describes four interconnected factors to be taken account of in identifying the child's protective environment. These are:

1. The value attached to children;
2. The status of women and carers;
3. The social connectedness of children and their carers;
4. The extent and quality of the protective safety nets available.

Each of these factors operates at the level of the individual, the family, the extended family, the community, the state, and society. Boushel sees the framework as an essential tool for both effective intervention in abusive contexts and in effecting social change. She also sees the framework as being true to the spirit of the Children Act 1989 in promoting partnership and culturally sensitive practice. The term 'the child's protective environment' is used

> ... as a way of signifying the range of structural, cultural personal and interpersonal factors which combine to make the child's world a more or less safe and fulfilling place. It is maintained that an understanding of this wider environment is essential to the assessment of risk and to the development of appropriate and user-empowering protection plans. (Boushel, op. cit.)

The Assessment Framework

The year 2000 saw the publication by the Department of Health of the 'Framework for the Assessment of Children in Need and Their Families' (DH, op. cit.). Practitioners in England and Wales are charged with maintaining a holistic and child centred perspective when undertaking statutory assessments of children in need or in need of protection. More than this, child protection practice is located within a wider context of

94

positive promotion of child welfare:

> Safeguarding children should not be seen as a separate activity from promoting their welfare. They are two sides of the same coin. Promoting welfare has a wider more positive, action centered approach embedded in a philosophy of creating opportunities to enable children to have optimum life chances in adulthood as well as ensuring they are growing up in circumstances consistent with the provision of safe and effective care. (DH, 2000)

The Framework of Assessment promotes an ecological approach which moves away from the previous 'checklist' approach of the 'Orange Book', (DoH, 1988) where assessment constituted a one-off snapshot or event. The Framework of Assessment promotes a view of assessment as a process, which will change and influence those involved.

The Assessment Framework itself provides a model of assessment that is multi-factorial. The Framework describes three domains which are represented as a triangle with the child's welfare in the centre. The three domains reflect the levels at which Boushel describes the child's protective environment as working, although there is less stress on the impact of wider social and cultural factors on the child and the family. The domains for assessment are:

- Child's developmental needs;
- Parents and caregivers capacities to respond appropriately;
- The impact of wider family and environmental factors on parenting capacity and children.

Hardiker's framework (Hardiker et al., 1999) is referred to in the DH publication, as a useful holistic model operating at different levels of intervention. The model describes three levels of intervention:

1. The first is vulnerable groups and communities where a community development approach can combat disadvantage (primary prevention).
2. The second is for families and communities experiencing early stressors where a social casework approach can address need and prevent deterioration (secondary prevention).
3. The third is for families subject to severe stress where remedial interventions can act as a last resort safety net (tertiary prevention).

Family centres operate at all these levels, perhaps with the same family at different stages in their lifecycle. Research commissioned by the DoH in the 1990s argued for a more holistic, integrated approach to child protection and family support.

> The research shows that agencies involved in child protection are often too remote from family support services, each having their own staff, ways of working and resources. Since the problems faced by children are complex, practical benefits can come from an approach which merges questions about the child's protection with others about support for the family. (DoH, Dartington, 1995)

Family centres are well placed to provide an integrated, comprehensive and effective approach to support and protection issues. The holistic framework suggested by Boushel can be utilized both to assess risk in child protection and examine families support needs to provide appropriate interventions to reduce stress and support the child within the family.

The Integrated Model

At St Gabriel's Family Centre all staff work in child protection and family support contexts in a range of different programmes in the centre. This results in wide ranging experience, skill and sensitivity to the issues children and families bring. A teamwork approach with a high priority given to supervision and support means that the distressing facts of child abuse can be heard, contained, understood, and managed. A reflective culture means that workers and families can learn from and process their experience. Involvement in long-term support programmes means that workers witness growth and change and are involved in the journey families make. The centre is working with both risk factors and protective factors for families and the balance between the two. This includes assessing the level of risk in child protection and working to change the balance by reducing stress and increasing support. It is important that current debates within social welfare do not continue the split in childcare between those who focus on protection issues and those who focus on prevention, support and work in the community.

A research project involving six family centres in Brighton and Hove, including St Gabriel's, found that all of the centres had high degrees of user satisfaction and were also able to engage the most marginalized and socially excluded families in effective work. All of the centres used an integrated model of family support and child protection work, although the balance of work and the location of the centres were very different (Warren-Adamson, 2000). The author of the research project concluded:

> A socially inclusive perspective reinforces the view that the functions described....containment, decision making, resource centre, community development, are real tensions which deserve to be contained within one centre, and that by settling for only one function opportunities are lost for families.

St Gabriel's Family Centre also has a child centred perspective, holding the child as central to all work undertaken. The UN Convention on the Rights of the Child (1991) is clear that children and young people have a number of rights which includes protection as one. Play and art therapy and consultation with children about a range of issues of concern to them, helps workers at St Gabriel's stay in touch with the child's world. Workers have also developed a range of skills in listening and communicating with children and young people at a range of ages and abilities. This provides the capacity for the centre to become truly part of the 'protective environment' for children with whom the centre is working.

St. Gabriel's has had variation in its focus along the support protection spectrum. What has remained central is a commitment to working with families in a range of ways and incorporating serious protection issues within a wider ethos and set of services. The aim is neither to collude with denial of harm nor to allow a narrow concept of protection to dominate.

Currently the centre offers a rich mix of services and interventions such as assessments, systemic based family work, therapeutic groups for children and adults, social support groups, toy library, parenting interventions, peer education, play and art therapy, individual counselling, pregnancy groups for teenage parents, and so on.

Case Study

What follows is an account of a piece of practice that aims to demonstrate integrated child protection practice within a family centre, using Boushel's framework. This case demonstrates how a wider holistic view informs individual practice and how a child protection focus need not prohibit the concept of the empowerment journey (Warren, 1997). A number of features have been disguised to avoid the possibility of identification.

Risk Assessment

St. Gabriel's received a referral from a social worker for a risk assessment on a family where a 4 year old child had been seriously injured. A medical assessment indicated that the injury was non-accidental. The parents were interviewed but neither took responsibility for causing harm to the child.

Following assessment of the attachment relationship between the child and her mother and stepfather whilst the child was in hospital, the local authority decided the child could live with her mother in a foster home with contact to the stepfather carefully supervised.

Risk assessments can be seen as towards the 'heavy' end of child protection functions and are clearly not readily associated with the more informal support functions at family centres. Parents in such situations may be angry, upset and feeling they have few or no choices.

The centre uses a formal approach to assessments within the framework of 'Working Together to Safeguard Children' (DoH, 1999). There are meetings to create clarity between agencies, to discuss what the assessment will involve, a clear statement of concerns, what the local authority want and what will happen to information. For this work the centre uses a team approach, and prefers to use a one-way mirror for live supervision. This is negotiated with the family and the reasons explained.

On the surface this position could be seen as limiting the choice for constructive work. Yet the idea that clear boundaries, and a clear statement of concerns can be associated with positive change has been argued in relation to child protection and in relation to work where the male partner is violent (Gouldner, 1985). The wider context is brought into the room. The power issues are not just about the power of the state over families but in this instance, the misuse of power by adults over children and men over women.

Krane and Davies (2000) and Healy (1998) argue for the 'productive and necessary use of statutory power for the redistribution of power within families' (Krane & Davies, 2000). It is essential, obviously, that the parents feel respected, cared for and 'held' emotionally during this process. There needs to be clarity that it is the harming behaviours that are not acceptable, not the individual parents as people.

Live supervision and the concept of a therapeutic team in a centre with good team support enables workers to handle the strong emotions engendered by child abuse and therefore helps the parents manage theirs. Reflective space for the workers is a critical part of the model and includes explicit examination of the values and preconceptions of the worker. Attention is paid to the 'narrative' developed in sessions and in listening to the parent's story. Krane and Davies (2000) argue that:

> The risk assessment trend has the potential to entrench oppressive relations of gender, race, and class in child welfare practice with mothers. We suggest an approach to risk assessment which incorporates a 'mothering narrative' might offer a more thorough evaluation of the condition within which risk emerges.

A series of sessions proceeded. These were with the parents together and separately. Boushel's concept of protective environments can be applied to this situation. The four sets of factors, linked to the degree of safety in environments for children were explored during the assessment. These are:

1. The value given to children (and particular categories of children);
2. The status of women and carers;
3. Social interconnectedness of children and their carers;
4. Extent and quality of protective safety nets.

This framework provided crucial information in assessing the risks in this situation. In this case the stepfather did not value this child and regarded her as a rival. He was dominating and, at times, abusive to his partner; he belittled her and undermined her self-esteem. She had been left unsupported, isolated and reliant on him. The assessment process enabled these factors to be examined and challenged. The wider view of communities and safety is applicable to an apparently individual situation.

Clearly it is implicit in the above that gender and power were very central to this situation. The assessment explored the power relationships between the couple and also wider views and attitudes. The protective environment model encourages exploration and analysis at all these levels. St Gabriel's takes the view that the wider structural position of men and women in society has to inform individual work.

Feminist perspectives are helpful. Indeed, historical evidence suggests that women as mothers have seen the state as an ally when faced with violence but understandably resent being treated in a condescending or patronising way (Gordon 1988).

One political solution here is to ally to the women while a more therapeutic practice stance is to help the couple on their relationship. The necessary stance has to straddle the two. Gouldner (op. cit.) argues for an also/and approach that synthesises the wider political with the personal practice rather than an either/or approach which insists one chooses. She has used this approach in the context of family therapy with domestic violence.

The sessions continued. The stepfather did not change. The mother made changes and disclosed information which convinced professionals that the stepfather was responsible for the injury. The key inhibitor to disclosing this had been that she felt she was to blame for introducing her partner into the household, and that she had therefore failed in her judgment and as a mother. This reflects the distortion of responsibility in abusive situations and the tendency for the socialisation of women to lead to inappropriate self-blame by mothers.

The worker was very clear that the mother was not responsible for the actions of a partner but she was responsible for making protective choices now. The sessions offered an ongoing process and trusting relationship that enabled her to make these choices. A statutory risk assessment context provided an empowering and therapeutic 'protective environment'.

The mother separated from the stepfather. She chose to continue sessions which proceeded without live supervision and became more explicit, personal and intimate. She identified the need for group support to sustain the change and develop her own confidence and skills. A forensic approach to risk assessment might have just made an assessment and followed this with recommendations. The mother in this case was engaged in a change process with a female worker she trusted. The integrated approach that St Gabriel's employs enabled the mother in this instance to make use of other services available in the centre.

Family Support

The Friday group programme at St Gabriel's works with women with children under five, who are experiencing significant stressors. 'Working Together to Safeguard Children' (DoH 1999) identifies a range of stressors that can have a negative impact on children's development. These include social exclusion, domestic violence, mental illness and substance misuse. Women participating in the programme may be unconfident, struggle with their children, have experienced abusive relationships, have a range of personal difficulties, be isolated and unsupported. Many also have enormous strengths and choose to join the St. Gabriel's Friday group because they wish to change the future for both themselves and their children.

The group offers nurture, food, care, containment, a therapeutic group for mothers, a children's group, parent-child interventions which promote child centered parenting and a range of other opportunities. The programme is very coherent with the promotion of a 'protective environment' for parents and for their children as outlined by Boushel.

Recently a study by Ethier et al. (2000) looked at the impact of a similar multidimensional intervention programme with families at risk for child neglect. The study indicated that such an intervention could not only decrease risk of neglect but that parents also showed improvements in family relationships, protectiveness, social support and inclusion, and personal development.

> Family centres have been criticized for having a narrow role acting as 'social regulators' for disadvantaged families living in poverty. (Cannan 1992)

The protective environment concept keeps the child as the focus yet inherently links the child's well-being and safety to a concept of the empowerment of women (and carers). This means that protection and individual 'policing of mothers' need not be associated. Within this model, protection requires empowerment.

The mother concerned made very good use of the programme and, as is practice, agreed through a review when it was time to leave. At this stage she was confident, living alone, her child had lived safely at home for a considerable period, she had not entered an abusive relationship, her child's schooling was arranged and she used the group to get ideas about and plan her future.

She wrote about her experience of the centre and it was produced as a document available for others to read at her request. A sense of the 'project user' as author. She considered being interviewed for a magazine, although in the end they withdrew.

In relation to these feelings of being author and speaking to the media, St Gabriel's offers support to parents – practical and emotional. It is a way for the service user to utilize new skills to participate more fully as a citizen if they wish. As parents develop in confidence, grow and change, it is common to find qualities and skills emerge that they did not know they

101

had. Often parents undertake training or find work.

The family left the centre, the mother undertook a college course and got a job. The project can sometimes make a contribution to course costs for users and has purchased cheap second-hand word processors to help parents. Of equal importance is having an environment that facilitates the development of these skills in people who are oppressed, poor and marginalised. The child continued to make positive progress and the family no longer needed social work input.

Conclusion

Family Centres can integrate support and protection work in an empowering and anti-oppressive way. Family centres are a critical part of the 'modernizing' agenda, addressing issues of social exclusion and providing a 'joined up' response to support, protection and inclusion. This ensures that children, young people and their families who are involved in child protection processes in family centres have access to as wide a range of opportunities and possibilities for change and growth as possible.

However, family centres are located within a context themselves, and they can only provide part of the child's 'protective environment'. There is also a need to change community and organizational cultures. Social justice for children and young people requires systemic change at all levels. An innovative example of a community based protection project is the First Stop Keeping Safe Project in Brighton whose development is described next. The First Stop Project arose from St Gabriel's work in the 1990s.

References

Belsky J. (1980), 'Child Maltreatment: An Ecological Integration' in *American Psychologist*, Vol 35, pp. 320–335.

Boushel M.(1994), 'The Protective Environment of Children: Towards a Framework for Anti-oppressive, Cross-cultural and Cross-National Understanding', in *British Journal of Social Work*, Vol 24, pp. 173–190.

Brofenbrenner U. (1979), *The Ecology of Human development: Experiments by Nature and Design*, Harvard University Press, Cambridge, London.

Cannan C.(1992), *Changing Families, Changing Welfare*, Harvester Wheatsheaf, Hemel Hempstead.

De'Ath E. (1988), 'The Family Centre Approach', The Children's Society, London, pamphlet.

DH. (1999), *Working Together to Safeguard Children*, HMSO, London.

DOH. (1995), *Child Protection: Messages from Research*, HMSO, London.

Ethier L., Couture G., Lacharite C. & Gagnier J.P. (2000),'Impact of a multidimensional intervention programme applied to families at risk for child neglect', in *Child Abuse Review*, Vol 9, No. 1, pp. 19–36.

Farmer E. & Boushel M. (1999), 'Child Protection Policy and Practice: Women on the Front Line', in Watson S. & Doyal L. eds. *Engendering Social Policy*, Open University Press, Buckingham.

Gill O. (1988),'Integrated Work in a Family Centre', in *Practice*, Vol 2, No. 3, pp. 243–255.

Gordon L. (1988), *Heroes of their Own Lives*, Viking Penguin, London.

Gouldner V. (1995), 'Feminism and Family Therapy', in *Family Process*, Vol 24, pp. 35–45.

Hardiker P., Exton K. & Barker M. (1999), 'Children Still in Need, Indeed: Prevention Across Five Decades,' in Stevenson O. ed. *Child Welfare in the U.K.*, Blackwell Science, Oxford.

Healey K. (1998), 'Participation and Child Protection: the Importance of Context', in *British Journal of Social Work*, Vol 28, pp. 897 – 914.

HMSO. (2000), *Framework for the Assessment of Children in Need & their Families*, HMSO, London.

Holman R. (1992),'Family Centres, Research Highlights' National Children's Bureau, London.

Krane J. & Davis L. (2000), 'Mothering and Child Protection Practice: Rethinking Risk Assessment,' in *Child and Family Social Work*, Vol 5, pp. 35-45.

MacLeod M. & Saraga E. (1988), 'Challenging the Orthodoxy: Towards a Feminist Theory and Practice', in *Feminist Review*, Vol 28, pp. 16–55.

Parton N. (1985), *The Politics of Child Abuse*, Macmillan, London.

Parton N. (1991), *Governing the Family*, Macmillan, London.

Parton N. (1997), *Child Protection and Family Support: Tensions, Contradictions & Possibilities*, Routledge, London.

Roberts D. (1992), 'Families & Family Centres – Child Abuse & Reluctant Consumers', M.A. Dissertation Kingston Polytechnic, unpublished

Thorpe D. (1994), *Evaluating Child Protection*, Open University Press, Buckingham.

Tzeng O., Jackson J. & Karlson H. (1991), *Theories of Child Abuse & Neglect: Differential Perspectives: Summaries & Evaluations*, Praeger, New York.

U.N. Convention on the Rights of the Child.

Warren C. (1986), Towards a Family Centre Movement: Reconciling Daycare, Child Protection & Community Work', in *Child Abuse Review*, Vol 1, No. 3, Summer.

Warren C. (1991), 'The Potential for Parent Advocacy in Family Centres,' MPhil Thesis, Southampton University, unpublished.

Warren C. (1993), *Family Centres and the Children Act 1989*, Tarrant Publishing/DOH, Arundel.

Warren C. (1997) 'Family Support and the Journey to Empowerment' in Cannan C. & Warren C. eds. *Social Action with Children and Families: A Community Development Approach to Child and Family Welfare*, Routledge, London

Warren-Adamson C. (2000), 'Family Centres: their Role in Fighting Social Exclusion', Interim Report of the Family Centre Action Research Project, Brunel University, unpublished.

Warren-Adamson C. (2000), 'We Must Not Bypass Family Centres', in *Community Care*, October 2000, No. 1342, p. 15.

9 Justice, Child Protection and Family Centres – Part 2 (Outside)

TERRI FLETCHER and MO ROMANO

First Stop Keeping Safe Project – Promoting Safer Communities for Children and Young People

> Though there are no easy answers to the problem of child abuse, there are ways forward. We are convinced that involving the community in protecting and safeguarding children can make a real contribution to reducing and preventing child abuse. But this involves a move sideways from purely professional practice to one that includes the community. (Macleod & Saranga, 1997)

Part 2 will look at the process and development of an innovative project which was set up to address child sexual abuse prevention in a community context. It explores the theory and thinking behind the project and the reality of putting this into practice on a housing estate in a South Coast city. The model, as developed by First Stop, argues for a holistic and systematic approach to child safety in the community, synthesising child abuse and child safety agendas and involving the community in the process.

Stage 1 – Theory and Thinking – Background

The 1990s has seen a growing interest in community work initiatives in favour of children and their families, for example, the promotion of child-friendly communities in the UK, NSPCC's Full Stop Campaign (1999), Heaton and Sayer's attempt to link social work's protective agenda with the wider interest of community development (1992), Henderson's broad focus on safe communities (Henderson 1995).

105

This account of community work intervention draws its inspiration especially from Boushel's idea of a *Child's Protective Community* (1994) and Finkelhor's (1984) framework, identifying stages of inhibition for the abuser from, in order, a) the inner person, b) the protective family, c) the protective community, and d) the child. In focusing on the protective community and the child, the First Stop initiative is not alone. Garbarino drew our attention to the need to link protection and communities (1987) and more recently Baldwin and Carruthers (1997) have illuminated community work practice in this context. What is distinctive about this project is that it proceeds from the external, developmental role of a family centre, and it attempts to tackle child protection head-on.

The First Stop concept began to take shape in 1993, following a series of discussions between the manager at St Gabriel's Family Centre, the head of the local Child Protection Unit and a Local Authority community work manager, about the prevalence of child sexual abuse. Of particular concern was the high rate of registrations on one of the town's large housing estates, which at the time had consistently just over half of the child sexual abuse registrations for the Brighton area as a whole and was recognised as having the highest rate of sexual abuse registrations in the County. This led to a proposal about preventing child sexual abuse through a process of Community Awareness and Education, a growing perspective in the exploration of alternatives in child protection. Recently, the Government document, 'Working Together', recognises that there is untapped potential within communities to protect children:

> Members of communities also possess strengths and skills which can be harnessed for the benefit of vulnerable children and their families. (DoH, 2000 para 3.88)

However, at the time of developing the pilot, these ideas were only just beginning to gain ground on the political and social agenda. The focus for change was still centred on the individual and often failed to recognise the potential for developing responsibility within the wider community to protect children.

Establishing a Community Partnership

The community work manager called a large inter-agency meeting on the estate to draw together and mobilise interested parties to look at how to prevent child sexual abuse in the community. This idea attracted a lot of interest and support from local agencies and some residents. A working group was established to take the project forward and to manage its overall development. This group had wide representation including Health, Education, Police, Social Services, Child Protection Unit, Playlink, Probation, Health Promotions and a local group – Women Survivors of Sexual Abuse. Most important, two local parents also joined the group.

One of them was a former beat police officer who lived and worked on the estate, and the woman, who we will call Mary, was a local resident and mother of four. She came with her own personal issues and agenda about sexual abuse and became a key player in planning and developing the project. This partnership framework and agency support has continued throughout the project's life and has been crucial to the project's development and success.

The Working Group was convened by the Social Services Department as the lead agency in this field, with overall responsibility being taken by the Community Development Manager for the local authority. The project was named 'First Stop' by the group to reflect that this could be a first port of call for parents wanting to prevent abuse. Additionally, a number of sub groups were formed to plan and develop specific areas of work.

The intention, to pilot the project for one year from September 1994, depended on securing the necessary funding to employ a project worker. In the event none was forthcoming and in 1994 Terri Fletcher joined the project as a student social worker on placement.

The Planning Process: Developing the Principles and Objectives.

A trawl of the literature provided little practical material on prevention. However, it did reveal the problem of child sexual abuse is widespread. It has been estimated that up to 60% of the population has received some kind of unwanted sexual attention as children.

Most Prevention Programmes Do Not Focus on Sexual Abuse Or Recognise the Role of the Community

And yet, most harm reduction strategies focus on environmental issues such as road and fire safety. The majority of prevention programmes do not deal with sexual abuse, or have tried to prevent further abuse after it has already happened. Prevention programmes which do address sexual abuse have mainly been focussed on children in schools giving them too much responsibility for preventing their own abuse, but have not looked at community or social attitudes or emphasised the importance of involving parents.

It was also recognised that in most cases of sexual abuse, the abuser is someone who is known to and trusted by the child. This suggested that in some communities the 'incest taboo' may be weak and that the boundaries of safe and unsafe sexual behaviour in relation to children may be unclear.

This view is reinforced by Finkelhor's research on preconditions for sexual abuse, which was very influential in our early planning. Four factors were identified which occur before a perpetrator sexually abuses a child:

- Motivation to abuse;
- Overcoming internal inhibitors;
- Overcoming external inhibitors;
- Overcoming the resistance of the child.

As previously noted, many prevention programmes have worked at the fourth level of Finkelhor's model, focussing on protection skills and knowledge enhancement for children in schools. However, evaluation studies of such programmes in the United States and Australia have indicated that an integrated approach in school and community was needed. Briggs and Hawkins found that the effectiveness of such programmes is largely dependent on parental involvement in reinforcing safety messages at home and that teacher involvement is also highly significant to positive outcomes (Briggs & Hawkins, 1994).

The Taboo of Child Sexual Abuse

The research showed that parents do not have enough information about the facts and nature of sexual abuse to protect their children. Parents also find it difficult to ask for such information or to discuss their concerns because of the taboo against talking about sexual abuse. This in turn helps to perpetuate unhelpful myths and stereotypes and can put children at risk.

Finkelhor's (1984) study of 521 parents of children aged 6 to 14 in the USA concluded that the majority, 71%, had not discussed the topic of sexual abuse with their children and that even where such discussions did occur, parents often failed to mention important aspects of the problem. For example, the misconception that children are most at risk of sexual abuse from strangers persisted in the study group.

This view was echoed by a study which interviewed those with most knowledge of the subject, child abusers themselves. An article entitled 'What child sex offenders tell us' concluded with the following 'advice' from offenders:

> It is evident that parents are not given enough information to keep their children safe, especially when they leave them in the care of others. Parents, teachers and other professionals need leaflets with specific suggestions, given out freely in schools, libraries, doctor's surgeries and other public places. Without good safety programmes and informed adults, children will continue to be vulnerable to the sexual abuser. (Child Abuse and Neglect, May 1995)

Consulting with the Local Community

How then to apply this theory to practice. At this stage we decided to consult with the local community to see if the research findings would fit with the views of local parents. With the help of local health visitors, family centre workers and Playlink pre-school visitors, a survey was circulated to parents to find out their perceptions of child abuse and what information they might need or want in order to feel more confident about protecting their children. Over fifty local parents agreed to take part in the survey.

The findings mirrored those of the literature review. Parents overwhelmingly talked about protecting children in terms of stranger danger warnings and these were the messages that had been passed on to children. Their fears for children's safety were mainly centred outside of the home; the most prioritised concerns being road safety, children playing out unattended and secluded play areas.

Parents expressed the need for more information, particularly in talking to children about keeping safe from abuse, which was an area of great difficulty for most of them. Parents did however have clear ideas about what they thought might help. The clear message was that parents felt they needed more information and skills to protect their children from abuse. This research and consultation process and the views and experience of the Working Group led to the development of the main principles in setting up First Stop.

Principles of the First Stop Project

- A partnership model between local agencies and residents;
- To break the taboo in talking about child sexual abuse;
- To focus on the strengths of the community, rather than on problems within particular families;
- To encourage the idea that it is adults' responsibility to keep children safe;
- To change the culture of a neighbourhood and to create a culture of knowledge and protection in order to reduce opportunities for child abusers.

The general objective of First Stop was to reduce and prevent child sexual abuse on the estate through a process of community education. The project would aim to break the secrecy about sexual abuse by raising awareness of the extent and nature of the problem and by promoting discussion and encouraging the community to take action to keep their children safe.

The project aimed to increase external inhibitors in the community to abuse through education campaigns in school and the community to raise awareness of the problem of child sexual abuse. Within this framework, we were clear that children could not be made responsible for protecting themselves and that the perpetrator should be held accountable. Non-abusing adults in the community were seen as the best allies in helping to protect children and prevent abuse.

The project would also work on promoting a strong message that child sexual abuse is not acceptable to the community and that adults are responsible for keeping children safe. First Stop would work from the premise that the majority of adults want a safer community for children and could act as protective adults for children given the right support, skills and information to do so. Involving parents and communities in the process of protecting children were therefore seen as key elements of a child abuse prevention strategy. How to involve communities in this process in a way that was meaningful, accessible and supportive was a central issue in taking the work forward. The review of the research literature suggested that there was no example of a campaign of this type in Britain, that is a systematic attempt to inform a culture of the reality of sexual abuse – analogous to campaigns on smoking, drink driving or AIDS.

Developing a Methodology: Process and Dilemmas

From the outset, the project was planned with a distinct community work focus in mind. It would use the well-established network of community groups and official agencies such as schools in order to develop public awareness through community education. This would be based on a partnership between parents, residents and professionals within the community. Furthermore, the professionals were very keen that 'discussions within the community should be open and honest'. There was also a strong drive to promote the principles of empowerment and ownership by the local community.

There was a high degree of commitment from the interagency planning group but the process did not always run smoothly. This was a period of mutual learning and co-operation which involved a steep learning curve, a willingness for all to take account of new perspectives and a lack of professional dogmatism. A particular challenge was integrating the personal and group dynamics associated with child sexual abuse with those linked to community development.

This was reflected in a number of concerns and disagreements which were debated within the Working Group. Firstly, there were fears about adverse publicity and stigmatisation of the estate and how this would affect the people living and working on there, particularly since a number of the agencies had already experienced this. There was also concern about an increase in disclosures from children and adult survivors as a result of the project; not only because of the resource implications, but because some workers themselves felt uncomfortable in dealing with this. A central dilemma was how to involve parents in the project and encourage local ownership, when clearly child sexual abuse is a subject which many people – parents and professionals – find distasteful, would rather did not exist and would prefer to ignore.

The difficulties of getting parents in the wider community involved was reflected in Mary's own experience of the Working Group. As professionals we wanted to promote participation, but the style and culture of the group did not always lend itself to this. Mary confided that she found the meetings formal and intimidating, full of jargon which did not relate to her experience. Although she was a committed member of the group, who expressed lots of opinions and ideas over an informal cup of tea, she found it very difficult to participate during meetings because she felt that she was not an 'expert'. We ended up doing much of our planning in her kitchen.

When we asked some of the other professionals how they experienced the meetings, many of them shared Mary's view. We therefore addressed this as a group, and changed both the venue and style of the meetings.

The issue of how to engage with the wider community on an issue as sensitive as child sexual abuse was one which was hotly debated in the early stages of the project, with two views emerging:

1. That the project should address the issue of sexual abuse head on from the outset, both in its publicity and approach.

2. That we should take a broader view incorporating other forms of abuse against children as well as sexual abuse.

At heart, the difficulty was to engage parents in an issue which they themselves had not identified as an area of concern in their neighbourhood; while at the same time recognising that child sexual abuse might never be place on the community agenda because it is too uncomfortable a subject.

There was however, some basis for optimism for the direct approach in the positive evaluation of the Zero Tolerance Campaign in Edinburgh. This was a city-wide advertising campaign to challenge social attitudes towards physical and sexual assaults against women and girls. Although the Zero Tolerance campaign offered no examples of the type of work with the community envisaged by First Stop, it was very influential in terms of the design of the project's poster and publicity campaign. The issue of the media was carefully planned and as a group we were clear in giving the message that the estate had been chosen to pilot this child abuse prevention project because of the strong network of community groups.

A Framework for Practice

The following methodology emerged:

- A community poster and leaflet campaign, with hard hitting child sexual abuse information and messages; for example,
- Work in schools about the broad issue of 'Keeping Safe' based on the Protective Behaviours model;
- A community training package about child sexual abuse for parents and professionals.

The poster and leaflet campaign was designed and developed by the publicity sub-group, influenced by the Zero Tolerance campaign, and was funded and produced by the East Sussex Police. The training pack for parents, was largely designed by adapting existing training packages for professionals around raising awareness issues relating to child sexual abuse.

Protective Behaviours

The Keeping Ourselves Safe programme in schools was based on the 'Protective Behaviours' personal safety and empowerment model. This was developed in the United States and adopted state-wide as a school based child protection programme in both America and Australia. Protective Behaviours is based on the exploration of two key themes:

> We All Have The Right To Feel Safe All Of The Time.

> Nothing Is So Awful That You Can't Talk About It With Someone (You Trust).

The programme is based on the positive starting point of feeling safe, what that feels like and acknowledging our feelings. It recognises that safety is an individual and internal concept and links safety with adventurousness, taking it beyond the restrictive sense of locking doors. The process encourages children and adults to become more aware of 'Early Warning Signs' in our body which tell us when we are feeling uncomfortable or unsafe. It also helps people to recognise whether this is a 'fun to feel scared' feeling like going on a roller-coaster when we have choice and control, a 'safe risk' when we make an informed choice or an unsafe feeling when we need to take action to keep ourselves safe. (dependent on the developmental stage of the child). The development and use of support networks of 'safe adults' is a key element of the process, which further promotes empowerment to take protective action where necessary.

Protective Behaviours was chosen over other school-based programmes because of the emphasis on the development of individual and community safety strategies and networks rather than prescriptive measures of safety and because the programme is a non-threatening way of addressing a range of safety situations including child sexual abuse. At this stage all local school staff were offered two days training on Protective Behaviours so that it could then be integrated in the school curriculum.

First Stop Gets Real Money

Money came from the Joint Finance Group (now Primary Care Group) for initial 3 year funding for the project on a pilot basis. Terri then joined the project as the full time worker. It was decided that the project and its worker would be managed by the Children's Society because it was felt that this would be perceived as a neutral agency which local parents might be more willing to get involved with. It also had a proven track record in managing child protection work, which was a crucial factor in terms of credibility with local agencies and ensuring safe practice. At this point discussions also began to try to secure a secondment from Social Services to enable an experienced worker to join the project to provide support for survivors of sexual abuse who might come forward as a result of the campaign. In the event, this took several months to finalise and Mo Romano finally joined the project, six months later and her role evolved into a far more integral part of the project's development and work in the community.

In preparation for the next stage, the project secured a local base within the community, as up until this point the project had been largely planned from St Gabriel's Family Centre, located in the middle of town. We were now ready, or so we thought, for the next stage, launching into the community.

Stage 2 – From Planning to Practice

The Publicity Campaign - Mentioning the Unmentionable

The project began its move into the neighbourhood with a poster and publicity campaign designed to raise awareness and introduce the First Stop Project to local residents. We had already made some contacts through local workers through Mary's involvement and through the survey which was carried out with workers from Playlink, the Family Centre and Health visitors. The worker personally went around the estate putting up large posters on every (legal) empty area of wall space until the whole

114

estate was covered in brightly coloured posters proclaiming the need for action on child sexual abuse.

At the same time, hundreds of leaflets were distributed via the local schools with similar messages about a community responsibility to stop Sexual Abuse. At this stage we had no idea whether we would be inundated with calls, either of the Mr Angry variety or from people whose families had suffered the effects of sexual abuse. I waited for the deafening roar, but it was the silence which deafened.

A follow up discussion at the local family centre elicited the following range of comments:

> Why this neighbourhood; what are you suggesting?
> I don't think you should give leaflets like that to children to bring home.
> There was no one to help me when I was abused, I think it's a good idea.
> It's a bit in your face isn't it?

It was interesting to note that even those parents who had responded positively to the survey and had in fact said that they wanted more information on protecting children, were somewhat hostile to the poster and leaflet campaign. This probably said as much about the process as the content of the launch.

Getting the Message Across

Thankfully, the project also received very positive press coverage, due to careful planning and some sensitive contacts. We were helped at this stage by an article in the community newspaper – we sponsored the production of one edition and thereby secured a front page spread. The headline read **'(Neighbourhood) Leads the Way!'** Positive re-framing is all. We don't for a minute think that this fooled the locals, who regularly asked at community meetings whether their estate had a bigger problem with sexual abuse than elsewhere, and if not what were we doing here? This required some careful handling since we wanted to be honest but not alarmist.

This was a crucial time for the project. Making contacts is the bread and butter of community work and we cannot overstate the difficulties of this task, in the context of introducing a project that is concerned with child sexual abuse. Picture, if you will, the scene, as the project worker visits a parent and toddler group, to make contact with local mums. All is going well until the point when the worker has to describe what the project is about. Crunch time, the issue can't be fudged. The worker gives it to them straight and suddenly the parents go very quiet and remember something they need from the shops. This is so often the understandable response.

People in the Community Tell Their Stories

Sometimes people would stay and talk, usually if they had a story to tell. In the first few months we had many conversations with survivors of abuse, many of whom were disclosing for the first time and with parents whose children had been sexually abused, many of whom said that they felt let down by the formal child protection system, which they often felt had failed to protect their children. Some of these parents were referred on to other agencies for support, but mostly, they just wanted someone to talk with and listen to them. At this stage the majority of contacts were made by individual chats and home visits and we began to think that a possible way forward might be a 'tupperware party' type approach to prevention, where a small group of parents came together in each other's houses.

Child Protection Within the Community

During this initial stage (and subsequently), we also had several child protection referrals from people who either did not want to talk to Social Services, were not sure if the concerns they had about a child were 'bad enough' to pass on, and simply wanted a 'middle' agency to talk things through with. In all cases parents were supported in passing on information, where necessary to Social Services colleagues and this was, perhaps surprisingly, accepted as the safe thing to do. It quickly became apparent from talking with parents that most of them had very little knowledge of how the formal child protection system works, unless they had first hand experience of it. Many parents were not clear about the role of other agencies in the child protection system and assumed that social workers and the Police were the sole players.

Moreover, there was and is a lot of myth and fantasy about what happens when abuse is reported to statutory agencies. Parents fear the consequences of reporting often with justification – reprisals from neighbours in the form of verbal and or physical harassment being a common and real concern. We were also told that it was local practice to firebomb the houses of suspected paedophiles, so people were reluctant to make allegations. Conversely an allegation of sexual abuse can be a powerful weapon for someone who is bearing a grudge. While all of this was positive in terms of our contact with the community, most of these people, having unloaded their concern did not want any further involvement with the project, and we did not want to become best known as the 'grassing up project'.

One parent, however, did come forward to get involved, which under the circumstances was a brave thing to do. She told us that the great fear for many parents was that other people would make assumptions about their involvement. Are they abusing their kids? Are they grassing up other people? Have they been abused? And mostly we suspect parents did not come forward because they were a) too busy looking after their own children, b) would rather not know anything about sexual abuse, it being a particularly distasteful and difficult subject, and c) did not think it had anything to do with them. It is always a good benchmark to ask ourselves if we are expecting more of others than we would be prepared to do ourselves. It is doubtful if many of us would be tempted by the offer of an invitation to a meeting about preventing child sexual abuse, unless we had a particular reason for being there. It was also unclear what we were actually asking parents to get involved in, since we were a campaign and not a service provider. What if they decided that the answer was indeed to run paedophiles out of the area? It was interesting that as soon as the project 'launched' into the community, one of our staunch supporters – Mary – withdrew her involvement in the project. This was largely due to family pressures, but we have also discovered that there is often a shelf-life for people's involvement.

The paradox became ever clearer, that while our aim was to promote safety, the community was telling and showing us that they were feeling unsafe about the project, and we felt unsafe too as workers. It was time for a rethink.

The Re-launch: The Project Open Day

The first breakthrough came with the idea of holding an Open Day, to raise the profile of the project, demystify what we were about, give people information, bring together agencies and parents and have some fun! Suddenly, with a practical focus, it became much easier to get people

117

involved, the Working Group once again became an animated forum of activity as local agencies took on different tasks for the day.

The day was planned and organised around the Protective Behaviours process being taught in local schools. The two themes 'Nothing is So Awful that You Can't Talk with Someone About It' and 'We All Have the Right to Feel Safe' became the focus for an information room about prevention and protection strategies and a 'Safe Space' room with hand massage and relaxing music. All local agencies co-operated in running the day and in bringing along local parents. Playlink the Youth Centre, Health Visitors, Survivors Network and local schools all ran stalls; the Family Centre closed for the day and were the star performers in a production of 'Little Red Riding Hood Tries Again' based on Keeping Safe strategies.

We provided a cheap lunch and refreshments which were served by a local mum and the Social Services manager for the area. Crèche workers from the local family centre ran a children's area. Local parents were also involved in making an Open Day banner, a backdrop for the play, a poster, badges and in distributing publicity. Local shopkeepers donated prizes for the raffle and displayed posters.

The day was a great success and well attended, because we had provided an event which was primarily fun, free and safe and the focus was not exclusively about child abuse. It also worked because of the partnership between different agencies and parents of the neighbourhood. This made it a real community event and lent us some much needed street credibility.

There developed a sort of borrowed goodwill, which still continues. It was also a great opportunity to ask parents what they wanted which in order of preference was more information on what children are doing in schools, seeing a video about protecting children, information on talking to children, being in a discussion group, having a discussion at home, being part of a parents advisory group.

The Open Day was a turning point because it gave clues as to how we might begin to integrate community approaches with child protection and was an example of working in partnership with both parents and other agencies. Some local workers asked for training in dealing with disclosure. A session was also arranged at the local Junior and Infant schools to give parents more information on the Protective Behaviours programme being introduced into schools. Twenty four parents attended this session, despite the school's prediction that we would be lucky to get four or five parents to come. This was largely achieved by standing outside the school gates for a whole week to invite parents to attend, and providing a crèche and refreshments.

The other major success was the development of a Parents' Forum from the six parents who had expressed an interest, all of whom were contacted post haste.

Developing The Parents' Forum

Our initial aims for the Parents Group were to provide a forum for discussion on child safety issues, to advise the project in its planning and process and to get involved in organising publicity and events. The parents, however, primarily wanted a space to talk about their own issues and feelings, particularly as most of them had unresolved personal issues about abuse. This was difficult to manage as we struggled to keep the meetings on a business-like footing when clearly the parents often wanted a support group; this also made it difficult for other people to join.

Although the meetings could often feel frustrating and meandering, these discussions were in fact very informative because they gave us a lot of information about 'where people were at', in terms of their views and ideas about child abuse and what they felt the community should do. Many of the group favoured a 'Megan's Law' approach in naming and shaming paedophiles, which we talked them through, and then out of, over a series of discussions.

The parents all undertook some Protective Behaviours training. Some of the parents took on general admin tasks such as sorting out the library of books and videos. Over time parents also co-facilitated presentations on the project's work for other family centres and made many suggestions about possible areas of work, many of which were taken up and developed.

Whilst it sometimes felt a bit chaotic, the group did in fact achieve a lot during its lifetime. This included getting the Council to provide spring bulbs to plant on the estate, to raise pride and confidence in the community. They also had a tree donated from a local garden centre to mark our first Child Safety Week which was planted in a square of baked hard earth outside the building, which had been empty for years. This is still sprouting despite predictions from the caretaker that it would be vandalised within days. The parents also organised and took part in our first Child Safety Week event, running an information shop, working with us in local schools and acting as advocates for the project with other local parents.

119

Amid the successes there were also some very difficult situations which arose in the group; one woman had an abusive partner and dominated the group with her story which she would tell at every opportunity. Another parent was accused of sexually abusing a child and had to be excluded from the group at least for the period of the investigation. Two of the group members began a relationship which was often played out in the meetings. Another parent was allowing her son to be in a risky situation with another adult and we had to work with her on some difficult issues which eventually necessitated involving Social Services. By working with people in an honest and respectful way and by positively challenging the group the worker was able to deal with the issues and maintain the group cohesion, even though there were moments when the group wanted to judge and exclude other members.

The group reformed many times and after a considerable time eventually folded, partly because of the lack of clarity about its aims and partly because people had developed and moved on. Many of them still keep in touch and one who has recently got a 'managerial' job told the family worker that she felt it was her experience with the group that had given her the confidence to apply. Another parent went on to do a teacher training course and a third has recently successfully claimed damages for the crimes of child sexual abuse committed against her when she was a child.

Stage 3 – A Safer Approach

Linking Child Abuse and Child Safety

The Parents Forum were particularly influential in developing our thinking and approach to working in the community. One of the first things that the group recommended was that we rewrite our project leaflet, using more positive language. From the lessons learned in our campaigning stage, the response from parents and the feedback from the Open Day, we concluded that a head on approach would not work in this community setting. We needed to find a safer way of talking to parents about difficult issues. While the vast majority of parents agree that children should be protected, no-one wants to acknowledge the possibility that their own children could be at risk. Some parents have unresolved issues of their own and feel unsafe talking about sexual abuse, and some simply find it too distasteful. What parents are prepared to talk about is Keeping Children Safe and this might include road safety, children playing out unsupervised and almost certainly bullying and stranger danger.

At this point we began to consider extending the use of the Protective Behaviours process which we had been using in schools for some time, to work in the community. We began talking to parents about Protective Behaviours and provided some training with a very positive response. Starting from 'where people are at' and feel safe is the most effective way of gradually introducing more 'loaded' abuse issues, within a safe framework. Protective Behaviours appeared to be a programme which could encompass all these issues and is acceptable to parents.

Protective Behaviours had been adopted from the beginning as the method for teaching safety awareness in schools. At this point, in the search for a broader, less threatening approach to community education, we realised that the Protective Behaviours process could be extended to raise community awareness and responsibility. Looking at child abuse within the wider context of 'Keeping Children Safe' sounds more positive and proactive and intrinsically has community support. This also allows us to think about child sexual abuse not as an 'out there' phenomenon, but as something which we need to think about in the context of ensuring children's safety, in the same way as we would more naturally and comfortably think about safety strategies for crossing the road.

This broader view of protection fits with Boushel's Protective Environment model (Boushel, op. cit.) which gives a good indication of factors associated with safer communities for children and reflects the complex systems and beliefs which influence a community's protective capacity. The view that preventive interventions need to influence a broad network of relationships and processes surrounding the developing child is widely held. Equally, sexual abuse programmes are more effective when they take a wider view, which encompasses bullying as well as sexual abuse. This is partly because this approach is less stigmatising but it also gives children and adults more opportunities for practising the skills they have learned. Following this re-framing process, it became clear that we also needed to develop direct services to get safety messages across in a way which was more supportive to families.

Working Together to Keep Children Safe

Since adopting Protective Behaviours as the framework for approaching safety in the community, it has created many opportunities for working with parents and other agencies under the slogan of 'Working together to keep children safe' and provided a basis for community training. All agencies in the neighbourhood, a number of parents and many children have undertaken Protective Behaviours training. This in turn has helped to create a common language and approach on the estate and resulted in a number of partnership initiatives. Using Protective Behaviours as a community safety currency also means that we have been able to develop a systematic approach to child safety.

Involving Parents

Our aim in working with parents is to support them in keeping themselves and their children safe by providing information, an opportunity for discussion and building links with other parents and community resources. It is important to recognise that parents can 'get involved' in a number of ways and at different levels. Some parents may choose to come to Keeping Safe groups, workshops and courses for information and support around child sexual abuse and specific safety issues. This type of safety work has to be very flexible to meet the needs of the group and might cover issues as ostensibly diverse as stress, bullying or sessions on paedophile behaviour. Our experience is that those parents who stay involved with the project often remain in contact for informal telephone support over long periods of time. These are often the group of parents who become the 'movers and shakers' and themselves develop and grow with the project.

For the majority of parents, however, their 'involvement' is likely to be more casual. Some parents come along to help make 'Keeping Safe' resources for children, or may help us with children's activities in school or drop-in to the summer under 5's play scheme. A still bigger group we may only ever see at the school gates or during Keeping Safe Community events. The great benefit of working in partnership with other agencies is that the messages can also get across to parents during their ordinary contact with other workers and thereby thinking about safety becomes normalised and part of everyday life. We continue to develop new ways of involving parents in response to parents' feedback and building on what we see working. A recent development is a universal home visiting scheme which parents have requested to talk on a one to one basis about safety issues for their family.

Our Keeping Safe work with children has concentrated on schools, key community resources in making contact with the greatest numbers of parents and children. To support teachers in this work we have co-ordinated drama and art workshops at the Primary schools in partnership with teachers, the Youth Service and the Child Protection Unit to introduce and reinforce Keeping Safe messages. Although our resources are limited, we aim to visit each of the five schools in the area at least once a year.

A safer babysitting course for young people from 14 upwards was undertaken in response to concerns about the increasing numbers of young people perpetrating against children they look after, parents who want a 'safe' babysitter and the risky situations which young people often find themselves in.

Evaluation and Dissemination: Does It Work?

The First Stop journey has been a constant process of learning and evaluating and we have tried to reflect this in the development and planning of the project. As with any prevention initiative there are some real difficulties in measuring changes in attitude and culture and things which do not happen as a result of what you do. A further difficulty is the cost factor; we have until recently been unable to secure any funding to undertake any evaluation of the project, especially since our funding has only been secured from year to year. Within these limitations, we have utilised a number of methods to evaluate the project's work.

We have monitored the rate of child protection registrations over time. A recent comparison of child protection statistics between the neighbourhood and others has shown a positive link between the length of time that the project has been operating and a distinct reduction in registrations for physical and sexual abuse in the area it operates. We acknowledge that such statistics need to be interpreted with caution. We also monitor numbers of people attending activities and changes in attitudes and behaviour of adults and children over time.

Often the most powerful evaluation of the work is what people say and do. For example a parent stopped a worker by the school gates to say that her son had been able to talk with her for the first time about his feelings about a domestic violence situation at home, after doing a Keeping Safe session at school.

A recent evaluation survey with parents and workers suggested that there was general support for the project and our role in promoting links with other agencies was particularly valued. Workers felt the project had 'helped local people to acknowledge child sexual abuse exists' and that 'parents who know about it are more able to discuss issues of child sexual abuse' although some felt that it had 'opened old wounds for some people'. A general comment was that it needed to reach more people. Parents from the Forum also gave us their written views of how they felt about the project. For example:

> Sexual abuse is an emotive subject even when it doesn't touch our lives. When it does, it's devastating. Protective Behaviours won't stop abusers from perpetrating but it can help children from becoming victims by educating them along with service facilitators, teachers, parents and the community. (Paul)

> I feel more valued as a person and a parent. I use Protective Behaviours for myself and my child. I am now becoming involved with my son's school and finding out if it is working at the school. I will in the future be going into the school to work with the children. Before First Stop I was more worried about stranger danger. I now realise that this is only made worse by the media. (Karen)

This year we asked children aged 5–10 to give us some feedback on work that we did in the schools this year for Child Safety Week. For example:

> What I have learned is not to bully anyone or anyone bully me. People called me Paki.
> I learned that if I have got some worries I can tell my nan, sister, auntie and anyone in my family.
> To be safe and if you need help ask someone.

All this gives us optimism that we are now on the right track. The last year has culminated in a local conference organised by the project called 'Making a Difference: Working Together to Keep Children Safe'. The principles of partnership work and community involvement which underpin the project were reflected in the range of agencies and local parents who supported the conference (160 local and national delegates) and presented their work and views on the day.

Locally, we are involved in a process of looking at how our approach to children's safety could be adapted by other communities across the town, hopefully resulting in a corporate child safety strategy for the town.

Summary

Some of the key milestones in our journey towards developing safer communities for children have been outlined, but bear repeating for those thinking of embarking on similar ventures.

Firstly, it is crucial to have the support and involvement of other agencies and the community and to get them on board from the outset.

Secondly, it is important to base your intervention and practice on a good understanding of theoretical principles and research in child protection and abuse prevention. However, practice needs to be developed within the context of sound knowledge of the community in which you are working and working alongside local contacts and networks. First Stop's development was helped considerably by having a worker seconded to the project from the local Family Centre with her wealth of experience and knowledge of the area.

Thirdly, it is important to be aware that if your aim is to mention the unmentionable, then people may not thank you for mentioning it! The vast majority of people agree that children should be protected, but there are many issues, dilemmas and fears associated with talking about child abuse, and these need to be worked through and addressed over time by parents and workers.

A more positive and safer approach to child protection in the community is to reframe this within a Keeping Children Safe model and to link child abuse with other forms of child safety, which are more readily accepted. Keeping Child safety on the agenda through community meetings, groups, discussions and events is also key.

To encourage communities to get involved in Keeping Children Safe, it is important to find ways to do this which are safe, inclusive and accessible. We have found the Protective Behaviours process a very useful and non-threatening way of looking at child safety issues and one which is adaptable to a range of settings and situations. It also allows for a common community currency when talking about child safety issues.

References

Baldwin N. & Carruthers L. (1998), *Developing Neighbourhood Support and Child Protection Strategies*, Ashgate, Aldershot.

Boushel M. (1994), 'The Protective Environment of Children: Towards a Framework for Anti-oppressive, Cross-cultural and Cross-National Understanding', in *British Journal of Social Work*, Vol 24, pp. 173–190.

Briggs F. & Hawkins R.M.F (1994), 'Follow-up Data on the Effect of the New Zealand School-Based Child Protection Programme', in *Child Abuse and Neglect*, Vol 18, No. 8, pp. 635–643.

DoH. (1999), *Working Together to Safeguard Children*, HMSO, London.

Finkelhor D. (1984), *Child Sexual Abuse, New Theory and Research*, Free Press, New York.

Garbarino J (1987), 'Family Support and the Prevention of Child Maltreatment', in Kagan S., Powell D., Weissbourd B. & Zigler E., eds, *America's Family Support Programs*, Yale University Press, Newhaven and London.

Gordon L. (1988), *Heroes of their Own Lives*, Viking Penguin, London.

Heaton K. & Sayer J. (1992), *Community development and Child Welfare*, Children's Society/CDF, London.

Henderson P. (1995), *Children and Communities*, Pluto Press, London.

MacLeod M. & Saraga E. (1988), 'Challenging the Orthodoxy: Towards a Feminist Theory and Practice', in *Feminist Review*, Vol 28, pp. 16–55.

10 Aotearoa/New Zealand – Family Centred Practice from a Mental Health Perspective

LYNNE BRIGGS

Introduction

In New Zealand social work practice in mainstream mental health services has a clinical focus. It provides assessment and intervention services for children, adolescents, adults and families with mental health problems. Social workers are usually members of multi-disciplinary teams and work with other health professionals. This means that mental health social workers need to be able to recognise the symptoms of mental health disorder as outlined in the Diagnostic and Statistical Manual of Mental Disorders-the DSM (American Psychiatric Association, 1994). However, effective social work practice also means that alongside an ability to identify mental illness the worker must look beyond the diagnosis and symptoms in order to understand the impact of social, psychological and cultural factors on the client's overall functioning.

This chapter recognises the need and importance for social workers to be familiar with, and able to use, guidelines for assessment and treatment of people with mental health problems. The work of the Family Mental Health Service is described and two case studies have been used to demonstrate how the DSM-IV (1994) can be a potentially helpful tool as well as being compatible with social work values. Thus, the focus of this chapter is on assessment rather than intervention.

Background

The Family Mental Health Service (FMHS) is part of the Child, Adolescent and Family Mental Health Services of Heathlink South, a large South

Island HHS (Health and Hospital Services). Heathlink South is a specialist mental health HHS that services the city of Christchurch and the surrounding Canterbury towns. Initially the FMHS was established under the *Hospitals Amendment Act* (1976). This Act provided a broad framework for the establishment of several community based Family Health Counselling Centres (FHCCs). Between 1978 and 1985 three centres were established in and around the city of Christchurch to service a population of nearly 400,000. A fourth centre was also established in Rangiora, a small farming community with a population of 22,000 people in North Canterbury. While Rangiora is only 20 kilometres along the northern motorway it is separated from the greater Christchurch metropolitan area by the Waimakariri river and farms.

All the Centres were set up to be staffed by Social Workers with secretarial support. A psychologist was also included in the initial staff establishment of the first and largest Centre. It was envisaged that these Centres would offer psychological assistance aimed at increasing the mental health and overall social well-being of individuals and families in the communities in which they lived.

Radical health reforms have occurred in New Zealand over the past fifteen years. These reforms brought about many changes in the way public health services are now funded. The FHCCs were not immune to these changes and the service has been restructured and relocated numerous times. Eventually the community houses were closed and a large base set up in the northern part of the city. This base is located in a busy inner suburb of the city close to the main arterial route to enable people to access the service by either private car or public transport. A number of outreach clinics were also established in the four corners of the city and in the surrounding rural areas in an endeavour to remain community, rather than hospital, focused.

Staffing establishments have increased considerably over the years. The team is now more multi-disciplinary and consists of fifteen Social Workers, four Nurses, two Psychologists, one Medical Officer/Counsellor, one Maori Health Worker, one physiotherapist and four secretarial support staff. Although there is no resident psychiatrist on the team three psychiatrists come into the service and offer regular consultation and clinical review for children, youth and refugee clients. If necessary, adults are referred for psychiatric consultation and medication to the Adult Community Mental Health Teams. Once stabilised they are referred back to the FMHS case manager for ongoing intervention and follow-up.

The FMHS intake system includes screening referrals to ensure potential clients would meet criteria, as defined in the DSM-IV (1994), for a Axis 1 diagnosis which includes the V-Codes. The age range of clients accepted into the service is 0-65 years.

In 1998 the Family Health Counselling Service formerly changed its name to the Family Mental Health Service. Service delivery includes:

- a self-referral service for families or individuals concerned about their mental and social well-being and who would meet criteria for an Axis 1 diagnosis;
- acceptance of referrals from specialised Mental Health Services and Primary Community Services;
- offering consultation to community agencies in regard to families with mental health problems;
- the provision of a comprehensive assessment and treatment of presenting clients or referral to appropriate specialist services;
- the provision of appropriate group programmes for identified mental health difficulties;
- the provision of group programmes emphasising good family relationships.

Prevalence of Mental Illness and Mental Health Problems in New Zealand

New Zealand Mental Health Services concentrate on the three percent of people with serious or enduring mental illness. The equivalent figure for children and young people is estimated to be five percent (McGeorge, 1995). A further 17% of people who usually do not require treatment from main stream mental health services can be found on the case load of social workers working in primary health and voluntary social services (Mental Health Commission, 1997).

Although traditionally mental health services have focused on illness and impairment there has been a move to a recovery approach that is consistent with the principles taught in social work training. Using this recovery model clinical social work in mental health settings focuses not only on the individual and the family, but on the systems that contribute to the person's illness.

Treaty Implications

New Zealand was founded as a modern nation on the Treaty of Waitangi (a treaty between the 'Tangata Whenua', the indigenous Maori people and the British Crown). Maori clients are entitled to mainstream mental health services with access to Maori Mental Health Workers. Maori have a holistic view of health and identify four dimensions – taha wairua (spiritual), taha hinengaro (mental and emotion), taha tinana (physical) and taha whanau (family).

The Blue Print for Mental Health Services in New Zealand (Mental Health Commission) states '...the concept of recovery can be easily applied to holistic approaches because recovery does not need to happen in the individual; the people and system that contribute to the person's illness also need to change also to enable that individual to live a better life' (1998:15).

Approximately 6% of the client population attending FMHS would define themselves as Maori. The FMHS has one Pukenga Atawhai. This worker carries out cultural assessment with Maori clients and their families presenting to FMHS. The Maori Health worker also offers cultural consultation to the case managers in the service and follows Maori clients back out into the community as part of discharge planning.

Clinical Social Work Practice Within the Multi-Disciplinary Team

Internationally, the contemporary practice of clinical social work has been transformed over the years by an ever widening clinical domain and by substantially altered contexts for practice (Brandell, 1997). At times it is difficult to determine where clinical social work differs from treatment offered by other professionals as social workers are just a likely to be case managers as any other mental health professional.

Good client care is reinforced through co-operation among multiple disciplines represented on mental health teams. Multi-disciplinary teams include psychiatrists, psychologist, nurses, physio and occupational therapists as well as social workers. All share the provision of a range of clinical services to clients and their families.

There are a number of models for case management that are used in mental health services. For instance the generalist model is where the social worker as case manager is responsible for all the case management functions and activities for a group of clients. This is the model that operates in the FMHS for all clinicians.

Although each clinician in the FMHS is responsible for carrying out assessments, treatment planning, clinical review of clients, discharge planning for professional accountability we are also accountable to each other as members of a multi-disciplinary team, to the standards of our professional body and to the service standards of our employer.

Furthermore, social workers are responsible for ensuring the client and the client's family are involved in the treatment planning; for ensuring the treatment plan is regularly reviewed with the multidisciplinary team and for keeping their supervisor informed of progress. The social worker is also responsible for liaison with other services such as general practitioners and other mental health and community services.

Social Work Practice and the DSM-IV

The DSM-IV was developed for clinical use in clinical, educational, and research settings. The diagnostic categories criteria, and textual descriptions are meant to be used as guidelines that are informed by clinical judgement. Making a DSM-IV diagnosis is the first step in treatment planning. To formulate an adequate treatment plan, the clinician will invariably require additional information about the person being evaluated beyond that required to make a DSM-IV diagnosis (DSM-IV, 1994).

There are arguments for and against the use of the DSM throughout the social work literature. Some authors contend that important information is lost when using clinical classification systems (Mattaini & Kirk, 1991:262). Whereas others (Karls & Wandrow, 1992; Lutz & Florey, 1993) see advantages in using it as a tool that can help organise observations about one aspect of a client's life. McQuaide (1999) in reviewing both the pros and cons of using the DSM, concluded that it has the potential to be both a useful and dangerous tool. Thus, it needs to be used with a perspective that is compatible with social work values.

The debate will continue and there will always be arguments for and against the use of systems such as the DSM-IV among the social work community. However, at the FMHS on completion of an assessment the FMHS social workers are expected make a DSM-IV diagnosis. In doing so other relevant collateral information about the client is also collected to ensure the biological, social, psychological and cultural factors that may be affecting the clients mental health are taken into account before the diagnosis is made and a treatment plan implemented.

To assist this process a wide range of psychometric tests are carried out by appropriately trained clinical psychologists and social workers in the FMHS. However, there are some main tests and instruments that are routinely administered by all FMHS staff following a clinical assessment with children and adolescents. These tests are described in the next section.

Collateral Information

Child Behaviour Checklists (CBCL/4-18, YSR and TRF Profiles)

The Achenbach (1991) child behaviour checklists are widely used screening measures of general behaviour and functioning in child and adolescents. The observable behaviour of children tends to differ from one context to another, for example between home and school and home, thus no one source can substitute for all others. The Achenbach (1991) child behaviour checklists for ages 4-18 years were revised and renamed from pre-1991 editions to improve co-ordination of data from parent, self and teacher report forms. The checklists are design to tap competencies and problems that are reportable by parents, youth and teachers respectively.

The CBCL uses a hierarchical factor structure that consists of eight correlated first order or narrow band factors (Withdrawn, Somatic, Anxious-Depressed, Social, Thought, Attention, Delinquent and Aggressive) and two correlated second-order or broadband factors (Internal and Externalising). From a theoretical perspective, the broadband syndromes have been conceptualised as reflecting different levels of anxiety. Internalising is associated with excessive anxiety and externalising represents insufficient anxiety or inhibition. According to Achenbach (1991), the two broadband syndromes are not mutually exclusive and often co-occur within the same child (i.e., are positively correlated).

The *Parents' Report form* (CBCL) is a four page form designed to obtain descriptions of competencies and behavioural/emotional problems of 4-18 year olds as seen by parents and parent surrogates. The design of the form is such that most parents would be able to read and understand the questions. If there is a question about the parents ability to do so then the clinician would need to read the questions to the parent and record their answers for them.

The *Youth Self Report Form* (YSF) is designed to obtain adolescents' reports about their own competencies and problems. The YSR is formed for chronological ages 11-18 years. The format, although similar to the *Parents' Report Form*, differs in that it is written in the first person and adolescents are not asked to report whether they attend special classes or have had to repeat any classes. The YSR is also designed to be self-administered by youths. However, if there is a question about reading and understanding ability then a clinician can assist them to complete the form.

The *Teacher's Report Form* is designed to obtain descriptions of children's academic performance, adaptive functioning and behavioural/emotional problems, as seen by their teachers. The 1991 scoring profiles include normative data for 5-18 year old who are attending school (Achenbach, 1991b). The TRF is designed to be self-administered by teachers. FMHS clinicians contact teachers before sending out a letter with the TRF explaining the reason for the request. A copy of the parental consent is also sent.

Draw A Person, Quantitative Scoring System (DAP, Naglieri, 1998). The task of drawing human figures is a non-threatening means of obtaining an estimate of intelligence. The present DAP has been developed to meet the need for a modernised, recently normed, and objective scoring system to be applied to human figure drawings produced by children and adolescents. It is especially useful for children who are resistant to more traditional examination procedures. The DAP can be administered for either screening or individual assessment. The scoring system can provide reliable information to supplement other intelligence test data.

Child Depression Inventory (CDI, Kovacs, 1982). The CDI is a 27-item self-rated inventory that measures symptoms of depression among school aged children and adolescents. Since its initial development in 1977, the CDI has been subjected to lengthy psychometric examination in normal and clinical children's populations and has an acceptable test-retest reliability and concurrent validity. The scale discriminates youngsters with the psychiatric diagnosis of major depressive disorder as opposed to those with other psychiatric conditions or non-selected 'normal' school children. As the CDI has been translated into many languages other than English it maybe useful for working with children from other cultures.

The CDI can be used as a screening device in a number of settings such as outpatient clinics. As with any test there is a chance that the CDI can give can produce false positive or false negative results. However, the combining of information from the CDI with a clinical interview minimises such problems and gives the clinician a more comprehensive and ecologically valid view of the child than might be obtained from just one source.

Case Studies

A primary theme in contemporary social work practice is the facilitation of the client's coping mechanisms and strengths to solve difficulties. Social workers in the FMHS have a responsibility to assess clients, make a DSM-IV diagnosis and to facilitate the most appropriate course of treatment. The collecting of information to do so requires skills in questioning that are respectful and that acknowledge the client's many strengths.

Social work intervention within the FMHS reflects the shift in focus that has occurred in mental health services over the last decade. That is, intervention has competency-based health orientated models that emphasis family strengths and resources as its main focus. Once the assessment process is completed the social worker has therapeutic freedom to work with the client in setting agreed upon treatment goals and the intervention approach used in achieving them.

Taking this approach into account at times social workers in mental health services do need to act to protect someone from risk of danger to themselves or others. This may mean difficult decisions have to be made to provide alternative care for people which may not necessarily be the choice of the client or their family. Nevertheless, careful and ethical social work practice can assist facilitate necessary clinical decisions and ensure actions are clear and unambiguous.

In the next section two case studies are utilised to illustrate how the DSM can be a useful tool in planning how to work with people. To ensure client confidentiality is maintained the names and circumstances of the cases presented are changed. However, they are cases that have been seen by FMHS social workers.

Youth Referral

Ann Jones, a 14 year old school girl, was referred by the Psychiatric Emergency Service (PES) to FMHS. The referral stated Ann had presented to PES the previous afternoon with mother with thoughts of wanting to die. She had made several similar presentations in the past to

134

PES. As on previous occasions, following investigation PES found that while Ann stated she felt like dying she was not actively suicidal and had no specific plans to harm herself. PES were satisfied that Ann's mother could guarantee her safety so she was sent home again on the understanding that she attend the FMHS for follow-up.

Assessment at Family Mental Health Service

Ann attended for assessment with her mother. She presented as an anxious slightly built healthy looking 14 year old girl with blunted affect. Although she appeared very sad Ann was able to make eye contact and engage in conversation. She was well orientated in time, place and person and there was no evidence of psychotic or manic symptoms. She reported feeling irritable more than sad a lot of the time. Her cognition appeared to be within normal limits. She denied having any sleep or appetite disturbance. Ann reported a loss of interest in most things in her life and that even watching TV was beyond her as she could not concentrate enough to follow the programmes. Her motivation and energy levels were low and she stated several times during the interview that she had nothing to live for and that life was not worthwhile. There was no evidence of recent alcohol or drug use although she did admit to having smoked mother's marijuana once.

Ann reported feeling down since January when she had last presented to PES. Over the past six weeks she had felt increasingly suicidal. When prompted to explain this feeling further she could only state she would like to be dead although denied having any suicidal plan or intent for suicide. This feeling had culminated to the extent that she had been sent to see the school counsellor because of her inability to participate in class activities. Ann stated she hated school, had negative interactions with her peers and teachers and that the teachers picked on her all the time. After telling the school counsellor how she was feeling the counsellor had contacted her mother and advised her to take Ann to PES.

Her mother reported that Ann has had difficulties with depressive symptoms ever since she was 11 years of age. Her low mood first appeared about the same time her natural father had left the family. Further exploration revealed he spent some time in prison for robbery, assault and causing serious bodily harm to another person. Ann could recall having witnessed violence between her mother and father repeatedly throughout her childhood. She remembered her father as a very angry and violent man. She also recalled clearly the two occasions when she had been the recipient of her father's violence. Ann and her mother were very afraid of him and reported feeling relieved when he had been sent to prison for several years. Although he has since completed his prison sentence they have had no further contact with him and believe he is living somewhere in the North Island. Ann said she had no wish to ever see him again.

Following other presentations to PES Ann had been seen several times by the school counsellor. The counsellor had then referred Ann and her mother to a local community agency in an attempt to assist them deal with relationship issues between Ann, her mother, and her mother's new partner. Ann reported she did not like him and that he was as bad as her father. She reported he argued a lot with her mother, had 'funny' friends calling late at night and smoked marijuana in the house. She had refused to attend any sessions with him.

Ann was very angry with her mother for letting him live with them and for spending their limited finances on marijuana. Her mother did not see it this way and reported it differently. She also stated Ann's constant irritability precluded any discussion about it. Furthermore, this relationship had recently ended and when presenting at FMHS only Ann and her mother lived in the house. However, Ann's mother was considering moving to a caravan park in order to reduce their cost of living thus giving her the opportunity to clear some outstanding debts. Ann was not at all happy about this proposal. Of note, Ann's mother also reported she was taking prescribed medication for her own depression and anxiety.

In summary, Ann presented as an anxious sad 14 year old with symptoms that were consist with a DSM-IV diagnosis of a major depressive disorder. On assessment she appeared to be at a low risk of suicide and she denied any suicide intent and plan. Her anxiety levels needed further exploration. Given the exposure and actual experience of her father's violence to her and her mother the possibility of PTSD (post-traumatic stress disorder) also needed to be considered. At that stage the greatest stressors in her environment were the lack of appropriate interactions with peers and teachers, the anger she felt toward her mother and the overwhelming sense of worthlessness she was experiencing. Ann's main aim in life is to feel better.

Use of the DSM-IV

During the assessment the social worker was able to use her knowledge of the DSM-IV to assist her make sense of the information she was getting about Ann and her circumstances. For example, the essential feature of a major depressive disorder is that for a period of at least two weeks either depressed mood or the loss of interest or pleasure in nearly all activities is experienced. In children or adolescents the mood may be irritable rather than sad (DSM-IV,1994: 320). Ann had certainly expressed feeling both for several months and with increasing intensity over the past six weeks.

Ann's story was corroborated by her mother and the school as they had also noted a withdrawal from activities and an increase in low mood and irritability. From the assessment the social worker had gained a picture of how Ann was functioning. The following provisional diagnosis was made:

Axis 1	Major Depressive Disorder.
	Parent Child Relational Problem
(V61.20)	
Axis II	No diagnosis
Axis III	No diagnosis
Axis IV	Family financial problems
Axis V	GAF=50

While use of the DSM-IV had enabled the social worker to reach some conclusions about Ann's current mental status she was also able to take into account other precipitating and maintaining factors. That is, she was able to see how the major disruptions Ann had experienced in her short life may have impacted on her current functioning. In keeping with the social workers diagnosis and following agency protocols the following intervention plan was put in place:

1. Psychiatric consultation;
2. A trial of anti-depressant medication;
3. The ongoing monitoring of Ann's mood and anxiety levels;
4. Administration of the Achenbachs, a CDI and a DAP;
5. Initially, family counselling to reduce the conflict between Ann and her mother;
6. Further therapeutic intervention to be decided after collateral information in scored and feedback to Ann and her mother is completed.

Results from the psychometric tests administered revealed that although Ann's overall total score on the CDI was not of clinical concern (T=62) her score on the negative self esteem was in the borderline range. The total test classification on the DAP indicated her intellect ability was in the high average to superior range.

The results from the *CBCL/4-18, YSR* and *TRF Profiles* are discussed below. From the *Parent Report Form* reported competence indicated Ann was low on activities and social interaction but working well at school. Internalising areas of clinical concern were withdrawn and anxious/depressed, while somatic complaints were in the borderline clinical range. With the exception of a high score on delinquent behaviour the results from the *TRF* were overall consistent with the mother's report. The *YSR* revealed self reported competence was low on both measures. Internalising areas of borderline clinical concern were anxious/depressed and thought problems.

Overall, these results are consistent with Ann's presentation to FMHS and indicate that she has the intellectual ability to achieve academically. Discrepancies between the scores and her academic achievement suggest that her mental health may be impacting upon her performance.

Following psychiatric consultation Ann was placed on a trial of fluoxetine. Initially her mood did lift as counselling progressed and she began to take an interest in school work again. Ann began attending one-one sessions with the social worker. She appeared motivated to make changes and worked well on problem solving and conflict resolution. The relationship between Ann and her mother improved significantly and she reduced her anxiety levels by making use of some relaxation techniques.

However, it soon became obvious that Ann continued to have difficulties. She began missing school, reported feeling helpless and believed that everyone had given up on her including the school and her mother. In addition to this she ceased taking her antidepressant medication for about two weeks without disclosing this to the social worker at the time. Of her own volition she had also re-started it. She reported a recent episode of feeling despairing and lonely and having thoughts of self harm, thinking perhaps she would overdose on her mother's medications. Despite regular counselling sessions at the FMHS she was not responding to all of our efforts. Although not in immediate danger to herself or others at that time a further psychiatric consultation was requested with a view to discuss other intervention options that may be available for Ann.

After some considerable discussion with Ann and her mother she was referred to the Youth Day Programme run by the Youth Speciality Service. She was considered appropriate for admission to that unit and has been transferred over. On completion of the programme she will be referred back to FMHS to assist her make an adjustment back to school.

Ann's case demonstrates the usefulness of the DSM-IV for diagnostic purposes. Had her low mood not been treated Ann may well have been successful in attempts to kill herself. Ann's case also reminds us that the psychosocial factors cannot be ignored. The impact of her environment on her overall functioning was important thus it needs to be remembered that the Axis IV should not be neglected.

Child Referral

Ten year old John Clark was referred to FMHS by his GP because his father was concerned about his decreased concentration and increasing disruptive behaviour at school over the past few months. The GP remarked that while John looked pale and withdrawn he had made good eye contact and engaged in conversation while in the surgery. The GP noted that recent changes in family circumstances had occurred and he thought that maybe John was having difficulties adjusting to these changes. He also noted John had previously been seen by a psychiatrist in the private sector due to behavioural difficulties at school. Some IQ testing had been done at that time with the results indicating John was a 'gifted child'. His behaviour problems were then seen as boredom in the classroom as he was reading well beyond his reading age and working at a level well above his peers. However, this was three years ago and the GP was now requesting that the FMHS see John to assist him overcome his recent problems.

Assessment at FMHS

John attended for assessment with his father. He presented in long baggy shorts, a sweat shirt and was not wearing any shoes despite the winter conditions. John's father felt his attire was a demonstration of his unhappiness of having to come for assessment. John appeared tired, slightly bored but comfortable in the assessment environment. After a short time he seemed to engage in the process. His weight and height were appropriate for his age. He said he ate well and his father confirmed this. His mood appeared euthymic and affect was appropriate. His vocabulary, though at low volume, was sophisticated.

Cognitively John was orientated in time and place and he reported feeling reasonably happy. He was well able to formulate appropriate responses to any questions directed to him. John saw his main difficulty was getting to sleep at night and, at times, controlling his temper. His father confirmed the difficulty with anger and reported that while generally John was a softly spoken child on some occasions he could be very explosive.

His father reported John was the result of an unplanned pregnancy. He also reported John's mother had a stressful antenatal period which was complicated by the onset of gestational diabetes. Labour was induced followed by a long and difficult delivery. John was successfully breast fed but was a poor sleeper. His father described John as a demanding child who cried a lot. Developmentally he seemed well ahead of his peers in language development, shape recognition and manipulation of objects. He also walked and ran earlier than most children.

John has had several changes in his life dating back to the separation of his parents nearly six years ago. Of note was his request at the beginning of the year to live permanently with his father whom he appeared to have close relationship with. John stated his reason for this request was because he was sick of moving around all the time. Not long after this change his mother, her partner and John's sister moved away. This presented a further change for John as, although separated for several years, until this move his parents had continued to live close to each other so the children would have regular access to both of them. Over the school holidays John had gone to stay with his mother and sister. However, John had returned to his father midway through the holidays because of an argument that had developed between him and his mother's partner.

Both of John's parents had achieved well academically and are employed in professional occupations. Based on the results of the earlier testing of John's intellectual functioning it was expected that he would also do well academically. No report was made available at the time and the private clinic they had attended had since closed down.

While John's father reported his disruptive behaviour at school it does not appear to impact on his academic performance. John's teacher reports he finds him a difficult child to manage in the classroom. He states John does not do as he is told, disrupts other children while they are working and appears unable to focus on and complete some tasks. He just gets up and wanders around the classroom at will.

Although this is not new behaviour it has increased over the past 12-18 months. John's response to these matters is that his constant tiredness prevents him from behaving and doing better at school. He also sees the tiredness as the reason he cannot be bothered to complete set tasks, instead he loses interest, becomes bored and looks for something else to do.

John tends to relate better to adults than children and has no real friends. School reports indicate that he tends to isolate himself in the playground and he only participates in classroom activities if he feels like it. He dislikes playing team sports and clearly makes this known to other team members. Out of school activities include mountain biking with his father, roller skating and reading.

John's father indicated that a further move is planned as the firm he works for is willing to transfer him to the same city where John's mother and sister now live. John appeared pleased about the possibility of being closer to his mother and sister again.

Overall, John was not clearly symptomatic in regard to anxiety or depression although he did say he worries about some aspects of his life, and he feels sad at times. The continued changing of cities and swapping from living with one parent to the other may have had an unsettling effect on him. The constant moving around also provides some understanding regarding his lack of close friends and his disinterest in attempting to make good peer relationships.

John's main concern centred around his reported inability to sleep at night which leaves him feeling tired the next day and thus prevents him from completing tasks. This stated lack of sleep puzzled John's father as he thought John went to sleep within an hour of going to bed. Furthermore, when checking on him before retiring himself John was always asleep and he has to wake him up in the mornings for school. John's father estimated John got around ten hours sleep most nights.

Use of the DSM-IV

Superficially, John's presentation would suggest a well functioning child who was able to engage in the assessment process and converse well. However, as his story unfolded a clearer picture of John's overall functioning began to appear. That is, the social worker could see that his behaviour difficulties, though not new, had increased in intensity and was now clearly affecting his academic and social development. His ability to pay attention in class or remain focused on his school work was decreasing, He would begin a task then leave it unfinished and move onto something else. Although on a one-to-one situation John was able to engage well (as demonstrated throughout the interview) his ability to make and sustain peer relationships was very limited. It was also known that at times he had temper outbursts.

That John had experienced multiple changes in his family arrangements to date were undeniable as was the resentment he felt toward his mother's new partner. Both are factors which certainly may have impacted on his overall functioning. However, the behaviours John was exhibiting were also consistent with some of the features of a Attention-Deficit and Disruptive Behaviour Disorder (ADHD) as defined in the DSM-IV (1994:

78). Drawing all this information together the social worker tentatively made the following provisional diagnosis:

Axis 1	Attention-Deficit and Disruptive Behaviour Disorder (predominately inattention type)
Axis II	No diagnosis
Axis III	No diagnosis
Axis IV	Educational problems
Axis V	GAF=45

A completed comprehensive assessment is essential before making any recommendations for treating a child with ADHD. Thus, the main treatment goals at this stage consisted of the following:

1. Administration of the Achenbachs, a CDI and a DAP;
2. Further psychometric testing if indicated;
3. Psychiatric consultation;
4. Feedback to parents test results.

The results from the initial psychometric testing are discussed below. John's score on the CDI showed there were no clinical concerns regarding depressive symptoms. The test classification on the DAP indicated his intellectual ability was in the deficient range.

Results from the CBCL/4-18 showed his parents were consistent in their reporting of John's functioning. Both reported overall competence across school and social activities. Internalising areas of clinical concern were withdrawn, somatic complaints and thought problems with anxious/depressed being reported in the severe clinical range. Social and attention problems were rated as being just below clinical concern. The scores on social problems, for example, not being liked, being teased, not getting on with peers were inconsistent with their earlier reporting on the competence scales where the quality of peer relationships was rated as being in the average range.

The TRF rated competence levels within the normal range. Internalising scales had a high score on aggressive behaviour, high scores for social and attention problems and lower, but still of clinical concern, for anxious/depressed.

Overall, these results were consistent with John's presentation to FMHS. Although at this stage further testing is required before any conclusion could be clearly reached about John's intellectual ability his score on the DAP was disturbing. This is particularly so given his parents understanding that John is a gifted child.

John's case again demonstrates the usefulness of the DSM-IV for diagnostic purposes. While much more information is needed before a final decision about John can be made, had the social worker just looked at the psychosocial factors she could easily have seen John's plight as a result of disruptions in his family life and concluded that his emotional needs were not being met. Indeed such factors certainly will have played a part in his overall functioning. However, given that ADHD is the most common psychiatric diagnosis given to children presenting to child and family mental health services (Barkely, 1990) careful assessment taking all factors into account needs to be undertaken.

In John's case antenatal factors need to be considered as John's mother had developed diabetes during pregnancy followed by a difficult delivery. Such factors need to be taken into account as they can be associated with other mental health disorders that are first diagnosed in infancy, childhood or adolescents. For example some of the Pervasive Developmental Disorders have some aspects in common with John's presentation. Furthermore, the unusual development of a sophisticated vocabulary gave the appearance of a 'bright child'. In John's case this contrasted greatly with school performance reports and results on the DAP. This means more specific testing is required to make a final diagnosis.

In summary, revised treatment goals for John include the completion of Connors rating scales. These scales, which were developed to assess the impact of medication on children with ADHD, are also widely used as a screening tool for ADHD (Conners,1997). Discrepancy between an apparently gifted child and the score on the DAP raises the issue of learning disability, possibility on non-verbal intellectual functioning. Referral to the FMHS clinical psychologist for further IQ testing will assist clarify these issues and assist intervention planning.

Once a diagnosis has been confirmed then intervention can begin. At that stage it is the responsibility of the FMHS social worker to implement an appropriate treatment plan. This may or may not involve the use of medication. One type of intervention that is known to be effective in the treatment of ADHD is parent training (Anastopoulos & Barkely, 1989, 1990). However, any treatment for children must be undertaken within a socio-cultural and scientific context. Thus, regardless of the intervention approach used it will involve working closely with John's parents.

Conclusion

This chapter has looked at clinical social work practice in a Family Mental Health Service. Two cases studies have been presented to illustrate how the use of the DSM-IV (1994), a full clinical assessment taking into account psychosocial factors alongside some psychometric testing can assist the social worker put together and formulate a clear comprehensive picture of their client. Thus, theories in use include systems theory through to intrapsychic factors. Without all these factors being considered, particularly when working with children and adolescents, there is a high probability that any intervention may be ineffectual. For example, the fact that John has now been in the school system for five years with the label of a 'gifted child' who is not working up to his potential is an example of how looking at just one side of the picture means important information may been missed out.

References

Achenbach T. M. (1991), *Teacher's Report Form*, Center for Children, Youth & Families, University of Vermont, VT 05401.

Achenbach T. M. (1991), *Parents' Report Form*, Center for Children, Youth & Families, University of Vermont, VT, 05401.

Achenbach T. M. (1991b), Integrative Guide for the 1991 CBCL/4-18, YSR and TRF Profiles, University of Vermont, VT 05401.

American Psychiatric Association (1994), *Diagnostic and Statistical Manual of Mental Disorders*, 4th Edition, Washington, DC. American Psychiatric Association, Washington.

Anastopoulos A. D. & Barkely R. A. (1989), 'A training programme for parents of children with Attention-Deficit Hyperactivity Disorder', in Schaefer C. E. & Briesmeister J. M. eds. *Handbook for Parent Training: Parents as Co-therapists for Children's Behaviour Problems*, Wiley, New York, pp. 83-104.

Barkely R. A. (1990), *Attention-Deficit Hyperactivity Disorder: A handbook for Diagnosis and Treatment*, Guilford, New York.

Brandell J. R. ed. (1997), *Theory and Practice Clinical Social Work*, The Free Press, New York.

Conner, C. K. (1997), *Connors' Rating Scales – Revised: Users' Manual*, Multi-health Systems Inc, Canada.

Hospitals Amendment Act (1976).

Karls J.M. & Wandrei K.E. (1992), 'PIE: A new language for social work' in *Social Work*, 37, 80-85.

Kovacs M. (1982), *Child Depression Inventory*, Multi-Health System, Inc., New York.

Lutz M.E. & Flory M.J. (1993), 'Instruments and psychometrics: a response to Mattaini and Kirk', in *Social Work*, 38, 229-230.

Mattaini M. A. & Kirk S. A. (1991), 'Assessing assessment in social work', in *Social Work*, 36, 260-266.

McGeorge P. (1995), *Child, Adolescent and Family Mental Health Services*, Ministry of Health, Wellington.

McQuaide S. (1999), 'A social workers use of the Diagnostic and Statistical Manual', in *Families in Society: The Journal of Contemporary Human Services*, July-August, Vol 8014, 4, 10 (7).

Mental Health Commission (1997), *Blueprint for Mental Health Services in New Zealand: Working Document*, November, Mental Health Commission, Wellington.

Mental Health Commission (1998), *Blueprint for Mental Health Services: How things need to be*, November, Mental Health Commission, Wellington.

Naglieri, J. A. (1988), *Draw A Person, Quantitative Scoring System*, The Psychological Corporation/Harcourt Brace Jovanovich, Inc., New York.

National Association of Social Workers (1989), *NASW standards for the practice of clinical social work*, NASW Press, Washington, DC.

Dr. Lynne Briggs, Family Mental Health Service, Private Bag 4733, Christchurch, Telephone: (03) 354 1502 Fax: (03) 354 1524 Email: Lynne.Briggs@healthlinksouth.co.nz

11 Aotearoa/New Zealand – Working Differently with Communities and Families

ROBYN MUNFORD and JACKIE SANDERS, with
ANN ANDREW, PETER BUTLER, RIPEKA KAIPUKE,
LELAND RUWHIU

The embracing essence of our whanau/family/community will reinforce the development of our children, and young people are the leaders on the morrow.

Introduction

This chapter will focus on a neighbourhood centre in a community in New Zealand. The philosophy and practice of the Centre are based on community development principles. This chapter will explore some of the contributions that these centres can make to enhancing community wellbeing, strengthening naturally occurring networks (Munford and Sanders, 1999) and integrating informal educational activities within social and community work practice. It will examine some of the principles which guide the work within such centres and some of the challenges these centres face. In doing this, it will examine the ways in which community development practice can be seen as an example of informal education with families and children.

The Centre is called a Whanau Centre - whanau (pronounced farno) is the Maori (indigenous peoples of New Zealand) word for family and incorporates all extended family members within a definition of family. This word conveys the essence of its approach and the focus on working with families and the contexts within which they reside. Those using the Centre come from a wide range of cultural backgrounds – Maori, Pakeha (the Maori name for Europeans), Pacific Islands peoples (New Zealand has a large population of Pacific Islands peoples who come from countries such as Fiji, Samoa, Tonga and the Cook Islands) and those from Asian countries.

Introducing the Neighbourhood within the Context of New Zealand

Living in New Zealand

Before providing further details on this community we need to situate it within the context of New Zealand and the events over the last several years. New Zealand has two major islands (north and south) and has a population of nearly four million with the population concentrated in the North Island and in urban areas. The population is becoming more ethnically diverse with Maori the indigenous people of New Zealand and other minority groups such as Pacific Islands peoples and Asian peoples making up a growing proportion of the population. These populations have young peopleful age structures and have potential for growth over the next decades (Statistics New Zealand, 2000). Currently the Maori population comprises 14.5% of the total population.

It is important to note that New Zealand has a constitutional founding document, the Treaty of Waitangi (Te Tiriti o Waitangi), which protects the rights of Maori and validates the existence of Tauiwi (others who came to New Zealand after Maori) to live in this land. The Treaty specifies that the relationship between Maori and the Crown will be based upon the three principles of partnership, protection and participation. This document has had a chequered history with disputes over land still taking place and Maori still struggling to retain their language and to practice their own cultural beliefs in this country.

These debates continue and the current social and economic statistics and the discrepancies in areas such as education, employment and health are a telling indication of how many Maori remain marginalised and do not experience full participation in their communities and wider New Zealand society. However, alongside this struggle and a point which is central to this chapter is the fact that over the last decades Maori have, despite the immense challenges, achieved much success. The struggles around the regeneration of the language and culture and the development of innovative educational strategies to achieve this through kohanga reo (language nests) and kura kaupapapa (language immersion schools) have

147

received world-wide acclaim from other indigenous peoples who struggle to have a place in their societies.

Over the last fifteen years the standard of living for many New Zealanders has declined as a result of major structural adjustments undertaken by successive governments. These adjustments have been driven by a neo-liberal framework that emphasises individual over collective responsibility. The changes have been accompanied by government policies that place greater responsibility for resources and decision-making on families, individuals and communities (Munford & Sanders, 1999). Many families and communities have struggled to cope with these changes. The impact of these struggles have been documented in a series of reports (Podder & Chaterjee, 1998) and regular economic forecasts from research companies. This economic analysis demonstrates that New Zealand now has the greatest gap between the richest and poorest households of any developed nation and this gap has increased over the past 15 years. Podder and Chaterjee (1998) show that over 80% of families are receiving a smaller share of the country's wealth and income compared to 15 years ago. A recent report from the market research company AC Nielsen, shows that the number of households earning less than $20,000 a year increased from about 18% to about 22% and households earning over $120,000 increased from about 3% to about 5%. All recent reports show that there are increasing disparities in this country between the rich and the poor.

Other recent reports such as the one by Howden-Chapman (2000) provide further documentation of the gaps between rich and poor in New Zealand and the impact that poverty has on key measurements of quality of life, such as health outcomes. This Report emerging out of earlier reports (National Health Committee 1998) provides further disturbing evidence of the links between lower socio-economic backgrounds and poorer health status. So, the life of families in the communities such as the one discussed in this chapter, is characterised by progressively reduced economic fortunes alongside the social and health stresses with which such changes are often associated. The current Labour-led coalition government has articulated an economic and social policy for closing the social and economic gaps between different sub-populations in New Zealand society. However, given the government policies of the last fifteen years, these policies will take some time to create positive outcomes for families and communities. In the meantime people continue to live in the communities affected by these broad policies.

Living in the Ross Community

The situation discussed above influences life in communities such as the Ross community. Neighbourhoods, community networks, schools and social service organisations have a key role in mediating the effects of government polices and have 'picked up' the pieces which have arisen as a result of the government policies from the past 15 years. For example, foodbanks that did not exist 20 years ago, have become a resource upon which many families now rely in order to feed their children. Emergency housing services for beneficiaries have increased and many now operate with waiting lists and have to ration their services. Advocacy services for beneficiaries and low income groups who are experiencing difficulties with welfare agencies and government income support services, have been established and their work is increasing (Fenwick et al., 2000). Communities such as the Ross community are particularly vulnerable because they have traditionally relied upon incomes from manual and semi-skilled employment. They easily fall victim to the consequences of government policies because they have little economic and social capital to fall back on once key industries close. Here, the impact of government policies and wider social and economic processes such as globalisation exact a high price in human terms as industries that employed many New Zealanders find they are no longer financially viable. The social capital that a community centre can create and harness becomes significant in terms of capacity building in the community and these centres may provide a much needed buffer from the effects of government policies (Burton et al., 2000).

The Ross community is a suburb in a city of about 75,000 (Statistics New Zealand, 2000). It has a large population of young families; many of these are sole parent families and many experience periods of short and long term unemployment. The total population of the community is around 9000 and there is a high proportion of families with children living in the area. Many of the households rely on income support from the state as their main source of income. There are a high number of rental properties in the area (note that New Zealand has a high proportion of private ownership with the purchasing of one's home being a goal for most New Zealanders).

In the Ross community there are a large number of Maori families and Pacific Islands people. This community is the most ethnically diverse of all communities in this city. Many poor families live here because they cannot afford to live anywhere else. The community has experienced the effects of the closure of key industries in the region. For example, meat processing plants were downsized and closed in the 1980s. Another key industry (a pharmaceutical factory) was situated within the community and had a key role in supporting community initiatives such as educational and recreational activities. The social networks that became associated with these work environments provided a strong form of support for families and individuals. People still recall fondly the social events at the meat processing plant which spilled over into weekend activities within the Ross community. These industries provided a range of supports for their workers, such as transport to the workplace and of course they also brought money into the community through the regular wage payments. No comparable new industry has come into the area since the closure of these two key employers. Small-scale industry surrounds the area but generally employment is in the city or some distance away in other communities. In a country with a poorly developed public transport system, issues around access to and from work constitute major barriers to workforce participation.

Given the high levels of unemployment, there are significant numbers in casual and part-time work and large numbers receive their primary income from state benefits. Many in the Ross neighbourhood struggle to maintain an adequate income for themselves and family members. These kinds of neighbourhoods experience a range of issues such as health related problems. A report by Howden-Chapman et al. (2000) integrated recent studies on the links between social inequality and inadequate resources. This report confirms what we already know as workers and researchers in these neighbourhoods, that those living in poor neighbourhoods are likely to have poor health outcomes and that factors such as inadequate housing, overcrowding and poor nutrition will lead to poor outcomes in a range of other areas. Over time, these patterns of risk becoming entrenched for people living in these communities and they begin to expect that nothing will change.

While we need to foreground the above issues we want to emphasise another point here. The authors are currently workers and researchers in this neighbourhood and continually argue for the rights of those living in these neighbourhoods to be recognised as people, not as examples of the negative statistics portrayed in the reports cited above. While it is important to highlight the negative statistics it is also important to acknowledge that behind these negative statistics there are people who struggle to maintain dignity and create an adequate lifestyle for themselves and their families (Schmitz, 1995, Munford & Sanders, 1999). These are people who are deeply committed to values of family and community.

The Centre - Ways of Working - Key Principles

The Centre was established in the early 1980s as a response to some of the issues the Ross community was experiencing at the time. Particular concerns were the actions of young people from this area including threatening and anti-social behaviour both within this community and in the wider community, such as the city centre. The Whanau Centre now provides educational and recreational services for children and young people in this community (and others travel in from other communities to participate in these activities), school holiday programmes, some social work services (family counselling), parenting programmes and other short courses. A range of groups also use the Centre for their meetings and activities. The Whanau Centre is situated on a large area of land that is used as a playing field for winter and summer sport. The Centre has had a key role in establishing the touch sports programme (a game similar to rugby but without the tackles, for boys and girls in mixed teams) that attracts children and young people from all over the city. The Centre has strong links with other agencies in the area (cultural groups, churches, health and social service agencies). It works closely with the primary school in the area and together these two agencies form a significant part of the local landscape.

The Centre works within a community development framework and supports families in their own contexts. It utilises naturally occurring networks to provide support. In this context community development can be defined as:

- Working within communities and groups to identify why these groups may be marginalised and collectively to respond to and transform this situation;
- Identifying a vision of how things may be for the future and to work collectively to achieve this by focusing upon long term strategies;
- Working alongside groups to improve the social and economic lives of all community members;
- Assisting people to make their own decisions and to move from dependence to independence and from exclusion to inclusion;
- Enabling people to identify their own strengths and to meet their needs in a constructive manner;
- Building on existing community networks to achieve participation and connections between individuals and in the process achieve community control of services and resources;
- Enhancing opportunities for learning within the community networks that already exist.

(See Derrick, (1995), Ife, (1995), Munford & Walsh Tapiata, (2000), for extended discussion on community development models in Australia and New Zealand.)

This framework is closely connected with the strengths-based paradigm. The key elements of a strength-based approach as it relates to working with families are:

- Families cannot move when they feel paralysed by their problems and needs. Therefore it is essential that the process of giving support addresses the human need to feel competent. (Munford & Sanders, 1999);
- Families' strengths will form the fulcrum for the change process. Families do have strengths and within each family are the resources to bring about change. Families are the key agents of change;
- A strengths-based approach moves away from a focus on deficits and on the dysfunctional aspects of families. While not minimising the enormous difficulties families may face such as abuse issues, poverty, poor health, the strengths-based approach aims to focus on the competencies families have used to overcome and survive very difficult circumstances;

- Workers utilising a strengths-based approach assist families to achieve and identify competence in one area in their life that can then be used to find solutions for other difficulties they may be facing;
- The objective is to assist families to reframe and redefine situations and to become experts at problem-solving, and rather than being overwhelmed by the challenges they become progressively more able to take control of their lives.

The principles underlying a strengths-based approach are strongly connected to principles of community development and working with families and communities to identify strengths that can be harnessed to challenge and overcome difficult situations. and structures (Pransky, 1998). Maori often refer to these approaches as whanau-centred work. The staff in the Centre have all worked as community, youth workers and social workers over several years. Some of them have strong connections with the Ross community in that they either reside in the community or have relations and friends living in this community. The work of the Whanau Centre incorporates elements of these approaches.

This means that those coming to the Centre are recognised for the strengths they bring. The difficulties are not minimised but Centre workers focus on past successes and achievements and build on these to achieve positive change. They support families to articulate a vision and then to work towards this in manageable steps. They also focus on the assets the community already possesses and utilise these to develop other resources and activities.

Workers have a comprehensive understanding of the daily lives of those who use the Centre. They understand what it is like to experience long term unemployment and poverty and how difficult it may be to become involved in community activities when one has been marginalised for many years.

Workers are expert at harnessing naturally occurring support networks (Munford & Sanders, 1999) and community resources (including the wider community) and they share this knowledge and pass on their skills in community organising to those who use the Centre. Some who have used the Centre for assistance in the past are now workers in the Centre. These people encourage others to join Centre activities, assist in building connections between people and in the process develop their own skill and knowledge base.

Elliott et al. (2000) explore how community workers have a key role in building the social fabric of communities. They identify some key strategies that workers can use to assist in strengthening the social fabric of the communities in which they work. The Centre workers adopt many of these strategies. For example, they have a clear analysis of what happens when families and communities do not experience wellbeing and they may become involved in actions that highlight these inequalities. They have made strategic connections with policymakers and others who make decisions about communities and their resources. Workers work directly with communities to develop skills and enhance the skills of individuals.

For example, they offer programmes and activities that strengthen communication skills, build self esteem and encourage self determination. The workers participate in activities that will strengthen the physical infrastructure of the area, such as ensuring that there is adequate lighting in recreation areas so sports groups can use them for longer periods. The Centre itself is a key resource, an important part of the physical infrastructure of the community and provides many opportunities for people to interact with another.

Workers are flexible in their approach to community development and respond to the diversity of experience within the community. When appropriate they will visit families in their homes spending time in their own environment. This is particularly valuable for families who may lack confidence and have difficulty in attending the Centre. Over time these families usually become involved in Centre activities. A key goal of the Centre is to enhance participation in community life. This goal guides the individual and group work that is carried out by Centre workers.

A key strategy not be understated is the style of work adopted by the workers. They are non-judgmental in their work, believing that the individuals, families and groups they work with can achieve positive change and have a right to engage with services that strive to enhance their wellbeing. The principle of unconditional positive regard (Rogers, 1951) also informs interactions between workers and users of the Centre.

The combination of these principles with the high level of commitment of workers means that people using the Centre feel safe and confident that the Centre will not give up on them. The workers focus on the importance of working with young people to help expand their opportunities and encourage hopes and dreams for a better future. The strong relationships they establish with these families enables them to explore issues such as abuse and violence and to work with families to understand the origins of these practices and to continually reaffirm that they are not acceptable.

Parents are encouraged to share in their children's aspirations. The 'never give up' philosophy is firmly integrated in a practice that is based on reflective practice (Munford & Sanders, 1999). Workers continually reflect on practice with one another, with Centre users, and with outside support systems. These maintain accountability in their work, assist reflection on their approaches to their work and the models they use, and, keep them 'hanging in' with the people with whom they work.

Putting the Principles into Action

'Getting Back into the Game'

The first example describes the work being carried out with a group of at-risk male young peoples. We have called it 'getting back into the game' as for many of these young men sport is significant and the example provided here demonstrates how they could refocus their lives and 'get back into the game' and make significant changes in their lives. This group (13–17 year old young males) have been expelled from formal education programmes. Their days once consisted of 'hanging out' and 'hassling' people in the local and wider community, engaging in petty and more serious crime, drinking alcohol and taking drugs. Most had been involved with child protection agencies and many of their families had histories of long term unemployment, abuse and violence. Many of the formal agencies and others in the community had 'given up' on these young people and assumed that they were biding their time before they moved into the formal young people justice system and, for some, into the prison system.

The Centre had worked with these young people for a number of years in holiday programmes but attendance was sporadic and most were unable to remain in activities, such as sports teams, over a sustained period. They were living in families who lacked material resources and many were living on the margins of the community with little participation in community activities. Their self-esteem was low although they engaged in behaviours that hid their feelings of incompetence. Given their experience with the formal education system their educational achievement was inadequate and most had immense difficulty in concentrating on learning and completing tasks. Most could not read, write or complete even basic mathematical tasks.

The Centre was approached by a local high school to operate an alternative education programme for these young people. They agreed to do this and employed a teacher to run this programme in the Centre from nine to three each day. Other resource people have supplemented the academic programmes and ran life skills and recreational programmes. Given the history of these young people Centre staff have been extremely creative in identifying activities that would encourage them to remain in the programmes. They have built on existing community relationships. For example, given that a large number are Maori they asked a kaumatua (Maori elder) to share his knowledge with them. This is culturally appropriate practice and a prime illustration of how workers have used their knowledge of the young people and the community to develop appropriate programmes. They have provided clear boundaries and goals for the young people to achieve. A range of educational methods are used. Small group work, and individual work are used to support teaching in the classroom. A number of activity-based experiences occur, ensuring that there are many opportunities for physical activity, adventure and excitement, things that are important in refocusing the energies of these young men.

A strength-based and whanau-centred approach guided work with these young people. Workers wanted to ensure that they were given another opportunity to achieve. Working in the boys community they were aware of the challenges faced with them and understood the negative attitudes many of them held. While they were realistic about the limitations they were optimistic that they could make a difference and this belief guided their work. These young people felt angry towards many who had attempted to assist them in the past and they had little respect for social workers and formal service agencies. Workers had to spend a lot of time building up trust with them and this took place alongside educational programmes. Expectations on appropriate behaviour were clear but workers kept their promises and remained available, to stand alongside the young people.

Slowly over time trust has been built. Horizons of the young people have been expanded. Work will need to continue and as the trust is achieved others will become part of the network of support for them. Some of them have agreed to be part of the action research programme we are carrying out in this community. Their stories tell of the struggles to survive and also demonstrate that the relationships that these young people have established with the workers, (relationships built on keeping promises, providing support within a community context and being available at the right times, not just from 9 to 5), may just make a difference for them. As we write, the programme has its first graduate, one young male has returned to a mainstream school to resume his formal education.

'Being Available to Parent'

This example describes a programme for parents who are struggling with the daily tasks associated with being a parent. Many of these parents are poor, experience ill-health, are parenting alone and have had negative experiences with formal social service agencies such as child protection services. Many also have histories of violence and sexual abuse. We have called this example 'being available to parent' because our ongoing research (Munford et al., 1996; Munford et al., 1998; Sanders et al., 1999) has shown us that many parents are wanting to take on parental responsibilities and parent well but a number of factors may limit the extent to which they are able to achieve this. These parents may be dealing with their own issues and the consequences of past experiences and unmet needs. They may be struggling to survive on a daily level and it may be difficult to give enough attention to the parenting role. Many of these parents can tell you about the knowledge and skills required to parent well but given their circumstances they may find it difficult putting these into effect. Many have had negative experiences in the formal education system and so these programmes offer them the opportunity to recommence their learning in a safe and supported environment. Authors such as Schmitz (1995) also tell us that single-parent families may be subject to criticism because they fall short of what may be seen to constitute a good family. Parenting groups at the Centre help these parents confront and overcome these challenges.

The strategies adopted by those running parenting programmes at the Centre are underpinned by the same philosophies that guide the work with young people in the example above. There is a recognition that the confidence of parents has been undermined and it may be difficult for them to identify areas of competence. Given that they have felt unable to parent effort is focused on developing specific strategies to address the wider issues that are making the individual 'unavailable to parent'. Parents are supported to move to a position where they can identify with the parent role, where they develop their own style and where they can address the issues that negatively impact on their parenting. They do this in a supportive environment with other parents who feel unable to parent and the worker focuses on the importance of learning together and sharing skills and knowledge. The worker is not seen as the 'expert' but rather as a facilitator working alongside parents to develop more effective ways for parenting their children. The location of the programme at the Whanau Centre is important as it means that transport difficulties are not a major issue. The support given to children is also a key positive factor.

Unlike many other parenting courses this programme begins with identifying the context within which parenting takes place. It begins by encouraging participants to identify their own needs; the course is then structured around these needs. The course does not provide a series of techniques as it is likely that these will not work for these parents either because the wider issues have not been addressed or because these do not match the lifestyles of these parents. Once some of the wider issues have been explored and addressed, the worker will focus on identifying the competencies that the parent has demonstrated and use these to develop new skills and strategies for effective parenting. The worker acknowledges the parents' willingness to address their parenting challenges and their choice to attend the programme. Over time the group becomes an important source of support for those attending.

The Centre provides a safe environment for these parents to examine critically what is going wrong in their lives, to address very difficult issues (such as abuse and violence) to identify the barriers to change and explore how these may be overcome. The goal for the worker is to ensure that the participants leave the Centre feeling empowered rather than feeling incompetent and useless; a feeling often experienced after an encounter with a formal social service.

What is exciting for worker and participants is the translation of learning about parenting to other areas of their lives. For example, to use the competencies developed to establish more effective communication strategies with others in their lives. This enables them to gain confidence in challenging those who, without any evidence to support their views, often criticise the level of commitment these parents have towards their children. Moreover, participants in the programme extend their personal support networks by attending this programme and they in turn will support other parents who are struggling to make sense of the challenges that confront parents. The obstacles to empowerment for so many of the parents of the Ross Community cannot be overcome without their collective strength.

Challenges for the Ross Community and its Community Centre

Resources are scarce for the families living in this community and it is a challenge for the community to extend its human and social capital. Resources are also scarce for the Whanau Centre. Given the lack of economic resources within the community funding for the Centre must come from outside the Centre. There is a fine balance between time spent on the work and on acquiring funding. Workers spend significant amounts of time gaining acceptance for the Centre's work from the wider community. For example, the local authority continually questions why it should provide resources in this area and not in others. Centre staff spend much time writing reports about the positive effects their programmes have for the local community and for groups from outside the community who come to the Centre to participate in a range of recreational and sporting activities. Some of the debates with which they have to engage relate to decisions about who is deserving of local authority and state funding. There are many contradictions here. The Labour-led coalition government has a policy of closing the gaps between rich and poor. However, the funding associated with this policy does not always filter down to communities. Organisations such as local authorities act as gatekeepers and may choose to inject funding into areas where they believe that outcomes may more easily be achieved. The Ross community includes many families who are struggling to obtain material resources and have experienced long term difficulties associated with this. Any policies for closing the gaps require a long term commitment to addressing the consequences of inadequate living standards and the problems that accompany these.

Centre workers work on an individual/group level and on a wider community level. They focus on challenging punitive government policies and identifying strategies to replace these with more enlightened policies that will have benefits for communities such as the Ross community. The

159

balance of work is always a challenge and workers continually reflect on their roles and their ability to maintain their commitment to those who use the Centre. An advisory group and other networks are used to support the workers and to maintain the vision of the Centre.

Workers have a commitment to ensuring that the Centre does not become isolated from other community resources within the Ross community and outside this community. There is a danger that the Centre becomes the only resource for people living in this area as other agencies abdicate their role with families in this community. The Centre staff actively encourage other community resources to use the Centre for meeting clients. They may take on advocate and mediator roles with families so that families feel supported when meeting with workers from social service and related organisations. Workers maintain their strategic links with other services and they take time to tell these services about the needs of clients in this community and how they might work in an empowering way with these clients. The Centre staff have encouraged community members to be proud about living in the Ross community but at the same time they have also attempted to strengthen links with networks outside the immediate community. This is an ongoing struggle as many formal social service agencies and other neighbourhoods have a negative perspective on the Ross community. This view may remain unchallenged if they are not prepared to visit the Centre to find out about the range of positive initiatives with which the Centre is engaged. The workers spend time reflecting on what they have achieved and reinforcing that small achievements can contribute to long term positive change for communities such as the Ross community.

Conclusion

This chapter has identified the important contribution community centres can make to families and communities by integrating informal learning opportunities and social support. Traditional social casework methods may inadvertently focus on families in isolation from the contexts in which they carry out their daily lives (Cannan & Warren, 1997, Gilligan, 2000). In contrast, centre workers support families within the context of the community and this work focuses on enhancing the capacity of families and the networks within the community. Community centre workers begin at a different place from more formal social services agencies. They carry out their work within the context of community life and life long learning and view the community centres as a key resource for families and individuals. Community centres provide opportunities for participation and function to strengthen community networks.

The workers in the Whanau Centre will continue to face challenges as they strive to maintain their focus on community development principles and work alongside the community to build on the strengths from within this community. Workers will continue to be confronted with the challenges of working in impoverished neighbourhoods but will continue to have a key role in enhancing the capacity of the community. They will continue to manage the tensions within their work and attempt to challenge decision-makers and government policies as they carry on their work with individuals and community groups.

The challenge for Centre workers is to position their work as a viable alternative for families who require support to carry out their daily activities. The community work that takes place in community and neighbourhood centres can provide hope and opportunities for many families who struggle to find ways to participate in their communities.

Note that the Ross Community is a pseudonym.

References

Burton P., Richards R., Briggs M. & Allan H. (2000), *Striking a Better Balance: A Health Funding Response to Reducing Inequalities in Health*, Health Funding Authority, Dunedin.

Cannan, C. and Warren, C. eds. (1997), *Social Action with Children and Families: A Community Development Approach to Child and Family Welfare*, Routledge, London.

Elliott B., Mulroney, L., O'Neil, D. (2000), *Promoting Family Change: The Optimism Factor*, Allen and Unwin, St Leanoards, NSW.

Espiner G. (2000), 'Inequality in household incomes still growing', Sunday Star Times, 15 October.

Fenwick. A., Davidson D. & Briar, C. (2000), *Is Advocacy Helping?*, School of Social Policy and Social Work, Massey University, Palmerston North.

Gilligan R. (2000), 'Family Support: Issues and Prospects', in Canavan, J., Dolan P. & Pinkerton, J. eds. *Family Support: Direction from Diversity*, Jessica Kingsley Publishers, London.

Howden-Chapman, P. & Tobias M. eds. (2000), *Social Inequalities in Health,* Wellington Ministry of Health, New Zealand.

Munford R., Sanders J., Tisdall M., Mulder, J., Spoonley, P. & Jack A. (1996), *Working Successfully with Families*: Stage 1, Barnardos NZ, Wellington.

Munford R., Sanders J., Tisdall M., Henare A., Livingstone K. & Spoonley, P. (1998), *Working Successfully with Families*: Stage 3, Barnardos NZ Wellington.

Munford, R. & Sanders, J. (1999), *Supporting Families*, Dunmore Press, Palmerston North.

Munford, R. & Walsh Tapiata, W. (2000), (2nd edition), *Strategies for Change: Community Development in Aotearoa/New Zealand*, School of Social Policy and Social Work, Massey University, Palmerston North.

National Health Committee (1998), *The Social, Cultural and Economic Determinants of Health in New Zealand: Action to Improve Health*, A Report from the National Advisory Committee on Health and Disability.

Podder N. & Chatterjee, S. (1998), Sharing the National Cake in Post-Reform New Zealand: Income Inequality Trends in Terms of Income Sources, Department of Applied and International Economics, Massey University, Palmerston North.

Pransky J. (1998), *Modello: A Story of Hope for the Inner City and Beyond*, NEHRI Publications, Cabot VT, USA.

Rogers, C. (1951), *Client-Centred Therapy: Its Current Practice, Implications and Theory*, Constable, London.

Sanders J., Munford R. & Richards-Ward L. (1999), Working Successfully with Families: Stage 3: Child and Family Research Centre, Barnardos, NZ, Palmerston North.

Schmitz, C. (1995), 'Reframing the Dialogue on Female-Headed Single-Parent Families,' *Affilia*, 10 (4), 426-441.

Statistics New Zealand (2000), *New Zealand Official Yearbook, 2000*, David Bateman, Auckland.

12 Contemporary Debates in Centre Practice in Youth Justice and Community Development

ANDY LLOYD and NICK FROST

Introduction

This chapter examines the role and function of a specific British neighbourhood project, the West Leeds Family Service Unit, in the context of recent organisational change and how the rationale for this change relates to some findings of some contemporary social research. In particular the work of the Unit is attempting to make links between two areas of research, policy and practice which are often seen as separate and discrete – the fields of family support and youth crime.

West Leeds Family Service Unit (FSU) employs a multi-disciplinary team of staff which is based in a neighbourhood centre serving a culturally diverse and materially deprived community in inner city Leeds. In the immediate catchment area of the Unit 58% of children aged 0-4 are white, 24% of Asian origin, 9% Black African Caribbean and 9% from other ethnic groups. The Unit is core funded through a service level agreement with Leeds Social Services Department and also receives funding from the National Lottery Charities Board and Children in Need. The Unit aims to improve the quality of life and facilities for children under the age of 12, and their families. This mission is undertaken through the provision of a range of functions in community, group and individual settings. The work is designed to address local needs, with a strong emphasis on issue-based group work and activity groups for children. The Unit has a voluntary management committee and forms part of a national voluntary organisation, Family Service Units, which was established in 1948.

This chapter reflects on two main themes – first, the process of change in service delivery and how this relates to, and has been influenced by, social research. It will be argued that the relationship between change and research is a complex one. Certainly it is rarely the case that new research leads to changes in service delivery in a straightforward and uni-linear manner. Rather, change is influenced by a combination of political, economic and social factors – a process to which research can contribute, steer and influence.

In this chapter we wish to explore these issues further. We begin by examining recent research in relation to youth justice, which has been influential in helping to shape change in the Unit. We then move on to examine research into family support – relating this to key recent national debates. We then bring together these themes of research and change in our conclusion, applying our findings to a concrete family centre setting and the activities which take place within the Unit.

Recent Findings in Youth Justice Research

As we have already stated we begin by examining some recent research in the field of youth justice, which will help to establish one of the research contexts for the operational section of this chapter. Initially it may seem that the concerns of this research are a long way from those of a local family centre, but we hope to demonstrate that links can be made to family support policy and practice.

To begin with we examine a recent study by Boswell (1995), which investigated in detail the childhood experiences of some 200 men (aged 14-59) who were serving long custodial sentences. All were male and half of them had been convicted of homicide (murder or manslaughter). Boswell interviewed each of them asking about their early childhood experiences, with a focus on issues relating to episodes of abuse they had experienced. These abusive episodes were analysed in categories of emotional, physical, sexual or organised or ritual abuse. Boswell then checked any disclosure from the victims against social work files for verification of their version of the events. Only if there were clear recordings in such files to confirm the account given did she allow for the episode in her figures. One of Boswell's most significant findings is that 72% of the sample of 200 had experienced some form of abuse or a combination of the various abuse categories. Given what we know about the amount of undisclosed, unreported or unverifiable abuse which happens, it is likely that this figure is actually an underestimate. It follows from Boswell's important research that nearly three-quarters of the most violent children in this country have experienced some form of childhood abuse.

Boswell's findings are consistent with those of Cavidino, who, in his study 'Children who Kill' (1996), quotes Dr Robert Johnson's letter to the Guardian newspaper published on 22 February 1993. Johnson was at that time a consultant psychiatrist at Parkhurst prison and wrote:

> Last week I was asked to evaluate a violent prisoner who was becoming increasingly bitter and aggressive. 'Were you happy as a child?' is my standard question. 'No', he replied, 'my father tried to kill me'. At the age of three, his father suspended him from a 200 foot bridge by a rope round his ankles to within a few feet of the water below. His mother pulled him back up. (1996: 11)

Johnson goes on to note that this man was serving a life sentence for a violent crime and believed he would commit more. This anecdote resonates with the Boswell research which we have outlined above, and will no doubt ring bells with readers who have experience of working within the criminal justice system. As Cavidino starkly observes: 'Childhood trauma leads to violent behaviour not only in childhood and adolescence, but also in adult life' (1996: 12).

Thus, utilising this research, we can begin to makes links between early years experiences and the issue of crime. NACRO, in their publication Families and Crime (1998), undertook an analysis of research relating to families and crime. Their summary suggests that there is a range of factors which are significantly related to an increased risk of criminality in young people. According to the NACRO study these factors include:

- Economic deprivation
- Poor parental supervision
- Parental neglect
- Harsh or erratic discipline
- Parental conflict
- Long term separation from a biological parent
- Having a parent with a criminal record

Evidently some of these factors are difficult for social agencies to directly address: the most obvious is having a parent with a criminal record. Children either do or they do not have a parent with a record – and there is little that social agencies can do about this. There are, however, a number of issues which can be, and we would suggest should, be actively addressed with parents and families whilst the children in the home are young enough for there to be potential for change. If we leave action on these issues until the young person is, say, 15 and already has a significant offending career, the task in infinitely more difficult and the chances of effecting change is limited.

We believe that West Leeds FSU is ideally placed within the community to address some of these factors. If we seek to address these issues in a coherent and considered fashion then there should be an incremental increase in educational achievement, family cohesion, play within families and a decrease in school non-attendance and school exclusion, youth crime and social dislocation amongst young people in the area in which we work. With the exception of the factor we have identified we believe that West Leeds FSU, as a community based family centre, can have an impact on a range of social issues, which research demonstrates has an impact of later involvement in crime. The nature of these interventions will be examined, once we have outlined related family support research.

Recent Findings in Family Support Research

Family centre interventions often display an ideological commitment to improving the human condition through supportive and preventive service delivery. This commitment is central to the value base to those of us working in, or with, family centres. It is a value base which emphasises partnership between staff and service users, and attempts to empower users wherever possible. In the harsh world of funding bids and service level agreements, however, we are often asked to go beyond this fundamental value base to examine the issue of 'evidence' to help establish our practice and, in contemporary parlance, to address the issue of 'what works'. In this section of this chapter we wish to examine the research base for family support work and examine how this can be applied and operationalised.

Gibbons suggests that the effectiveness of family centres should be assessed by criteria such as:

> ...the extent to which they contribute to a neighbourhood's resources, and to the bonds between local residents; their contribution to decreasing social isolation among families and increasing social integration. (1990: 92-3)

Importantly, Pollitt (1988), suggests a methodology for directly involving services users in generating the outcomes used in evaluation and research. This method has been operationalised by Frost et al. (1995) in their study of Home-Start. Such a methodology is consistent with the value base of family centres which we have already mentioned. Rather than impose pre-constructed 'instruments' of objective measures designed in the academy empowering research methods should attempt to integrate service users into the research process.

In the UK as we enter the new century, the context for research-led debates around family support inevitably has as its starting point the Department of Health publication, 'Child Protection - Messages from Research' (1995). The publication has its roots in the Cleveland child abuse 'crisis' of 1987 (Campbell, 1988). Following these unsettling and well-publicised events the Department of Health commissioned a programme of wide reaching research which came to fruition in the form of 20 publications. These were brought together and summarised in the 'Messages' publication. However, 'Messages' went further than simply summarizing research and engaged centrally in a crucial child welfare policy debate which had been emerging throughout the 1990s. Thus 'Messages' became the trigger for a new debate which became known as the 're-focussing' debate. The recent focus, it was argued, has been on 'child protection' in the narrow sense, of ensuring that children were protected from inter-personal abuse or neglect by their parents or other caretakers. 'Messages' questioned this narrow focus – it was argued that this led to an investigatory mentality, often leading to no particular intervention or support for the family. This form of practice, it was argued, should be 're-focussed'. 'Messages' puts it like this:

> The research studies have questioned whether the balance of child protection and the range of supports and interventions available to professionals is correct. This is an issue area child protection committees

and professionals associated with this group must consistently raise about services in their region. (1995: 54)

The new focus should be more broadly on the welfare of the child and family – thus the key question shifts from 'how can this child best be protected' to 'what can be done to best promote the welfare of the child and family'? Again as 'Messages' argues:

> In fact a continuum exists between child protection, family support and child welfare. Agreement leads to better outcomes and agreement can be reached without recourse to the child protection process. (1995: 55)

Thus it follows that we must 'intervene with a lighter, less bureaucratic touch in a number of cases, integrate family support services both practically and conceptually more with child protection, and thereby release more resources from investigation and assessment into family support and treatment services' (Wendy Rose, Assistant Chief Inspector, DoH, 1994). Crucially it was argued that this approach was, in any case, mandated by Section 17 of the Children Act, 1989. Section 17 states that:

> It shall be the general duty of every local authority ...
> (a) to safeguard and promote the welfare of children within their area who are in need; and
> (b) so far as is consistent with that duty, to promote the upbringing of such children by their families, by providing a range and level of services appropriate to those children's needs.

Thus, whilst the child protection aspect of child welfare mandated by Section 47 of the Children Act remains important, 'Messages' argued that:

> An approach based on the process of Section 47 enquiries and Section 17 services might well shift the emphasis in child protection work more towards family support. (1995: 55).

The role of the voluntary sector, and potentially of the family centre movement, are crucial here. The Children Act emphasises this point when it states that:

Every local authority – shall facilitate the provision by others (including in particular voluntary organisations) of services which the local authority have power to provide by virtue of this section.

The role of the voluntary sector is potentially further enhanced by the fact that both Department of Health commissioned research ('Making Sense of Section 17') and inspections carried out by the Social Services Inspectorate (1999) which have been critical of the perceived failure of local authorities to develop a coherent approach to implementing Section 17 in a strategic manner. Given this context how can research help develop a clear role for a family centre?

Whilst the current policy debate context has been established by 'Messages' there remains a wider research backing for the shift towards family support. It this context we can examine only a small proportion of this research. We have chosen to focus on home-visiting and on some evaluative research commissioned by the West Leeds FSU relating to our own practice. This has the advantage of contrasting an over-arching study, bringing together a wide-range of research, with a specific local study.

The efficacy of home-visiting has been well-established in a wide range of research studies (see Seitz, 1990, for a summary). Famously the High/Scope Perry Pre-School Programme provided intensive home visiting and pre-school education over a two year period. The intervention group and a control group were followed up and at age 19 and 27. The intervention group were less likely to have been school drop outs, have been arrested, on welfare, to be illiterate, or unemployed than the control group. These are remarkable and very convincing figures.

The researchers suggest that for every $1 invested in early years programmes $7 are saved in terms of later state expenditure. These findings have been influential in terms of the policy of the current British Labour Government and their initiatives, including Sure-Start, which is similar to the Perry programme. In the British context there are equally optimistic findings drawing on home visiting programmes (see Frost et al. 1995, for example).

More specifically the West Leeds FSU commissioned some research to assess the impact of the Unit on the immediate locality. The West Leeds FSU was established in 1989:

to improve the quality of life of families with young children and increase the range of choices and opportunities available to them, in line with FSU's policy and practice on equal opportunities and participation.

The evaluation study finds that the centre had made contact with almost half of the local people with dependent children within the first three years of its existence. The centre had attempted to pursue an equal opportunities policy, but had attracted mainly women. The fact that the centre was dominated by females meant that it carried particular appeal for local Asian women, who were more likely to have used the centre than other local residents.

> Participants confirmed that they had established networks of support and friendship through their association with the Project. They felt less stressed and worried and their self esteem had been enhanced. They had increased confidence and for some this meant 'moving on' to employment and training courses. There was also evidence that the Project had successfully promoted child development, particularly with the under fives. (1993: 61)

The evaluation also found that:

> The Project was successful in establishing itself as an open access centre which provided family support without stigma and which complemented the services provided by other local agencies. (1993: 61)

The relationship between a non-stigmatising approach and access to services has been highlighted elsewhere (Frost et al. 1995). Crucially the West Leeds FSU has also addressed structural issues of inequality and racism:

> The project had been able to promote friendship and co-operation between adults and children and by its policy of confronting racial harassment, has encouraged greater tolerance within the community. (1993: 60)

Having looked at two themes of recent research – in family support and youth crime – we now move on to look at the actual practice of this particular family centre.

Current Policy and Practice at West Leeds Family Service Unit

Given this strong research background – linking youth crime research, family research and our own evaluative study – West Leeds has decided to make a strategic shift to ensure that our work as a family centre is informed by research and forms a coherent whole. The political context for this is both local and central. Locally the City Council have, in common with many other local authorities, worked towards a system of Service Level Agreements. This means that the Unit is given a number of measurable targets and these are monitored by the local authority. Ultimately the funding for the Unit is dependent on achieving these targets.

At central government level the policy of the Labour government has in many ways struck a chord with the work we are developing at West Leeds FSU. The government Green Paper 'Supporting families' (1998), links family support and the prevention of youth crime, as did the rationale for the introduction of the Crime and Disorder Act, 1998. In many areas the government are encouraging 'joined-up thinking' – which we aspire to demonstrate, all be it on a small scale, at West Leeds FSU. The area in which West Leeds FSU operates has a high incidence of youth crime. In recent years the area has experienced two high profile incidents of public disturbances. Given what has been outlined above it makes sense to develop a knowledge based approach to early years intervention. West Leeds FSU hopes that its approaches to the early years are helping to contribute to a long-term reduction in crime. At the time of writing it is far too early to evaluate how effective our approach will be.

How then can policy shift and develop to address some of the political trends and the research findings which we have outlined above? At West Leeds the following projects and methods of working seem to us to address a coherent agenda addressing many of the factors identified by NACRO and outlined above.

Advice Work and Anti-Poverty Strategies

Given the research as demonstrated, that poverty and poor housing are associated with crime (as well as many other factors in human unhappiness), West Leeds FSU have always had anti-poverty strategies at the top of its agenda. The Unit provides extensive advice work at two different localities. Additionally the Unit is active in a local network which acts as a springboard for co-ordinating activities across the locality and ensuring that we maximise the resources coming into the area. Whilst family centre projects can 'resolve' poverty it is important that anti-poverty strategies remain central to tackling family disadvantage and the link to crime. Such strategies provide the framework to family support.

Supporting Families

As we have seen, recent government thinking suggests that parenting is a high political priority. There can be little doubt that parenting is a difficult job. As Faber and Mazlish remark:

> I was a wonderful parent before I had children ...... living with real children can be humbling. (1980: 1)

The Government's White Paper, 'No More Excuses' (1997), which preceded the Crime and Disorder Act introduced the notion of a Parenting Order, which is designed to 'help and support parents control the behaviour of their children' (para 4.11).

The Parenting Order could be operationalised in a variety of different ways but one tested method is to offer a series of group or individual sessions on a weekly basis for approximately 3 months. At West Leeds FSU we already offer parenting groups and hope to develop them further in line with the Crime and Disorder Act. This raises many issues for voluntary organisations. To what extent should we be seen as operating as an arm of Government – implementing what could be seen as oppressive forms of control over parents, already struggling in adverse socio-economic circumstances? At West Leeds FSU we have, perhaps controversially, decided to bite the bullet. This decision was taken on the basis that Parenting Orders are going to happen anyway, and that we should do what we can do make them work in the most empowering way possible for parents. A further advantage of this work being undertaken in the voluntary sector is that being one step removed from the statutory sector, we have an opportunity of developing a non-punitive approach.

At West Leeds FSU we have a strong history of work with single parents. This group have had a high public profile in recent years with cuts in benefits and a 'back-to-work' culture. West Leeds FSU does not accept the notion that single parents' households are de facto damaging to children. There are many circumstances when children are receiving a less abusive and more consistent quality of care in a single parent household than in a two parent household where conflict and abusive adults are present. Indeed we have already seen that one of the indicators of delinquency is parental conflict.

However, it is clear that the task of parenting is a highly pressured one and that there are occasions when single parents, who often live in poverty, would benefit from extra support and help. The Single Parent Support Scheme (SPSS) based at West Leeds FSU does precisely that work. It trains volunteers and then links them with single parents to act as a support, friend and encourager. Since 1992 over 75 volunteers have been trained and more than 80 families have received support. The tasks are many and varied but the key element is that of offering the parent the encouragement to move forward and develop self-confidence. There is strong research evidence as we have seen in relation to the positive impact of home-visiting schemes.

Play Work

At West Leeds FSU we have always seen play as a central part of our strategy. Play is a vital part of allowing children to develop to their full early years' potential. This issue links with later educational advantage. For example, a school local to West Leeds FSU has found that nearly 20% of children in their reception year are significantly delayed in language skills. They speculated that this could in part be seen as the result of using the television as an extra 'parent'. It must be stressed that this is not deliberate, systematic neglect or abuse. Often parents do not have the energy, self-confidence or skill to play effectively with their children. Our current work shows that parents themselves have limited play experiences from their own childhood to call upon. They therefore have to be allowed to discover play for themselves before seeking to play effectively with their children. It is time that we acknowledge as a society that playing with children is not an innate skill generic to all parents. Many universities and other academic institutions now run degree or diploma courses in play work covering child development, stages and milestones, and appropriate play for age. Parents who do not have the appropriate skills to play effectively with their children should not be criticised but taught and encouraged. The West Leeds FSU Play at Home scheme (PatH) undertakes aspects of this work. Taking referrals from local health care and welfare professionals, it takes play into the home and encourages parents and children to play together. It is noticeable, but not surprising, that parents, once given the appropriate cues, spontaneously join in with the play.

Home/School Links

The NACRO report notes that:

> A lack of parental interest in children's education was correlated with future delinquency. (1998: 3)

Again there is a risk and a temptation in the media and politics to be overtly critical of parents who do not have good links with their children's school. They are seen as 'bad' parents who are 'failing' their children. Yet there are many reasons why parents are unable/unwilling to make and maintain good school/home links.

In the area around West Leeds FSU, many parents do not have English as their first language. An interpreter at parents' evenings and letters home produced in community languages as routine may see improved take up on parents' evenings. Issues of adult literacy and parents own experiences of schooling may create such a power imbalance that parents do not feel comfortable in a school environment and so they stay away.

Childcare, particularly for single parents, is always a difficulty and many times parents simply cannot attend parents' evenings for the lack of a baby sitter. Some children attend school hungry, having had no breakfast. This may be to do with abject, grinding poverty which many who live on benefits experience on a daily and weekly basis or may be a lack of routine which has come about, again not by abusive, deliberate intent but by exhaustion as a result of this daily grind. A scheme which would set about to improve home/school links and provide assistance with child care, routines and adult literacy provision, through the work of both education support workers and family aides, would reduce this separation of home and school.

Family Centre work can and have a central role in working with families to reduce the level of Youth Crime. If children have lived with abuse which has not been properly recognised and taken seriously, we will find that our children will continue to become involved in criminal behaviour. It is our responsibility as adults to address these issues rather than to individualise the problem and demonise our children. For, as Madge Bray says,

> A child's current behaviour often reflects an essentially sane response to an untenable set of life circumstances. (1997: 48)

The difficulty we are then faced with as a Family Service Unit is how do we complete the circle? The families we work with have children who are subject to child protection procedures. It is not unheard of, however, for the same family to have older siblings with some involvement in the criminal justice arena. This is not a different problem. This is two parts of a continuum and as long as social welfare professionals seek to separate youth justice issues and child protection issues, we will continue to fail vulnerable and needy young people.

References

Boswell G. (1995), *Violent Victims*, The Prince's Trust, London.
Bray M. (1997), *Sexual Abuse: the Child's Voice – Poppies on the Rubbish Heap*, Jessica Kingsley, London.
Campbell B. (1988), *Official Secrets*, Virago, London.
Cavadino P. ed. (1996), *Children Who Kill*, Waterside Press, London.
Department of Health (1995), *Child Protection: Messages from Research*, HMSO, London.
Faber A. & Mazlish E. (1980), *How to Talk So Kids Will Listen So Kids Will Talk*, Avon, New York.
Frost N. (1997), 'Delivering family support: Issues and themes in service development', in Parton N. ed. *Child Protection and Family Support: Tensions, Contradictions and Possibilities*, Routledge, London.
Frost N., Johnson E., Stein M. & Wallis L. (1996), *Negotiated Friendship*, Home-Start, Leicester, UK.
Gibbons, J. (1990), *Family Support and Prevention*, HMSO, London.
Gibbons, J. & Tunstill, J. (1997), *Making Sense of Section 17*, TSO, London.
Home Office (1997), *No More Excuses*, Home Office, London.
Home Office (1998), *Supporting Families*, Home Office, London.
Johnson, L. (1993), *Families in Partnership: An independent Evaluation of West Leeds Family Service Unit Neighbourhood Project*, FSU, Leeds.
NACRO (1998), *Families and Crime*, NACRO, London.
Pollitt, C. (1988), 'Bringing Consumers into Performance,' in *Management Policy and Politics*, 16:2, pp. 77–87.

Seitz V. (1990), 'Intervention programs for impoverished children : a comparison of educational and family support models', in *Annals of Child Development,* Vol 7, 73-103.

Social Services Inspectorate (1999), *Getting Family Support Right*, Department of Health, London.

13 User Participation in Family Centres in Greece

VASSO GABRILIDOU, ELPIDA IOANNIDOU and
EVI HATZIVARNAVA

Introduction

This chapter endeavours to account for family centres in Greece, which are run by the National Welfare Organisation of Greece, a quasi governmental organisation to which the Greek Government delegates much of the responsibility for delivering services in the field of child and family social work. The National Welfare Organisation was born in the midst of the upheaval of the Greek Civil War that followed the 2nd World War. In 1947, with the initiative of the Queen of Greece, the Welfare Organisation of the Northern Provinces of Greece – where the Civil War was taking place – was set up, later to be called the Royal Fund, and finally renamed as the National Welfare Organisation. Today, the National Welfare Organisation is a legal entity, run by a Board of Trustees under the supervision of the Ministry of Health and Welfare. Its revenue is derived mainly from a state subsidy. It has however some income from other resources too such as the sale of products, member contributions and European Union Funds. It runs a variety of activities and programmes aiming basically at child protection and family support through a large number of services throughout Greece. Amongst its programmes and services, its Family Centres – around 270 in urban and rural areas – hold a prominent position.

Origins of the Family Centres

The National Welfare Organisation's family centres developed out of two different traditions in the Organisation's service provision; the 'Children's Houses' in the rural areas and the 'Urban Centres' in the urban areas. The first 'Children's Houses' were established in 1950 with the purpose of providing support to the large number of children who were repatriated to their families and villages after being protected in the Organisation's residential institutions during the difficult years of the Greek civil war (1946-49).

> The Children's Houses provided day-care educative activities for children and youngsters such as short-term training courses in areas related to the rural local economy but also to everyday household needs, evening courses for the illiterate, athletic activities etc. However, right from the beginning it became apparent that children could not be helped unless one gave equal support to their environment, that is, their family and their village. As it was reported 'The Children's House' used the children as a means to reach the villagers and as agents of the new methods that were to be applied for the improvement of the living standards of the village....it sought, in particular, to make the best use of resources that were available in the area.[1]

The same report, referring to a text on the internal functioning of 'Children's Houses', reveals the close connection between the Houses and the local community and the emphasis on client-participation. The text gives direction to the person in charge of the House to take a strong interest in the affairs of the village and particularly in matters of hygiene and improvement of living conditions, actively to involve the parents in the children's matters and the Children's House and to make use of volunteers as 'friends' of the House in order to assist in the training of the children, to use their personal transport for cases of need, to help children organise themselves in a system of self-government and to disseminate the objectives of the Children's House amongst the villagers.[2]

Evidence from reports shows that the Children's House became, in fact, an agent of change in practices and attitudes in the local community. For example, the House's farming lands were used as nursery gardens for new or improved quality plants that were distributed to the villagers who received them free of charge if they agreed to cultivate them according to the House's instructions. The House's training technicians, with the help of trainee children, repaired the villagers' houses free of charge if the villagers provided them with the necessary raw material; the young girls who attended lessons in home economics with their teachers went around the

---

[1] Unpublished report of an unknown author.
[2] Op. cit.

village houses in order to show the applicability of their knowledge and to disseminate it.

The 'Urban Centres' started at a later stage. The first one was set up in 1958 as a response to the increasing deterioration, due to urban migration, of living conditions in certain districts of the large urban centres. Their purpose was to identify and deal with the needs of the inhabitants of the communities in which they functioned. Through collaboration with other local services and agents, they developed a variety of educative activities (i.e. house economics, sawing, carpentry, typing, traditional dancing, library, study room) and social activities (i.e. theatrical activities, social events). Legal aid was provided in certain cases, while a home nurse visited the families and took care of the transfer of patients to the hospital or the provision of medicine or gave advice on hygiene issues. The inhabitants could also use the centres in order to cover personal needs, for example, they could use the centres's sewing machine or the carpenter's equipment for certain hours per day or certain days per week.

Through the years, both the 'Children's Houses' and the 'Urban Centres', which were by nature flexible mechanisms, diverted their orientation and activities, adapting themselves to new circumstances. So, the 'Children's Houses' limited their training and local development function and became rather more like further education and social units which embraced all villagers. The 'Urban Centres' started to engage social workers in their daily activities.

The names changed too. By 1985 the name 'Community Social Centres' was introduced for both the 'Children's Houses' and the 'Urban Centres', while by 1993 the name 'Family Care Centres' was adopted in order to signify the importance of family as the focus of attention in the work of the services.

However, the discussion on the role and scope of the family centres has by no means ended. Questions are raised such as: to what kind of families should the Centre focus its attention? Should it be every family or those that are mostly in need? What is the role of family centres? Are they primarily 'prevention' mechanisms? If yes, to what level of prevention should they turn their attention (i.e. primary, secondary or tertiary level)? And, what kind of activities seem most appropriate for a family centre? Is it more effective to have as the point of reference 'the family' as a whole or the 'age-groups' that constitute it? Could or should the role of family centres in the urban and rural areas be the same or different? Changing circumstances with regard to financial resources and personnel have also shaped the recent discussion: Is it possible to run family centres in small villages in a cost effective way? How can Family Centres improve their effectiveness?

Current Trends

At the risk of generalising, we would argue that the following recent developments and trends characterise the National Welfare Organisation's family centres. There is a trend towards continuous development of family centres in urban areas. On the contrary, in rural areas due to decreasing village populations but also cost effectiveness considerations, family centres are closing down. Alternatively, more flexible structures are sought for small villages, for example, the development of family centres in rural areas that operate as a base for the provision of services in nearby villages consistently but periodically.

Another trend is towards increasingly focusing on families in need, families in crisis and socially excluded families and not families in general. However, there is a strong feeling that activities for particular socially excluded groups should avoid group segregation and, on the contrary, be integrated within the family centre's total activity and aim at improving inter-group communication. There is an emphasis on the 'preventive' role of the Centres.

There is a trend towards the provision of more specialised social welfare services (counselling, group support) and an emphasis on local collaboration and partnership with other local agents and particularly the Local Authority. Local resources and energy are sought in order to develop and support the centres' activities and increase effectiveness. There is an emphasis on strengthening user participation.

Introducing the Family Centres of Polichni and Toumba of Thessaloniki

The Family Centres of Polichni and Toumba are located in Thessaloniki, the second largest city of Greece. Thus these centres have grown out of the tradition of the above described 'Urban Centres'. The municipality of Polichni is a poor labour district of Western Thessaloniki, with around 50,000 inhabitants. The area was developed without urban planning after

1922, when the Greek-in-origin refugees from Asia Minor (the present Western coast of Turkey) and Caucasus, along with a few internally migrated Greek people, inhabited the area. Even today, around half of the municipality's land remains outside the city plan. The residents are mainly industrial workers, while in the last five to six years around 350 Greek Pontian families from the ex-Soviet Union migrated into the area.

The Family Centre of Polichni

The Family Centre of Polichni, set up by the National Welfare Organisation in 1962, constitutes the main social welfare service in the area. With the philosophy of 'integrated social action' and an interdisciplinary approach it develops – through constructive relations and collaboration with other local agencies, local committees and the Local Authority – a variety of activities of supportive and preventive nature that respond to expressed local needs and in particular, family needs. With its activities, it provides important services that help the family strengthen its role and relationships, preserve its unity in its natural surrounding and improve its quality of life.

Present Day Activities

Its present day activities include: day care facilities for children of pre-school and school age of working parents but also of families with socio-economic difficulties, social work on an individual/family basis, including selection and support of foster care families. There are also social work support/initiative/interest groups (for example, volunteer women's group, foster care parents group, school-children interest group), adult educational groups, support programmes for the elderly, cultural and social activities (for example, speeches, social events). There is also participation in local committees and other locally co-ordinated actions with a social purpose.

Toumba Family Centre

Toumba is a more middle-class area with around 160,000 inhabitants. In fact it is part of Thessaloniki's Municipality. According to the family centre's experience and inhabitants' knowledge, the main problems of the area are related to difficulties in interpersonal relationships, divorce and family abandonment, school difficulties, drug addiction and difficulties related to the integration of recently migrated Greeks from the ex-Soviet Union and Albania.

The Toumba family centre was set up in 1971. Its present day activities are very similar to those of Polichni and include day-care facilities for children of pre-school and school age. There is social work on an individual/family but also group level (for example, parent support group, school children interest group) as well as adult education activities. The identification, collaboration, and involvement of volunteers is a component in the family centre's activities but also in voluntary social initiative groups. Collaboration with local agencies in the identification of local needs and problems and the formulation of proposals and plans of action is significant. There are also cultural and social events.

Example of Activities

The development of two particular activities – one from each centre – will be presented below as examples of the pedagogical and empowering role of the Family Centres in the local community.

Polichni Family Centre and the Development of a Day-Care Programme at Karatasou Area

The Karatasou area is part of the Polichni Municipality. However, it is rather cut off from local services being around two kilometres away from the Municipal Authority's offices and the Polichni family centre. No other social welfare service was available in the area during the family centre's intervention. It is a district of poor housing and inhabitants of low educational and socio-economic level. It is estimated that around 50% of the population lives below the poverty line.

In 1995, the Polichni family centre, with its community oriented philosophy and method of work, and in an effort to identify and deal with some of the problems of the Karatasou area, encouraged and co-ordinated local groups and agencies to express an interest in local matters, and to participate in the process of problem identification and generate resources and ideas in dealing with the problems of the area. Thus, local gatherings were organised in order to sensitise and motivate the local population and identify local needs.

Through further collaborations with local agencies, the specific difficulties of the families of the Karatasou area were researched. In particular, in collaboration with the Polichni's Women's Association, the families with children of pre-school age was identified as a group most in need. In July 1995, a local committee consisting of the Polichni family centre, the Polichni's Women's Association, the Church and the Municipal Authority, formulated a proposal for the development of a day-care programme for pre-school children in the Karatasou area and asked the National Welfare Organisation to extend, with the support of the Municipal Authority, its family centres' activities into this particular area by developing the programme and taking the responsibility for running it.

In the discussion that followed, each of the two partners – that is, the National Welfare Organisation and the Municipal Authority – assessed their resources and capacity in relation to the proposed programme. However, it became apparent that more accurate information was required about the area, and the inhabitants' needs with regard to the programme but also their other needs and priorities and their views about the kinds of activities they wished to see develop in the area. So it was decided that a small survey should first take place.

The survey was implemented in October 1995. It was organised by two sociologists and one social worker from National Welfare Organisation. The main objective of the survey was to identify local needs with regard to the care of pre-school children. However, other local needs were searched and the possibility of implementing other programmes, besides the day-care programme for children, was discussed. With the initiative of the Municipal Authority, the inhabitants were informed about the survey and its objectives and those interested were asked to visit the research team at a particular place and in particular days and hours. Fifty questionnaires were completed mainly from parents with children of pre-school and school age. Out of the fifty families, forty seven had children of pre-school age. In 54% of the families both parents were working and in 36% only the father worked. However, from those non-working mothers, 75% stated that the main reason of their not working was the problem of child care. Twenty-four pre-school children (2½–5½ years of age) were identified as immediately needing a day-care facility between the hours of 7am and 4 pm. Though parents thought that other programmes and facilities in the area were important, most of them (90%) considered that a day-care programme for children was a priority. The researchers, taking into account the expressed local needs and the family centre's resources and experience, suggested that a range of activities could be immediately developed in the area, including a day-care programme for 25 children of pre-school age, an adult education programme, parental counselling on an individual and group basis (once a week).

These activities would be run by the Polichni family centre in the particular area as 'satellite' activities, a method of intervention often used by the National Welfare Organisation's family centres. The two main partners – the National Welfare Organisation and the Municipal Authority – agreed to support each other in the development and running of the suggested activities. For this purpose they signed an agreement in which the specific obligations and responsibilities of each partner were laid down. Under this agreement:

a) The Municipal Authority agreed to provide the premises where the activities would be developed, make the necessary adjustments in the building in response to the requirements of the activities and be responsible for any repairs that may be needed in the future, provide part of the necessary equipment and cover the running expenses (for example, electricity, telephone), cover the cost of children's lunch, and provide the necessary auxiliary staff.

b) The National Welfare Organisation agreed to take the responsibility for the administration and running of the activities, provide two full-time day-care workers and other part-time personnel for the activities, provide part of the necessary equipment, provide all the necessary educational material, and cover the cost of children's breakfast.

A local committee consisting of three people from the National Welfare Organisation, three people from the Municipal Authority and one parent would have the responsibility for the selection of children in the day-care programme.

The activities in the Karatasou area started to operate in March 1996. The clarity of the roles of the two main partners, the participation and support of the local people, groups, and agencies in the development of the activities, the clear knowledge of the local needs, the input of people from different disciplines and experiences, the implementation of a 'step-by-step' careful process of development, and an effective policy of communication at the local level, were all the elements that the family centre's personnel considered as important in successfully fulfilling the objective of developing a day-care programme in the Karatasou area. However, since then they have increasingly considered that the active participation of the users themselves has been the most important component.

Toumba Family Centre – Development and Implementation of a Parental Support Programme

The development of the discussed parental support programme in Toumba family centre took place in October 1996 with the initiative of the Centre's social worker and after collaborations with the schools and other local agencies. It was evident from these collaborations that there was a total absence of such or similar programmes in the area though it was recognised by everyone that such a programme was much needed. Parents in urban environments often live isolated from their wider family network, while other local networks have lost their strength. The upbringing of children is not an easy, straightforward story. Parents have questions they cannot answer and difficulties they cannot solve. At the same time, due to technological developments, they are recipients of many different and often contradictory messages which they feel powerless to assess. They feel the need to be supported in their role and be accepted as parents.

The family centre, in response to this need, planned and developed a programme for parents of pre-school children with the title 'Develop your confidence and your resources'. The programme's objectives were:

- to support parents in matters related to the upbringing of their children;
- to strengthen their self-discipline and encourage democratic attitudes and behaviour towards their children;
- to develop a social network amongst the parents and a climate of collaboration and solidarity;
- to help them in their all-round development in order to function as active and responsible citizens.

Fifteen parents expressed an interest in the particular programme, including one father. They fell into the age-bracket 21–40. They had all completed secondary education while three had completed higher education too. They were all working. The parents were interviewed by the social worker in order to assess their particular needs and develop a programme that was responsive to these needs. Two methods of intervention were used,

185

group work and individual work, for those parents that felt they needed such support.

Using Group Work

The group, which was co-ordinated by the social worker, met once every two weeks. The specific objectives of the group work were:

- to develop a climate of trust and acceptance amongst the members;
- to develop the parents' skills through group discussions initiated by the Social Worker who followed a specific text;
- to allow parents express their personal difficulties with their children and reduce the emotional stress that these difficulties produced.

During the school-year 1996-97, the group met fourteen times and discussed issues that were related to human behaviour, communication, encouragement and self-control. At the same time, in order to further develop the group's cohesion and strengthen initiative, sense of responsibility and self-decision, certain social events were organised by the parents, such as a social event on the occasion of the New Year, and an evening out. By the end of the school-year, the parents expressed their positive evaluation of the group work and discussed with the social worker the possibility of carrying on the group work during the coming year, but this time on a different basis. The proposal was that various experts should be invited to discuss particular issues of interest to the parents.

The group indeed carried on its work during the school-year 1997-98. Parents defined a list of more specific issues that they wished to discuss. Experts were sought who could voluntarily come and contribute. During the year, 12 meetings with experts took place. The issues that were discussed fell in four thematic areas:

- The role of art (for example, music, theatre) in the child's development;
- Health-nutrition – the role of prevention;
- Various psychological issues (for example, jealousy, competition between siblings);
- Sociological issues (for example, the role and impact of television in children's lives).

Again, during 1997-98, as in the previous year, certain social activities were organised. It is worth mentioning that the parents took an active part in the setting up a 'Clothes Bank' with the collaboration of local shops and industries, in order to support poor families in the area. At the end of the year, the parents positively evaluated the group work and decided that the objectives of this particular group were completed and that new groups with new objectives could be developed, enriched with new members.

Individual Work

Support was provided to four parents facing particular family and inter-personal issues including problems related to self, and to communication. Altogether, during the two years of intervention, 38 interviews took place with the social worker with the objective of improving the parents' self-confidence and parental and family skills. The social worker, evaluating the implementation and results of the programme, expressed her satisfaction, pointing out the steady participation of parents in meetings and events, the increasing involvement of parents in defining and redefining the objectives of the programme and in the process of planning, implementing and evaluating activities. They showed great improvement in their confidence in handling issues and situations within and outside the group.

The parents themselves expressed improvement in communication with their children, the development of skills of collaboration and solidarity within the group but also with other groups (for example, through the operation of the 'Clothes Bank'). The satisfaction expressed in writing by the parents themselves in a self-evaluation exercise with comments like:

> I received help that I had not thought of or taken any interest in before.
> I managed to improve the self-control of my own behaviour.

We must note that a formal system of planning and evaluation that is applied in activities developed by the social services of the family centres of the National Welfare Organisation was used by the social worker in charge of the programme. The above two examples reflect the philosophy of work of the National Welfare Organisation's family centres. The first example shows the merits of collective effort at the local level and what one can achieve by working together and negotiating agreements. It is a partnership practice to solve, through community support, family problems. Family solutions are seen as part of community solutions and communities are encouraged to take things in their own hands. The second example shows how social skills can be developed through practice, participation and shared responsibility.

Conclusion

We have attempted to show how Greek family centres have evolved, emerging from their post-war history and sensitive to the needs and life-style of its users, the terrain of the country, and the developmental style of the National Welfare Organisation of Greece. Key themes have been the fusion of education and social work support, and empowerment through self-determination and participation in the centres themselves.

14 Make Your Experience Count: Social Work as Informal Education
DI HOLLAND

Yeovil Family Centre is an integrated family centre receiving funding from NCH Action for Children, Social Services, Somerset Education Services and the Health Authority. The staff consists of a Project Manger, an administrator, three project workers, a specialist social worker and a sessional worker. The only full time worker is the specialist social worker, but all staff are employed and managed by NCH, Action for Children. The work provided includes open play sessions, community education groups, parenting support groups, working with children who have been abused or are very troubled, family work, individual play therapy, supervised contact, group work.

Make Your Experience Count (MYEC)

Make Your Experience Count is one of the community education groups and is an integral part of the work provided in the Family Centre offering a good platform for consumers at the centre to move on. The following are direct quotes from group members:

> It has been a challenge but given me a brighter future to look forward to.
> Now I feel I can do things on my own again.
> I can look at life more positively.
> I still can't believe that two hours a week for ten weeks can make such a difference to my life.
> MYEC came at a perfect time in my life and really helped me to start again on my way.
> Attending MYEC was one of the best decisions I've ever made. It opened my eyes to a lot of things and gave me back the confidence I seemed to have lost.

Make Your Experience Count was established in South Somerset as a community education course in 1987, primarily targeting women returners who wanted to make changes in their lives, by thinking about a start or return to education, training, volunteering or work. This was at a time when it was thought that women returners would be required to fill a gap in the jobs market. The course aims to identify and assess the strengths and skills that people have gained from experience. It enables them to make informed choices about the opportunities available to them, and plan and prepare for moving onto other possibilities.

It was and still is a ten week course (2 hours per week plus some work at home) with a free crèche provided, offering all who attend the chance to explore alternatives in work, education, training, voluntary work and in home life. It was, and is achieved by encouraging the building of self-confidence and self-esteem through recognition of the group member's own skills, qualities and strengths. It is especially beneficial to those who have few or no past formal qualifications. Originally the course was established on an ad hoc basis and tutors were recruited from past group members for groups establishing in new areas.

However since 1987 the course has become an Open University Community Education Course in association with Somerset Education Services. There was close collaboration between the original tutors and the Open University with whom they shared all their original group materials. Through the work of the same tutors the course has become accredited by the SouthWest Access Federation for one credit at Level 1. It may not seem much but to many in the groups it will be their first positive learning experience and certificated achievement. In Somerset the course cannot be provided except by Make Your Experience Count accredited tutors (now part of the Return to Learn team), who were Make Your Experience Count students themselves, so ensuring that quality standards are maintained.

The ten-week course consists of six core sessions including the final one. These begin by moving the group through a continuous process reflecting on experience as a way of identifying strengths and skills and moving onto identifying and setting personal goals before planning for progression to further opportunities. They provide each group member with the opportunity to consider their own personal development, skills and feelings surrounding their past experiences. It also encourages creativity, communication and self-reliance. The first five sessions provide the springboard from which they can move on.

Getting Started – introducing group members to each other and to the course. It includes opportunities to start negotiating course content, to agree initial ground rules, and to reflect on the roles people play in their individual lives.

Who Are You – enabling group members to become more aware of themselves as individuals by expressing how they see themselves, and to value themselves and their personal experiences. This is done through the shoe box exercise which although daunting at the time generates a great deal of reflection, discussion and positive evaluation about it at the end of the course. Each member of the group is encouraged to bring a shoe box/ carrier bag with six things in it which represent them in some way or which are precious or which they value in some way. They are invited to show these items explain why they chose them, and talk about what it means to them. The emphasis is put on choosing things they are comfortable to share with others. Examples from past groups have included such things as: a swimming certificate, which was their only achievement until then; house keys, because they had previously lost their house when they left a violent partner; a benefits book which provided them with their independence for the first time; photos of family both alive or dead who were significant in their lives; books, music or hobbies.

What Have You Learned from Life – encouraging group members to identify what they have learned from their personal experiences of life and identified some of the strengths and skills that they have learned from their everyday experiences. One such example occurred when a group member shared her extremely vivid memories of being bullied at secondary school. She had never shared it with anyone and had as a result had an unhappy and unsuccessful education. But as a result of sharing within the group she felt able to deal with problems her child was having at school far more confidently. Incorporated in this session, which continues onto the next, is an opportunity for the group to look at experiences in their lives, through producing their own lifelines, both the positive and the negatives. This is a personal exercise not done during the session, which some find very hard to find anything positive about. However the group workers have found that the members, by focussing more on the process initially, have been able to look at their lives, or a section of it more easily. Instead of a straight line they have been very inventive; a bookcase with multi coloured book covers for different stages, with unhappy difficult experiences in grey, there to be

191

opened when ready; a snakes and ladders board, or a tree with continual new growth, and the rotten fruit on the ground to provide nourishment for the tree. The group members' inventiveness always amazes us. The shoebox and lifeline exercises on the whole always seem the most memorable, stimulating and exhausting exercises.

What Can You Do? – Raising group members awareness of the skills used in everyday life and helping them identify their own transferable skills. Many people attending Make Your Experience Count seriously under-value themselves and often have great difficulty appreciating that they have gained useful skills and should be able to acknowledge or 'boast' about them. The session looks at supposedly simple tasks such as shopping or decorating and analyses the tasks and the variety of skills needed to accomplish them. Time is also spent identifying skills the group members possess and enjoy using, which could possibly be transferred into other settings. An example of this is a love of gardening which has resulted in a qualification in environmental studies.

What Do You Want? – Enabling group members to identify their personal goals and also providing an opportunity to assess their learning half way through and what else they want. To some extent, the earlier sessions will have helped people clarify where they might want to go but this can be very daunting so this session provides them with an opportunity to take part in a completely unrestricted dream activity. The group is provided with all sorts of creative materials in order for them to produce a personal representation of their dream life, dream job or dream day. This enables them to identify the things that are really important to them and also the changes they wish to make in their lives. It provides the basic material from which they can start setting goals. On the whole they still consider their future targets as impossible but we are always amazed at how many do achieve them.

Final Session – Where Do You Go From Here? – Enabling group members to make achievable plans for change. Time is spent looking back at what they have learned and also looking forward at what they want to achieve. They have discovered that learning, no matter how apparently insignificant, can be important and that they can make informed choices about what the way forward is for them.

The middle four sessions focus on topics or themes which are negotiated by the group members.

- *Coping With Stress* – looking at the stress caused by change, and ways of dealing with it. When people are planning to make changes in their lives it is useful for them to look at how it will affect them as a person. It is important for them to find out what can help them cope with the stress that such changes can cause.
- *Looking For a Job* – considering different ways of finding out about jobs and applying for them. This session allows the group the opportunity to find out about sources of job information, how to set about looking for jobs, applying for jobs by telephone and how to write an appropriate letter of application.
- *Organising Your Time* – encouraging group members to reflect on how they spend their time at the moment, what they might like to spend their time on in the future, how they feel they can find time for the things they want to do which is also very important. When the group diarise their week they find the differing ways their time is divided a real revelation.
- *Presenting the Evidence* – looking at the importance of record keeping and ways of presenting evidence of strengths and skills, including portfolios and Curriculum Vitae's. Although the group may not choose this one as a separate session there is now a requirement with accreditation that everyone should have a CV in their folder. So the group workers will provide help in completing this throughout the course.
- *Presenting Yourself* – looking at the impression we make on other people, and preparing for interviews. This also involves understanding the importance of body language and the effects it might have on others.
- *Saying What You Mean* – enabling group members to become more assertive in their behaviour. This is always a very popular choice as many of the group members have such low self-esteem that this choice is very important to them. The session looks at reasons why people are assertive, non-assertive or aggressive and ways of altering their stance by considering different situations through simple role-play or through discussion with the rest of the group. One example occurred when a group member was extremely anxious about a review at the social services department, where she knew she would become very angry and aggressive, because she felt that she was not able to get across her feelings. So the group worked through what she wanted from the review, how she could voice this calmly, and what compromises she

would accept if her wants were not totally possible. After the review the social worker rang us to share her amazement that this person had been so reasonable and more understanding. Consequently both sides had moved forward with arrangements agreeable to them.

- *Getting the Right Advice* – enabling group members to gain access to advice and guidance that will help them to make informed choices. This can be through visits to a local college, a careers office, a learning advice centre or by a visit from an adult guidance worker.
- *Learning a New Skill* – providing the opportunity to sample a new skill and to reflect on how people learn. This can be anything within reason decided on by group negotiation and can involve such diverse skills as bread making, car maintenance, silk painting or a day's orienteering.
- *Organising a Visit* – providing the opportunity to gain first hand experience of a local organisation, which may be able to provide them with future opportunities, for example, working at the supermarket or local industry.

The Importance of Choice

The group choice ensures that the course reflects the group members needs and that their expectations will be met. It also helps to develop communication skills within the group, builds confidence and enables group members to be clearer about their own needs and goals. They also have ownership of the course, which contributes to its smooth running. All members keep a folder with all their work in it, which also provides the core for accreditation. Accreditation is not a compulsory element of the group but all our group members are encouraged to go forward for it as they are doing the bulk of the work as a matter of course.

Make Your Experience Count is an intrinsic and successful part of the work at Yeovil Family Centre and the setting up of a group within the centre is not dependant on outreach work as other such groups require. All our Make Your Experience Count groups are run with two accredited tutors. This ensures issues which are raised during the session can be dealt with in a sensitive and supportive way, either by withdrawal from the group during the session, or at a time after the session.

All such groups are provided with a crèche which is run and organised by qualified crèche workers. Adults are not prevented from coming to the group if their children won't settle in the crèche; and occasionally babies and youngsters have remained with the adults throughout.

The course is advertised within the centre, and at two infant schools where project workers provide a service. Information is sent to social workers and health visitors for referrals to the group. Finally, parents and carers attending the centre, whom staff consider are ready to move on, are approached personally about the group. The needs of these adults are carefully considered, especially, as they can be attending the centre for many different reasons. Some of their issues will have been addressed and they will be ready to spend time on themselves and able to consider their future plans.

Not everyone is carefully selected but the group members are made aware that because of what may have happened in their past, some of them may be unwilling or unable to look back at their past experiences, which is an integral part of the initial sessions. Therefore they would not be able to gain maximum benefits from the course at that time, although hopefully will consider it at a future time. Each member of the group always has a different starting point, and a set of individual life experiences at the outset, which makes it difficult to quantify hidden changes.

Although written work is involved, a lack of literacy skills has never been a limiting factor. With two group workers there is support always available throughout each session in whatever way is necessary. No group member has ever been prevented from being accredited because of a lack of basic skills. There is always a range of ability within a group. For example, one adult had great difficulties in writing and spelling and one worker had written dictated information on her behalf. The social worker had never been aware of this and the woman took a while to acknowledge it within the group. But by the end she had joined a basic literacy course, which further increased her confidence, which coincided with a less aggressive response to problems she was having with her children's school and in relationships with social services.

There is always time given to individual students outside the group and especially in the early stages the support strategies were essential to some students successful continuation and completion. For example, one student acknowledged that course members and tutors had supported her through discovery of a 'surprise' pregnancy but was able to progress from being withdrawn initially to reaching a surer sense of direction which included both motherhood and going to college.

The group is open to anyone although our centre remit means we work predominantly with parents, carers and their children up to age 11. However, the course has assisted people who have suffered from post-natal depression, nervous breakdowns, are in violent or unhappy relationships, survivors of childhood sexual abuse, parents who have children who have been abused, parents whose children are having supervised contact with ex-partners who were violent towards them, or for people who want to put past experiences behind them. Social Workers have also referred parents who are slightly out of our remit but they see it as a positive moving on for those people. The course is extremely successful especially in building self-esteem. By the end of the course students feel confident to make choices and know the next steps open to them including following their options.

Wider Education Links

Another link with education occurs with the two project workers who have been working with two infant schools in the area since the Family Centre was set up in 1989. Establishing a base for positive practice has proved difficult at times, particularly when the needs of the differing funding agencies, the staff at the respective schools and of course the consumers have to be considered. However, all members in this relationship have worked hard to overcome any of the problems that have occurred, resulting in a positive working relationship.

The project workers have a small amount of their part time hours allocated to the schools and the rest of their time is spent working in the family centre. The work carried out at the schools has evolved over the years, providing similarities and differences in the types of work offered, depending on each schools needs at a certain time.

Individual referrals are passed to the project workers from the head teachers, school social workers, and health visitors. Parents and carers may also refer themselves. The workers discuss with all concerned parties what is available and what would be best suited to their needs. This could be an introduction to groups already established at the various venues; such as toy library, parenting groups, community education groups, or to drop in play sessions at the family centre. The groups run at the schools, except for the toy library, are exclusively for families linked to the school. The referrals might also lead to individual work with the child, the parents, or both. The workers offer counselling, support or an advocacy role.

Some Practice Examples

A parent requested help through the head teacher, concerning specific personal problems. These were dealt with over a span of six sessions, followed by family attendance at play sessions.

Another family requested some support for their child because of anxieties about attending school and subsequent bed-wetting. The project worker worked with the child on strategies around difficulties in the playground, as well as some advocacy work with the school staff on the child's behalf.

Another self-referral came from a parent during a parenting group. The parent became extremely distressed about her management of her child's behaviour and was worried about possible consequences. With a great deal of discussion and support from the project worker, the parent referred herself to Social Services who provided ongoing support whilst it was needed. Other members of the family centre team can also handle referrals when their skills are felt to be more appropriate to the problem presented.

As already mentioned facilities offered vary between the schools. The toy library is based at one of the schools with an open door facility, available to all parents and carers of children under 5. It is open at the school twice a week and staff from NCH Action for Children are available on one of those sessions. This means families can borrow good quality toys for their children for a nominal membership fee, but can also discuss any issue that they are concerned or anxious about either in the informal setting of the group, or by arranging an appointment to see the worker separately.

Workshops have also been set up and have covered a variety of topics both educational and recreational, running as and when required. Examples of topics include – making children's books, art and craft activities, stress and relaxation, personal presentation, first aid and safety. Incorporated within these workshops all the family centre workers are involved in an annual pre-school celebration based at one of the schools. This allows parents the opportunity to view the organisations and services available for their pre-school children, whilst the children participate in the free play activities provided by the organisations. This event now involves up to 15 different groups and services as well as consumers and press. It is a positive fun way for such parents to learn about what is available for their pre-school children without having to visit every venue.

Groups within the two schools have varied considerably but have been particularly varied and popular at one of the schools, which has a nursery. Both of the schools run parenting groups but with a totally different style. One of the schools was involved in the piloting of, and has continued to use, a specific package. The other school initiated its own group with the joint involvement of a nursery worker and the project worker. They tended to be referral based groups for parents with children in the infants and nursery school who were experiencing difficulties in parenting and family relationships. But as said before the referrals were often made by the families themselves. The aim of the initial groups were to offer support, friendship, and advice on parenting issues, to offer time to listen to parents worries that may arise, to suggest alternative ways of coping, and to show that none of us are alone with our parenting problems.

The topics covered were those that the group members requested and follow-on groups requested a number of the same topics, for example, children's behaviour, bed time routines, eating patterns, safety, play. Interspersed with this were information giving sessions from outside speakers, for example, an asthma nurse, road safety officer, health visitors. Other issues, which were extremely important to an individual, might crop up during an already planned session. These would be dealt with at the time as necessary as they were often equally important to other group members as well. As group leaders the co-workers had made it clear from the outset that no one had all the solutions and others in the group would also be able to offer alternatives to try.

Following on from the initial group an interest was expressed for more. Some of these have run at the school such as Women and Health – a WEA course, and a Volunteer Support and Training Programme which is another Community Education Accredited Course all of which have been run by the family centre workers. Some also moved onto the Make Your Experience Count Course at the family centre or gained so much confidence that they participated in courses at the local college.

Many issues have arisen as a result of working within a school setting, not least of which were staffing, time and space. As with all the groups that the family centre runs there are always two co-workers in the school groups who have to spend time building up trust and faith in each other's judgement. This takes time particularly when the workers do not work together in any other capacity. But by working together it meant that even if one worker was ill or detained the group could continue. It also meant that if a sensitive issue arose one of the group facilitators could deal with the situation on an individual basis, allowing the rest of the group to continue with the session as planned.

The crèche was always an essential requirement when running groups but this often proved very difficult. Providing consistent qualified staff and space for the crèche as well as a separate group room is often difficult in a busy school. So quite often the crèche would be in the same room as the group – not ideal but not impossible to cope with.

Another issue, which was addressed between the heads of the schools and staff, was the issue of confidentiality. This was a major problem when some parents within the group could be in direct conflict with the school and therefore could be voicing feelings that the staff felt they needed to know. This was obviously much more of a difficulty for the worker from the school, but family centre workers have clear guidelines on setting out groundrules on confidentiality in groups which all members are made aware of and agree to. In fact the schools have often benefited from the group process allowing such parents to voice their conflicts and deal with them appropriately.

The schools also benefit in other ways from having such groups. They tend to form strong, supportive friendship groups, which they will turn to in times of crises. They can develop a more positive relationship with the school when past negative experiences of their own schooling, or lack of it would have prevented this. This enables them to help and support the school in different ways, such as in the parent teachers association or in helping in the classrooms. One group set up and ran a road safety session tailored to the nursery children as a thank you to the school. There are also benefits on both sides from a group such as the Volunteer Support and Training Programme where the group members have to do some voluntary work as part of the course and tend to seek placements within the school who in turn will provide references when they move into employment.

Although the work described is based in the schools there is always a crossover between the schools and the centre. This allows for staff supervision, exchange and sharing of ideas, and also for continuity of other work at the family centre. Supervision and support for the workers are vital where attitudes and values may be viewed differently by the different agencies concerned. Confidentiality has been one such problem, but this fear has been allayed by positive advocacy work when parents attending a group have been in conflict with the school.

In order to provide this service to the schools there is regular liaison with the workers, the heads and the project manager, to evaluate past activities and to plan for the future. These meetings are once a term. The heads also attend the management support group meetings, which provide a further forum for workers, funding partners, consumers, and any other interested parties. Evaluation and feedback from the schools and the consumers has been very positive and has been shown through new groups starting as people refer themselves because they have seen the outcomes for previous members.

The schools and family centre are never really totally separate because one family could take advantage of services available at all the venues. A family could come initially to a drop-in play Session, utilise the toy library at one school, obtain a place for a child at the other school's nursery, become a member of the school's parenting group and then move onto Make Your Experience Count at the family centre. There could also have been some individual support offered during this same period. The nature of the work is such that there can often be an overlap.

Conclusion

Two aspects of the educational dimension of family centred social work have been shown. In the first account, a simple but well organised programme shows how parents with little esteem and often lifetimes of negativity are engaged, over time, upon the first step of an educational experience. In the second account, two cultures which have often been seen to clash – social work and formal education in schools – are shown to complement each other with strong collaborative practice. Centre and school have become productively inter-related making sense of the various and varying needs of people who want to make use of both.

15 The Neighbourhood Centre as a Base for Social Action and Life-Long Learning[1]

JOY ADAMSON with MEMBERS of TOGHER FAMILY CENTRE, IRELAND[2]

Introduction

Togher Pre-School and Family Centre is a voluntary, community based project located in the heart of an estate in Togher, Cork City, Ireland, occupying an extended and modified three bedroom house. The centre provides for the needs of 2,525 local authority built homes that are situated in the Northern end of the Togher Parish. The centre developed from a long established community-based pre-school facility (1973). The pre-school work has always been characterised by a great sense of local identification and this laid the foundation for a large element of parental involvement. The primary focus of the work is on early childhood education and development in partnership with parents. At present, the family centre provides a pre-school, a crèche, after school activities for 4-12 year olds and adult development programmes using self-directed groupwork.

D

I was born in Cork and I'm living in...adjoining to Togher for the last 30 years. I come from a family of five boys and two girls and I come fifth...I had a child when I was 18 and I moved into the Togher Parish when I was 19. There was a local nun who used to come around to anyone who would see her and she would come and visit you. So she came a couple of times and I used to be dodging her – I didn't want to – I suppose from my point

---

[1] McCabe & Lewis 1998.
[2] This chapter consists of interviews transcribed almost word for word except for obscurities on the tape and a few major repetitions.

of view, I was 18 – had a young baby – things weren't going very well and I was in a bad relationship and so I didn't want involving with anything and so it took 6 months of her coming knocking at the door and her telling me that there was a family centre in the area and there was a lone parents group which would be support for me – twas the courage, I think, as well, trying to pick up the courage to come up here. So a friend of mine who happened to be living in the block next to me who was a single parent as well, the two of us decided, to get her off our back, that we would come up. So, I'll always remember, twas Christmas and she told us that Santa would be available for the children and at that time my daughter would have been seven and a half months old and my friends daughter would be nine months old. So up we came, to the family centre, and Santa was here and I remember Sister C. was here and she introduced herself.

The door was opened and because people were coming to see Santa it made it easier because there was loads of people coming and so it made it a little bit easier as well, but then, because at that time we – I would have been the youngest at that time – again I knew her, Sister C., and she made it quite plain to call her C., so eventually it was C. and we came back in January to the lone parents group. We would come in the morning from 10 till 12.

Yes, it broke the ice and then we came back after the Christmas holidays. Twas still a bit nervy, I suppose – you're looking at, now, we weren't long out of school, it was kind of, well we'll see what way it is. I think the option was that we could put the child into the crèche, have a break, get a break from her which was great for me. So, I remember coming down – it was Monday morning from 10 till 12 – was very worried about putting her into the crèche and when you were upstairs you could hear children and you were listening – you were straining towards the door – is that my child, is that my child? – that took a while to calm me down. From the support on the Monday and I suppose everybody in the centre, there was support for the lone parents...and at that time there was a lot of groups going on here in the centre so we were allowed to join in other groups, so I went into arts and crafts on a Tuesday, and maybe cooking on a Friday but the other people, the other members of the centre didn't have that choice...they had one group because at that time there was a lot of people using the centre so there was a lot of resentment towards us lone parents as we had the option of staying for two – so it was very hard to get it across that our Monday was a support. I could go on a Monday and I could get support after a bad weekend. I could say that I would have killed her; there were people there with me who knew what I was going through. I think a lot of the other people didn't realise that if my child was sick and trying to get that as well to the other members – cos I lived on my own at that time, in the top story of a block of flats and it means if she got sick there was no phone in the area I'd have to dress her, come down three flights of stairs in a buggy – I couldn't get up and I couldn't go – the others they had partners or somebody and I said to them look at it as there's a body. You've someone there and you can go out where I couldn't. I'm stuck. The only break that I had was when I used to come over to the family centre, or else I might go home to my parents house but say from 6 o'clock at night when I closed my front door that night, that was it. That was me stuck, and it took a while for people to comprehend was it was like I suppose at that stage – 11/12 years ago, they saw that if you were a young girl, pregnant, you get a house and some money, you're taken care of, so it was trying to break down those barriers in the family centre, it was kind of a bit tough as well. But the only thing is that like when we got involved in the groups we integrated with the other members and they supported us then when they got to know us and they were actually a better support group than the support group on the Monday. So it actually worked out as a support well for me personally, worked as a great support, and I made great friends and got great advice and everything. It was just the barrier that I was a lone parent, they had to kind of work past that.

At the time we had a social worker, not in the role of a social worker but as a facilitator, and she wouldn't have been there in all of the sessions cos at that time there wouldn't have been a nice feeling between the women and the social workers. We seen social workers as someone who'd take our kids and stuff...it took time to build up the trust, and again there was no break, it was every Monday, so like it wasn't a six or ten week course, it was every week every Monday for 2 hours. It was great.

When we went into the other groups and we were talking about parenting skills and we did a parenting course, it was written by a nun, and we done that course I think it was an eight week course. We were bad, we were shocking, terrible. If you didn't do AB or C then you were wrong...I think we had, we were more aware and were able to speak our minds and we were questioning things, again because the centre wasn't just lone parents, there was other members of the centre, we were integrated at this stage. We sat down one day, and devised our own parenting course...four years after starting. So we sat down and we decided what we wanted as a parenting course and I'll always remember that we decided that we wanted the first part of the course to have the right to say no, we had the right to treat ourselves to a cup of tea, hankies, anything. It was very hard at the time to comprehend that. Some of us let ourselves go, buying for the kids and the kids had loads, but our health was suffering and we hadn't, and when we sat down and looked at it we decided the children had enough and we needed to look after ourselves and if I got sick, well if the child got sick then automatically we'd go to the doctor but if I got sick then sure it would be alright, then we looked at, if I'm not well then who's going to look after my child, so we decided that we'd spend that part of the course looking after ourselves, so we went round Cork, we went for our breakfast, went for our lunch, to historical places in Cork we'd never been to. We went to Shandon and rang the bells. Some people had never been to Shandon in their lives...we had a child psychologist in as well...for a course that was supposed to last 12 weeks, it lasted 12 months, which was great. You missed it when you were finished. It was great. Got a lot out of it as well. But we gave as much as we got. No-one decided, like, the co-ordinator at the time would have been V. so we worked in partnership with her and she didn't make all the decisions.

We made it as a group, which was the way we wanted it done...and we had a social worker and we had a health visitor, a doctor...we would see along our life who we needed. We even role played going to see the social worker welfare officer. For me really what I got was...the welfare officer deals with special needs payments, your medicard form, for schooling and stuff like that and you hand in a form to them...and they can refuse you and make you feel very, very low, had a lot of power and we role played how you go down to the person and your rights and everything, and ..that person wouldn't have a job unless you were sitting there kind of sit down, don't give in and you have the right to appeal, so we were learning as well. That was a great benefit because we would be dealing with the social work officer at least once a month. So it was great to play act it, go in and not be afraid to pull up the chair and sit up straight and hand over your form and ask questions as well. And again the same goes for the doctor. You find when you're going to the doctor that you're sick but by the time you're going in he's chatting and you forget to say what's wrong with yourself. So what he taught us was to write it down and when you go in then hand him the bit of paper and hand him what's on the paper and he'll ask you from that, which is great...

When we were dealing with the parenting I was asked to get involved in activities in the family centre and one of the women who would have been against lone parents at the start I was after making friends with and asked me whether I'd give a hand with her with the kids one day per week and so I gave her a hand. I'm not very good at spelling and the reading. I would read to myself but wouldn't read out loud and it was story-telling we were doing and I was asked to read a book to the children and the sweat just poured out of me and I was very, very nervous but I got used to it eventually and I didn't know all the words and I asked somebody and they told me and from there I got involved in the out of school activities...and we branched out and set to doing arts and crafts and drama, so I started doing courses for myself for working with children, so I started branching out then as well...and we went to Belfast...we were linked with Bernard Van Leer at the time and they had a project in Belfast – the 1,2,3 house so we went to visit a group of us – there was 10 of us went to Belfast, was never so afraid in my life, going away, I was saying on the way in the train if there's a bomb scare I'm going back home, I'm going back home, but when we got up there they were very nice, different cultures, I see the work they do with the out of school kids and the money that's involved and everything and the College gave them a certification in after schools. We didn't have that qualification here in the South so when we came back we said we want to do this, we were voluntary people working and we felt we wanted this bit of paper. We felt it was time for a good couple of years so with the help of our co-ordinator here and the local college who got onto Belfast for the outline of the course, and they worked with us and there were three of us who did the play-leader, the first time done in Ireland, we did that here and it was accredited by NVQ and within that course we also did NVCA that's the Irish Vocational Council Awards so we done two so we actually got the qualification so it was great. At the time I would have been employed here on the community employment scheme. Because I was a single parent I was entitled to do this because they would have been married or their husbands would have been on the exchange, on the dole, and they wouldn't have wanted their wives to do it so that was another barrier.

But even I found from being a volunteer and my role in the centre being an employee, I found it very hard. I just, you know, you have to come within the guidelines and the rules and I found it very hard. As a volunteer I could say stuff you and walk out the door. I could have done that. I didn't have to take any crap from anyone. But it was a big change for me, like my hours had to be done, I had to be there at a certain time, I also was in

205

College at the time part-time and I also had the child, so I had three major things going on so I had a lot on.

Looking back...I suppose from the very first day we started off, I started a personal awareness course and from there I done my child minding course, then parenting course, went back to do the play leader, accepted to do a community...course and now I'm a tutor...I feel from being involved in the family centre I'm more outspoken...I'm in a lot of groups outside and bring the information back into the centre. I have no problem getting up and standing in front of a group of people, I have done that before, from when I started I couldn't see myself doing this. For me I wouldn't be as strong as I am without the support of the family centre because the support has been there every step of the way. I might have taken two steps forward and maybe one step back but there was always someone there to hold my hand, bring me along, learning to say no as well, I don't have to say no, I have the right to say no.

M

I'm from the area and I used to come here when I was young, I was about 3 (I'm 25 now). And now my own children come here. I'm working in the preschool downstairs and my daughter comes there, she's 3 and my son is in the crèche and he's one year – it's great – it's a way to meet people, like I know people's faces but coming up you get to know them.

All my friends used to come and I used to be down home so my mum she said we'll go and it was great 'cos we used to come up and we'd have play time when it was raining as well – it was brilliant, we used to love it and the kids love it now. My little girl, she learnt to talk properly, to draw, to get her own words, she helps me at home now, she came up here in nappies and now she's fully trained. She was very slow to talk and to walk, and when she came up here I passed her into D. and I said I'd stay and she'd say no go and see, and then I went and every morning, well I think she was 11/12 months old when I started bringing her up and she loves it...she's coming on fabulous...and with him he's able to speak now. He'll tell you now when he's wet, change his nappy and now he's after really getting strong.

I think it gave me independence and I was kind of relying on other people to help me like when I was moving into my flat and then I got the job, and I done everything myself, you know gave me back all my independence – definitely gave me a social life, I have a friend here. We go out once a week and going on courses, to the things I've always wanted to do but I never had the chance to, and it helped me with the kids too. I went to school with D. as well and B.'s been here for years, since it opened. And most of the girls from around I know and some of them are friends.

N

I was born the third child of the family, the baby of the family, of one brother and one sister, mother and father now deceased, six children aged 26 – 12 all born in B., lived in B. 19 years and in Togher for 26 years, married young as I said, I've been a member of the family centre for about 16 years.

I lived in the flats first and then I sent my children to the family centre which was only pre-school at that stage. I could see myself as Mrs Walton with all these children around me and I would be the perfect mother. You know and they say pass this and pass that and we'd be so perfect in every way, but Christ after having three children it wasn't at all like that, and I thought there must be more to life than this you know, so when D. was born...so friends of mine were coming up, so there was a women's group starting and we said we'll go have a look, so we went off down anyway and meeting a lot of women you know, chatting away, you know, some place to go, children run wild you know...met Sister C. then and she said why don't you and I say says why not we'll give it a go, first day dropped 'em in no problem, came up at 4 o'clock to get 'em, well will you come home with me and he told me no problems and he'd stay here for ever, this was the centre of the universe and he was delighted with himself...

I brought him, then there were a few other girls downstairs, and then Sister C. was here and she said should she make a cup of tea, and then we stayed and had a cup of tea, and it was just evolving then into a family centre, it was just like the next step, so of course Sister C. had a captive audience didn't she, so we'd have tea and a chat and we'd stay in the kitchen, and then she'd start to say well were we interested in groups, so groups to us, like, my God, what are groups? And she was saying on personal development, and like we were married, and so we didn't even know what personal development was.

So there was a meeting one morning...and anyway she started talking about all these courses and things, that they'd be facilitated by her. So our first personal development course was a major shock to us, wasn't it. We were all taught to be assertive and say no, Jesus we didn't have a clue, really we hadn't a clue, and like she was saying like, and we didn't know to say no, and we all came from the same position and we all thought we had to be like everybody else. So after our first personal development course we started to being ourselves, and our attitudes and a whole lot of things, so we kind of went on from there. That was the funny thing, and to talk about yourself, you know, that was very hard...you were, y' know, appendix to some other person, I was D.'s mother, T.'s wife, I was never me as myself as a person, you know so we learnt that too. The first year was personal development and then we did assertiveness and then we had kind of a break, little steps, d'you know, kind of getting to know yourself, your attitudes and your opinions, we didn't seem to have opinions either, d'you know, everybody kind of knew better than what we did, like they'd be saying you could be doing that and we'd say but we couldn't do it. Like those with babies they'd be running after the nurse or whatever, wouldn't make a decision for yerself... because the nurse said...twas hard.

Enjoyed it, as well as that, it was only one morning a week – Tuesday – and.what else would you be doing on a Tuesday? You know. Why not, yeh. It was free, the cup of tea was there, the biscuits were there, the chat was there, twas informal. It was like, that C., she kind of educated us without us knowing, she was educating us, d'you know, and we were ripe for it at the time, and..we just took to it..we done a parenting course then. That was the big one. We done it by the book, the...book, shock, horror, everything we were doing was wrong, everything...we were totally not good parents at all. It was very hard. We said to C. that we were all quite capable of sharing things and we'd be out in the kitchen sharing things amongst ourselves so we looked at parenting courses, so we studied for six weeks, sharing your life experiences like, about children going to bed at night, children that weren't eating, it started off quite small and it was only going to run for 6 weeks and it went for a year, because we realised that we had qualities that we didn't know we had, d'you know, and we were all doing the best we can and we were all individuals.

We gave ourselves rights, like the big one was I...like my child, love my child, my child doesn't have to be nice to my friends, don't be rude, and we realised that the children had rights as well, and there was no point forcing em...We got certificates at the end of it. We didn't actually do anything with it. Parenting course which had come up through the centre since, they have modelled themselves along the same lines.

While all this was going on as well, it created an awful lot of problems because while we were busy along getting ourselves educated, getting assertive, getting ourselves personally developed...what were our husbands doing? It was an awful shock to them, wasn't it. All of a sudden we were no longer the stay at home women, we were no longer like 'em. My husband, it was a fierce problem for him because like if he came in and said there's a child out in the road I'd get up or he'd say, it's raining and you have your washing out (not everybody's washing). So after, after doing the assertive course, especially, I could turn round and...we were no longer...accommodating...do you know...we started questioning things, why does the dinner always have to be at one o'clock?...it was very hard for them, and, this is my big one, I'd say, 'why are you angry? – do you want to say a bit more about being angry..' and he can't hack that at all like he'd be saying 'what the f... you been learning up that f....g nursery?' But once you get a taste for it you are inclined to do it. Even with the children, after our parenting course, we learnt like it's OK for the children to be angry, you know, and they have to express themselves...and they'd say, 'Daddy have you had a rough day, would you like to tell me what's wrong?'...'There's nothing wrong and I don't give a shite...' (Irrepressible giggles).

Two of my closest friends were lone parents but they weren't having the same problems that I was having because they were on their own. Other parents did, especially with husbands at work. Like the husband at work he expected everything to be there when he came in, you know, he expected me to be there when he came in and he couldn't understand that, like, I could be going somewhere, especially when we started meeting different people and things, you know, if the Minister's coming here or what. They'd have been happy if we'd stayed like their mothers, d'you know. The older Irish men expected it, and we would expect it ourselves, I mean, as soon as I started doing the course I realised, it's no life.. it's hard to explain what you need for your own individuality.

The parenting course was a big one; the personal development course was a big one. Sexuality was a big one, ourselves as women, because we tend to see ourselves as stereotypes, it was a big one with me, teams was another big one, being comfortable with your body and all that you know, saying no, all these kinds of things, looking at our relationships, did we want to be like our mothers and fathers, that was very hard for a lot of us, in that course it was very difficult...actually it was our first course with a man facilitator. ..he started off with how we first heard about sex, what sex meant to us and everything you know, and we were all just totally in shock, it was a very hard course, ran for 6/8 weeks...after that...the back to work course. We actually went out of here. It was held down at the community centre – 1989, it was, hard, and boring, work experience, hard dealing with work and the children at the same time…

V. came on board, formalised education a bit more, well, no, she didn't exactly represent formal, before like you would stay in your group then it opened up, all the groups were changed…you might be in different groups…it didn't bother me but it did some…it expanded a bit more…and got more people involved.

Could you reproduce Togher FC? You'd need another B…we were always encouraged to be around…more bottom up, we constantly need to be asking what the people want…we heard it in Dublin…users…I hate that word. …Did I tell you I went to Holland? Van Leer wanted people to go and do a presentation in Holland, so the names went into a hat, one member from each group…it was hard work…standing up doing a presentation to all these foreign people. It was a total off the wall experience, and knowing that you're capable of doing it, there was never a problem…take a chance and do it, going to conferences…going to the European anti-poverty network, 3/4 days on European training…sharing experiences, going up to Dublin to conferences…actually asking questions, d'you know, this is just……Well, I was kind of, I was always…it was there…untapped and I don't think formal education could have untapped it either, had to be done informally…

I done a non formal guidance course and we got our certs at the college last Saturday week…and I went for non-formal 'cos it was very relevant to my life, to what I'm doing, with working with young people…if you've been in prison like, to have someone from your own background, level like, makes an awful difference, rather than someone coming out of the probation service or social worker calling in, so I don't have that bit of paper so I think I'd go on and do a diploma…

R

I came from the next Parish, the one up the road, I moved there, I was actually re-housed by the probation, I got a flat, my first child was only three months old, and I was only 19, with a three month old baby, and I was with her father at the time, and moved in, full of hopes, happy families, y'know, so the parish nun came to the door and told me to come to the family centre, and then she came back again and I thought alright I'll go, just said I'd go to get rid of her, so she came back again and we weren't

210

after being there like, so she says to the girl next door, why don't you go up together, I've arranged for you to go up together, so I know the girl because we were at school together.

That was Christmas 1987 so I got involved in things, I started doing personal development course, assertive courses and then I became assertive and I didn't like what's going on around me so I wasn't happy in the relationship because you know we were together with the child, I tried to make it work, it needed two of us anyway to make it work, but I was the only one working on it, and I just realised one day I didn't want it and so we broke up...she was two then, when we broke up, it was one of the best things I ever done because I didn't realise I was being dragged down so much, financially and emotionally, mentally. It was like the minute he was gone it was like a weight of my shoulders...he had a drink problem, so I mean I was able to get things from the home, for me, I went out and got a job and...which has changed me so much, people have different view of me, they have more respect for me.

I started looking at my life, I think, what I wanted, I didn't know what I wanted, but I seemed to know what I wanted after splitting up with him, I knew what I didn't want. I came to realise that you don't have to be in this situation, I mean it wasn't easy, he wasn't going to go, there were solicitors involved, violence you know. I didn't just turn round and said I want to break up, you'll have to go because it meant removing him from the house, it took the solicitor, pressing charges against him.

In the end he did go like but it was hard, I didn't confide in anyone, I had to prove to myself that I could do it on my own, then when he was gone I had this challenge, didn't I. My baby was very demanding and very spoilt and then I started feeling guilty, so I spoiled her more, I was doing more damage.. and she didn't know discipline. I literally wanted to kill her, I was depressed, worn out...when will I end it all, I was that bad, I just saw no future...you're there at night and you have to decide everything on your own...and then I went to the marriage counsellor for about six months, through the centre.

I got involved from day one, you know the groups for the mothers, all sorts, I went to Dublin, for training days, and I had to leave the child and that changed me as I started to feel independent, meeting people and getting out, and I started to see that there was more to life than being a mother, you know, I was only 18 when I had her and I had to do something or I never would have lived, and then I met this guy...

211

C

I was born 30 miles from Cork – there was 16 in my family – 10 boys and six girls – I was sixth – at that time we used to go to Mass on horse and trap – I tell my daughter and she doesn't believe me – there was a man lived up the road had a horse and trap and every Sunday morning we'd see who got up first to get a lift – when we went to school, there was four of us and two of us would hide in the ditch while the other two tried for a lift and then we'd jump out and there'd be four of us. My dad used to cycle to work 30 miles from...and he never missed mass in his life...very holy person (father died) and then my mother remarried and we came to the city. My mother now lives out at west Cork...into Irish dancing and all that...had a second go at life...I got married myself when I was 19 and I had six children, I had one after the other which is great because I think you're young with your kids...

I live directly across the green here and all my kids came to the nursery, the six of them came here. I got involved in the play schemes because my own kids were in them. They didn't have much else here at the time because there was no classes going on here at the time...the early days of the family centre. So mine had all finished and off to school and then they started off the first course here – it was a return to work course – we had to go down to the community centre every morning from 9 –12 and in the end she sent us out and – it was how to be assertive – and they taught us a few things, y'know, which was great because I was always a quiet person. It was the first course I'd done...I just wanted something outside of work for myself – I decided I'd love to do it for myself – so I got myself some work experience in a butcher's shop – it was great for me to get back to work again.

It taught you to speak up, that what you have to say is as important as anybody...and I worked there for 5 years. And then I decided to do another course – cleaning at the school – I had put in for a course here last year but it was too late so they were looking for a caretaker here and I am caretaker here at the moment, because B. came and asked me and I said if I can transfer the course from across the way and I could so...It's fabulous here...and they do courses here in the evening so I can come to those, it's brilliant. It's brilliant because everybody is treated the same, with the same respect, there's nobody any better than anybody else...this is a place where people can come to talk, there's always somebody here, they always make time for people.

I'm doing a computer course also here at the moment. Most of the courses are here; there's a lot like car maintenance, for example. Because everybody needs a car, to get to work for example.

S

I was born in the north side of the city, came from a large family, married a girl from the south side and then about 15/16 years ago I moved to Togher, I was living in one of the flats in the main road and I eventually got a house.

Could be 12/13 years ago, I had one son and one daughter – 3 and 4 years of age – there was a summer playscheme, came up and I put my two kids in the playscheme now like, and I was told to register the kids at a certain point, and I took it for granted that it was all women like, so I came up here and I registered my kids, my first time being in the centre like, at that time we had sister C. – she had a fair say in it all then like – I got introduced downstairs – I had no interest in ever coming to this place, then Sister C. – she used to call at people's houses and she came to our house one day and she said where was I and she said why don't you come up to the centre? I just happened to come over one day and then I met V., like I was talking to a few of the members like what was going on here like, like it was a lot smaller then, but basically we just used to generally chat.

And we'd be in the kitchen and there's be two men and 18 women so I didn't see any reason for getting involved in the centre but then they did courses and I think the first course I did like would be woodwork, we were transferred to a school below – college of further education – and the family centre got donations like a fund for the men, then there was a pottery course come up, twasn't bad and all like, mixing with the females, blah, blah blah and all that like, we done a few things and all, like, so I got more or less involved in the centre, some left, more came, it got bigger and bigger like, then I got involved in the men's group...tried to get going just for men in the centre like, there was about 2/3 of us to start like (six years ago) We had a music class at night-time. That was very good because we got members' sons that come over..it was very good with guitar lessons and all, like, and then went on for a while and it faded out like, and then I as left on my own again, like, and we decided we'd have an open kind of group which would be male and female to do jewellery, art, music, keyboard. The

213

4 guitars were bought and there was me and three girls joined up like…it's very hard getting a group together because a lot of girls downstairs have commitments…but for me it was a great benefit…there was a girl called K. O'F. was her name – Dublin girl – she was an art teacher and she came in and she taught us – I was actually the first actually here – then we got a few other girls like and then there was a man, no there wasn't – so there was 4 of us plus the teacher, every Wednesday it was, one of the longest courses going.

K

I'm a parent member, voluntary worker – I've been involved since 1989. For the first few years I was involved as a – my step-daughter was the first to come here to use the pre-school services and my partner V. became heavily involved in the centre in Sister C.'s time so she was more involved directly in the centre at that time…so I was back at home while she was busy up here. I used to be very frustrated at times about the amount of time that was spent up here on the other side knowing the value of it, not only for V. but for the community. It is hard work at home when you're involved in a centre like this. I was employed at the time as a taxi driver – long hours and then I became unemployed in 1996 and I became more directly involved in the centre – we switched roles – so her involvement got less and when I became unemployed I took up that role of doing the roster for the pre-school centre. I became involved as a parent on the roster and got involved in setting up the first men's conference in Cork.

We got the conference up and running and the first meeting was amazing , it gelled, and history was made. I was very conscious at the time that I was parachuting in because other men had been involved in more practical aspects…and their perspective I couldn't take on because I didn't have any experience. I was conscious of that all that history that had gone on. …and then we had the conference which was quite successful. 60 men came to that and a booklet came out of it (McCarthy & Lewis 1996).

In the meantime I'd been trying to further my own education by applying for courses…at the last minute I filled in an application form for a degree and I discovered a course in early childhood studies at University College, Cork, which was exactly what I wanted, an ideal course for me…and I've been accepted and I've just finished my second year on that course. The centre has supported me with child care for this course…Without the centre's child care I wouldn't have been able to get in.

The centre didn't directly influence me but through doing the men's conference it boosted my confidence to do it. It's all back up.

Getting involved. Technically, men become involved in these things through the women – they open the door a bit – men have got to catch up. I tried to help the centre and then the centre helped me.

A

I've been coming here for 20 odd years and got involved here through a friend of mine. We at the time were involved in drum majorettes, you know, girls which was popular at the time, we used this place for training. For a few years I worked here in a voluntary capacity, fairly regularly and I was involved in the whole fund-raising and things that were happening, and the whole movement of it becoming a family centre. The earlier women's groups that were started here I would have been involved in those...and they started in adult education for women and literacy and I got involved in that, supporting families...got involved in a course in literacy management...I've never given up my literacy work here and I also get involved in the after school activities.

In the earliest years, I always think this was funny because in the sixties there was somebody talking about birth control and she almost lost her job, and now the younger women here wouldn't have believed that had happened. I have seen the place go from just a room downstairs which was totally pre-school (except perhaps we had cookery classes, not accredited courses). They were courses on personal development, people reflecting on who they were, it was a whole new thing that people were able to discuss, it was the pre-school worker who did it, at a time when women were just coming into their fore. It got us all thinking of ourselves as not being at home. We still manage to keep homes and look after families and that. This centre represented all that. Discuss things that were undiscussable. Safe place, I suppose. My kids used to say to me we're going to take a placard over to the family centre saying we want our mother back again. Some very special friendships, sisterhood. Here it was growing into different kinds of education. People were encouraged to go back to education, university, whereas earlier it was pre-school and maybe the women met for a cup of tea and then they started going to the groups,...I suppose adult education changed them. At one time it would be seen as sewing or cooking or something but now most of them have gone from that stage...and now we have university courses in the centre and people don't have the time to do four years in college but this way you can do it, unit by unit.

B

Well, my sister had been involved at the centre for years anyway. Her little son, he went to the pre-school here and when he had gone to school she still came here. She was well into networking so that's how I became involved because before that I hadn't a clue what it was. I was actually studying at the time myself – I was doing a child care course – work with the children here at the family centre. I came here on my work experience here – placement. It was nine years ago. I finished a year at college and then I did Montessori for a year then I was on my final year and my sister was actually saying that a job was coming up here…

I've actually had the job six years…Well the experience I have gotten here has been incredible. I don't think I would ever get it anywhere else. From my own personal development. It's made me more aware. From working with people, with the parents, I mean a lot of them have had very tough lives, hard times, I mean it's a lot to admire the way they get on and do things. Never judge a book by its cover, it's so true. It has been fantastic for me. I'm more sensitive and tougher at the same time.

It's fantastic working in the old community because I know that was the long term plan…I was the first person from the area to work here so it's fantastic but it's quite tough as well, you know when you're living in the community…a lot of times…you're in the street and they might ask you something and the day's finished and you don't want to talk about…I'm doing a child care course, early childhood and the modules are from birth to 6 years and we've been moved around to learn about each age group.

At times when people see you out in the community you have to behave in an appropriate manner and I would be very conscious of that, y'know, that if you're going out for a night, something simple like that…but it took a while to build up relationships with people, for them to get to know me, and the fact that I'm so young as well, I would have been only 20 when I would have started here so but it was the fact that I'd gotten the job because all the parents had gone for the job itself, I suppose. I was younger then and I suppose it didn't bother me as much. It would bother me more now – in fact a lot of people turned round at the end of the day and said 'I'm glad I didn't get the job because I wouldn't have been able to do it,' but there was a lot of obstacles I suppose because people were feared of the change…

216

My job?...working with children, working in partnership with parents, working with other staff, working as a team, working with outside agencies and also making sure you do training for yourself. We have team meeting every Monday and, like, it's from 2–4, first there would be...if there's any concerns about the children because we work with outside agencies....there's a lot of energy here, and y'now, you can get burnt out quite quickly, so we're going to put this into place, taking care of ourselves..., so we're going to have a points system and who goes for lunch because sometimes we wouldn't even take lunch...and maybe at the end of the month or two months there would be a gift voucher!!! ...I'm never moving from here...this will always be my community...and I do a lot for the community...summer playscheme...not to do with the centre...we make a lot of contact with parents in the community who would never come up here...and now their child is in the crèche...the centre is a safety net for people.

W

I was born in the city centre in 1942 and I was one of eleven and at that stage Togher was a market gardening place, twas a country walk, no houses, nothing here only green fields and my first child now, he'd be 35, we used to bring him out here for walks in a pram, twas nothing but green fields and market gardening..all little cottages would have doors and like living in the city, in the centre of the city, really now in the heart of the city this was a brilliant place then y'know and there's be football matches, twas known then, where these houses are built now, was known as then as the *heighties* because it was all lumps and bumps. It was fields like where you could get lost, there was a dip, y'know and there was a railway bridge then just a few yards south from here and that was West Cork railway line so you'd come out and you'd watch the trains which was yet another great asset like to people in the city, y'know, and because the only time you'd get a trip on the train was once a year to the seaside, you'd go to the seaside once per year, but that's all you could afford really because them times wages were very small and like I say, then I got married I went to primary school and I left school at 12 and that was the highest you could go and it was only doctors families and solicitors whose children would go on to secondary school, at that stage which was in 1954.

So I went to work and I got married when I was 21 and I had six children and I had my third child by the time I came to Togher (it was only starting to be built) and there was just 18 houses here and nothing else – there was fields and when I got the house first I always remember my parents saying don't go to the country we'll never see you. I also then also had a flat in the city so I said for God sakes, in half an hour we're into the city and it was actually built privately to be sold these 18 houses but they couldn't sell them and so the Corporation bought those 18 houses and then they expanded and built the estate.

So, then I had my 4th child here and my 5th child, who died, and it was at that stage that I got involved here – that would be 25 years ago – and twas a friend actually said to me can't you come up and get out of the house but the thought of babies just didn't appeal to me, like, I didn't want, but was best thing that I ever done, as I faced the problem I had, y'know, by not wanting to be in contact with babies, but sure after two weeks, five days a week, y'know, so I started coming here then and did voluntary work. The Centre, twas in the early stages, the child I had before him, was actually born too early for the pre-school, if you know what I mean like he's 29 now, y'know, like, I just had him at the wrong time like, if the baby that died had lived he would have been the first to come here.

So, it's a place that grows on you really, there's a great community spirit here really, there's great bonding and it sort of expanded, and the houses expanded, and like it went from 18 families living in the middle of a field to hundreds of families within about four years, y'know, it sort of grew gradually and you know how a community is so quiet and all of a sudden a house is built and people can't get used to it and can't cope with it...but I don't know what it was, but there was great feeling every time we saw another block of houses going up, y'know, and everybody, like, the minute somebody would move into a house, whoever was there before them, you'd see em running with pots of tea, you know settling in with a cup of tea and then, as you know yourself, you go to a new place and you have a cuppa it breaks a big barrier and you get sort of into unpacking. All in all, it's, I mean, this place is, how can I say, I don't know how, now, to, it's like the heart of it, of the area. It seems to draw, all the time...I say it's enticing energies people don't know they have, it's drawn it out of them, I mean, I've known people that come in here, I myself, like when I came in here first, and I saw every body doing crafts, I, like, they looked at me as if I'd two heads, as I'm saying to you, people didn't have the confidence then.

Well, I was more or less brought in by the hand, by a friend, a neighbour whose child was actually going here at the time, and she kept saying, c'mon out, y'know and after 2/3 times I more or less come up in the beginning because she said if I didn't come up she would torment me, like, she turned out to be a brilliant friend for what she done for me, y'know. I can remember the first day and I felt as if I had three heads because the people that were here were so comfortable with the place and they had a purpose to be here because they had a child here, but here was I coming into a nursery school with nothing, because, y'know, my other children were at school. So, it meant that I was on my own all day, y'know, but I had no baby to bring up here and, like, I couldn't, I said I won't fit in there, there's no way I'm going to fit in there when I haven't a child to bring up, but after the first day it was like I'd been here for months...I felt really at ease, and it wasn't anything that anybody said, it was just a feeling I got, like, it's OK for me to be here, it's OK for you to be awkward, 'cos we were awkward...when I was here for a day or two I discovered there was people that actually had no children here. I thought everybody had a baby, y'know, but no, twas people that just wanted to get their time...and I think that's where the women's groups started.

There was a bond made with women, even then. Now I know children are a great breaker down of any barriers but the children were in the room with the parents at the time because there was no other place for them, twas, only just the one room and the parents sat in the corner and the children were on the other side playing, so I think it was just little words like people said, that it clicked with ye, that they don't have to be here, y'know, they've no leader and its OK for me to be here. After a while it felt good that you had a reason to come up and to get out of the house 'cos, like, to be, honest to God, to be in the house on your own all day waiting on the children to come home from school. So my next baby was born 3 years after that and naturally enough he became a pupil as fast as I could, y'know, so there was another man then from the Southern Health Board who actually started a woman's group below over the bridge in the community centre. He was actually the first to start a women's group but I did wait for it to be founded down here because a lot of the women were women that had their children here, in the pre-school, and we started that off below there and then my last wee boy used to come here...twas just a very easy thing, whatever it was it was, like, a great bonding with the people.

Crafts, or might be only just bring up your knitting and sit down, y'know, or could be repairing toys, or could be painting a wall...everybody would know what colour our bedrooms were 'cos it would be on every wall, y'know. I mean anything we had I mean like twas funny like you'd look at the painting and say I couldn't put that in my room it's horrible, you know, and somebody else would say it about you, y'know, they were probably saying, oh my God...when you look back on it now like it's so funny, but it was great friendship and lots of those people are still friendly with one another today...and it just grew and grew and, like, in the beginning there was only a couple of mothers here and then there's over a hundred and that's a hundred at any one time, y'know, there could be 50 that get outside jobs and you're guaranteed that 50 would be replaced.

There seems to be a great turnover because people are learning that facilities are here, I mean, as I said to you at the beginning, I left school in 1954 and I would have loved to have carried on but I didn't understand it at the time but like it was like only when I got married and had my own family and I realised that my own children were going places how hard it must have been with eleven...and I got my first opportunity to education when I was 48...Just a housewife and coming up here and learning crafts, friendships, and then they started self-development...not too formal that because you hadn't got the education you were afraid of it, y'know, you didn't need any education...and what I like about it was they asked you what would you like to do, what did you want out of it, so you actually spoke in your own words.

So, development was more or less one of the first ones I really done and then first aid...and we sat an actual exam...where you had to, you had to sit down and like answer questions and it was the first time I think outside an interview twas something of education, and I felt that was a great help with the family because there was an awful lot of practical things in it...then I went down to parenting and then as time progressed and there was so many women in my age group that was living with teenagers a course started so it actually went up in steps, 'cos you got the basics from the pre-school downstairs. That was a course in itself.

Then you had first aid which was tending to them and then personal development, which you came out of it and said, my God, I'm just not Mrs so and so, or somebody's mother anymore, I'm still who I was, then, as I said, it was difficult like when all of a sudden you were landed with teenagers and their different outlook on life, their different needs and there was an awful lot of young mothers here and they were no more than teenagers themselves, 'cos we only had the basic education and then I started on an English class and twas for me brilliant like. And then we went into partnership, we had a great relationship with the schools, and they offered us a cert. in English and they sent tutors out, and anybody who wanted could join in with them on the day...so I done that and we done the City and Guilds communication...and it like gave us another insight into what our children were going through, and we were waiting on the checking of the books to see what marks we got, y'know, we were literally sick, y'know, and imagine what they were (going through) who were so much younger without your experience of life, and then this course came then in UCC and it was for women in the community.

I said I'd go for it and I went for the first year...it took me out of here and into UCC and it was just one night a week but then UCC supplied a tutorial which came back in here another day. So we had our tutorials here and our course up in UCC. So we did that for 12 months for our certificate and then they offered us to work for the diploma in it, and we said well we'll try it anyway, so tried it and got it and it gave us a different outlook on life, different outlook on life altogether (because) like we're not career women. If you're a mother you can't be a career woman, I maintain, to that extent but we could actually understand our children more when they were going through exams and when they were studying.

We discovered, like, well they can't be disturbed. We understood why they were moody...and we found during the diploma year particularly that our children had a great deal more respect for us because we had begun to understand them – that's the way I felt anyway, that we knew what they were going through...it solved a lot of problems outside of education. It broke down an awful lot of barriers. You understood what they were going through, what they felt. And if they were tired in the morning you often got up tired after reading for an hour. So I think it done a lot for family as well as for you. I mean when my husband knew I was going into UCC he nearly lost his life. He said you'll never be able to finish it. And I said I will. But if he'd said you never will be able to twenty years ago I'd have said alright, so I'm a mother. But I'd come so far that I knew that I was able for it...I suppose I had the energy for it because I was after getting such a taste for education which I'd never have got if I hadn't come here...you get a sort of a taste, a hunger, when you say I'd love to have done this, I'd love to have done that. And that I find here if you say to any of the members like I'm thinking of doing that course they'd say oh she'll walk through that, or, do you really think that's for you? D'you know you'll always get support and you feel that somebody else your own age, your own education, your own background, you can talk to them better. At times you'd say, I'm thinking of doing this, goodness I've never be doing that, d'you think I'm able for it? and straight away, the support. You've not got one person going through the door, you've two, d'you know, that's what I find anyway.

I think it comes from inside, inside yourself, and I think if it's something you wanted to do when you were young and you hadn't got the chance to do it, finances or circumstances, I think if it's always there then you'll do it. And if you get the opportunity, grasp at it. But some people are unfortunate enough that they never get into a community. I wouldn't leave Togher if I was paid. It's like as if you were born here, y'know, you get that sense of feeling that you're here for ever, you never want to leave it, and I know people who actually left Togher; I don't think they gave it a chance.

I'm on the management committee and I'm also find-raising and just do a lot of representing the place. I don't think I'm anything more special than anybody else, d'you know, that the management is made up of 50% community and 50% professional and that's the way we like it. I think because from the very beginning this was our centre, it's the Togher family centre – it wasn't the Southern Health Board centre, or the CCDI centre, and from day one we cleaned it, kept it on a voluntary basis, took pride in it, y'know..and when a professional came in they were never hid away in a room for a meeting, you were always introduced, whether you were on your knees scrubbing, you were always introduced to them as an equal, and I think that has a lot to do with it, and that has a lot to do also I think with the co-ordinator, and we've had two brilliant co-ordinators. If you haven't a good co-ordinator..it's a very, very hard role. In family life you can't get up every morning and say I'm going to please everybody today. We're her boss, yes...but it doesn't come into it, nobody wants to be anybody's boss. Even on day to day things, should we do that or this and she say, well, what do you think? And vice versa…she takes everybody into consideration. We all look after her...we say just sit down for five minutes…just sit down for five minutes! and she'd sit down...and she knows better now 'cos she'd be sat down and we tell her to go and have a bloody holiday for herself. I mean it's a big, big responsibility and there's an awful lot of work done that nobody knows, the work she does, the people on the ground don't know the planning that goes into this, and it is a big job but it's great then to know you always feel that you're somebody because when you're asked opinions…in a lot of places the decision is made...and you come in the next day and everything is changed, whereas here, there's planning, there's questions and answers. There's advice, both giving and taking, and I think that's what works here.

222

You don't go and introduce yourself as W. I'm part of management. I'm W. I'm a member...I think with new members the cuppa tea and a chat in the kitchen and the one to one. Usually people come up with someone. I mean in three years there's been one or two people who've said there's no body on the door but on the whole, and there has been a lot of building and everything going on...and like the public health nurse has brought in an awful lot of people, young mothers who wouldn't have the nerve to come in here but they come with their babies to the clinic. She's opened a baby clinic and they've come up and you could see shock on their face like when they've realised this place was here...I mean you'd say everybody in Cork knows where Togher Family centre is, but they're surprised that it's so big, that there's so much activity here...it's like there's a protection ring around it and anybody's in here feels safe...that's what I'd put on it anyway. I'll tell you this much. There'd be a lot more people who'd have social workers, counsellors, on tranquillisers, and that, if it weren't for places like this...these family centres are in a couple of areas in the city and I would honestly say this has broken down barriers of the stigma attached to social workers...we can link up...I mean I don't know because all this is done confidentially between (the co-ordinator). I know that if in my heart I needed a social worker I could come up and ask V.'s advice and she would either sit down with me or if I wanted somebody outside she'd get me somebody, but nobody knows it. That's a very, very private part of the centre. There are a lot of things I'd say we don't want to know about because they're somebody's private thing, but I'd say a lot of barriers have been broken down. More Togher Family Centres? Nobody would have the years to do it. We'd be old, old people on zimmer frames...I mean it's after taking 30 years and that's a very hard thing to explain to somebody, like there's things and I would honestly say, and they have been recorded from day one, you'd say we'd never have done them things...you have to have the right people, at all levels...and you need a good co-ordinator as well, somebody who you respect...And it's no good giving them a new building; I think they must work for it.

References

Freire P. (1976), *Education: The Practice of Freedom*, Writers and Readers Publishing Cooperative, London

Freire P. (1985), *The Politics of Education, Culture, Power and Liberation*, Macmillan, Basingstoke.

Ledwith M. (1997), *Participating in Transformation: Towards a Working Model of Community Development*, Venture Press, Birmingham.

McCabe M. & Lewis R. eds., and the contibutors (1998), *Lifelong Learning – the process,* Togher Family Centre, 6 Maglin Grove, Deanrock Estate, Togher, Cork, Ireland.

McCarthy D. & Lewis R. eds. (1996), *Man and Now – Changing Perspectives,* Togher Family Centre , 6 Maglin Grove, Deanrock Estate, Togher, Cork, Ireland.

16 Conclusion – Lessons from Family Centres: the Authentic Site for Ecological Practice

CHRIS WARREN-ADAMSON

Chapter 1 argued that UK social work had turned its back on the institution and sought status in fieldwork. In this text there has been an attempt – with the help of international friends – to assert the centrality of a certain kind of institutional practice, namely family resource centre practice. This chapter highlights the importance of centres as a legitimising and learning base for the emerging child and family practitioner and concludes with a call for an international forum of centre-based practice.

Social Work as Informal Education

The idea of the integrated centre is a rich mixture. It is argued that informal education is a strong thread in the integrated practice world which makes up this text. Distinguished writers have long made the connection between education and family support practice (Weiss & Halpern, 1988; Weiss, 1989; Heifetz & Seppanen, 1989; Seitz 1990; and Lightburn, 1994) and in this text it appears to be demonstrated in action. If this is so – social work practitioners as 'teachers' – we should also embrace the literature of community and adult education. (for example, Lovett, 1975; Brookfield, 1983; Lovett, Clarke, & Kilmurray, 1983; Houle, 1984; Brookfield, 1986; Jarvis, 1987; Westwood & Thomas, 1991). This educational strand of centre practice becomes even richer when linked with the contemporary idea of social inclusion. The acid test of social inclusion is in the way practice addresses the universal needs of families without relinquishing a commitment to those at the very margins.

Social Inclusion, and Family Centred Practice

One of the major challenges for integrated centres is to manage the child protection juggernaut on the one hand, and on the other, the advocates of universalism and community regeneration. The pull of child protection is well known to centres. However, it is equally important to connect with those who are driven by contemporary and powerful ideas for neighbourhood renewal, for example, see Atkinson's 'strategy for neighbourhood renewal and the welfare society' (Atkinson, 2000) and Barton's (2000) plans for the eco-neighbourhood. If centres do not join with, ally with, such perspectives, they will be marginalised.

However, there is a danger that Atkinson and Barton's visions, like Marx's view of the lümpenproletariat 150 years before, might in practice (and however inadvertently) result in the users of centres being rendered ineligible for participation in the new future. The under-class may be over-taken or just not considered worthy of the club.

Centres, then, occupy a difficult middle ground. By settling for just one aspect for the centre, for example, family assessment, practice becomes marginalised from the other agencies. Welfare becomes ghetto-ised. On the other hand, in settling for community development, those users at the very edge will drop off the agenda. A socially inclusive practice, however, contains these tensions in one centre. By putting it all together centres make social inclusion work (see definition in Williams, 1998: 15).

The Ecological Paradigm

The proposition of this text is that social work is best seen as an ecological, educational endeavour which finds some of its best expression in the practice of family centres and their equivalent, internationally. At a theoretical level, an ecological perspective is an increasingly accepted paradigm of practice. Major writers have long argued the perspective as underpinning social work practice (in the UK – Statham, 1978; in the USA – Bronfenbrenner, 1979; Hartman, 1978; Whittaker, 1983; Maluccio et al., 1986, Germain, 1991). Eventually it has found more recent and fuller expression in the UK (for example, Wren, 1995; Jack, 1997; Golding, 2000) and, at the launch of the New Millennium, the UK Department of Health, the Department for Education and Employment, and the Home Office are sponsors of a new Framework for the Assessment of Children in

Need (DH, 2000) which explicitly acknowledges the ecological perspective as its foundation for assessment. However, such a framework requires a healthy context in which to operate, as much concerned with process as with product. Unfortunately, office based practitioners of whatever status – unless engaged actively in a well resourced patch initiative – have little hope of engaging fully with the new framework for assessment. They will rely even more on the (family) centre.

An ecological perspective requires of practitioners a close knowledge, a direct experience, of the developmental needs and patterns of children and families, and skills in employing methods of intervention in individual, group, and community contexts. It is not a linear view of development but rather explains behaviour in terms of tandem development (Germain, 1991) and of transactions within and between systems. Most important, social work practitioners, by committing themselves to helping and controlling, are not observers but are part of that transaction.

It is ecological practice which appears to be mirrored in the accounts in this book. It is the editor's contention that this is foundation practice, and that this should be the priority experience for the emerging children and families practitioner (see Batchelor et al., 1999). The priority learning experience for emerging practitioners should take place in direct and exposed settings such as those presented in this text, not in the relatively distanced case-management position. This direct, client-in-context experience will give practitioners a much needed legitimacy when, further on, they secure their office-based and specialist jobs.

Putting It All Together

This distinctive family centred practice embraces knowledge and skills which draw from traditions of social work, community development, early learning, youth work and informal and adult education. It involves:

1. *Multi-level work*, one to one, small group/large group, undertaking support and guidance, training, informal and adult education and skills development, local change and providing information, promoting, collaborating, co-ordinating; programme development; and so on.

2. *Direct work*, with, a) children and young people, b) children and young people with their parents, c) adults as parents, d) adults in need of care

and support, e) adults as participants in communities, for example, local management of groups, f) adults as participants in their own education, training and work.

3. *Transitional work*, a) helping individuals to move on, b) making links between groups and organisations, setting up forums, c) mediating and brokering, d) resource finding, e) networking.

4. *Partnership work*, on the ground, for example, professional and user, professional and volunteer, supervisor and befriender, between paid and unpaid, between trained and untrained, between specialist and lay, as well as between professionals and between organisations and agencies of different size and levels of formality.

5. *Management and inter-disciplinary work* – pulling all this together so that no one tradition dominates another.

Recommendations

a) There is a need for a new thrust in children and families practice which re-embraces the institution and in particular recognises the family centre (day and residential) as the primary service setting and primary setting of learning for child and family social work; and

b) Consider the social work practitioner's foundation learning and expertise as built on the direct experience developed in the collective, hands-on setting of a family centre;

c) Develop the family centre as a central practice placement in the qualifying programme for child and family social workers;

d) Enhance the social work education curriculum by increasing the content in counselling and group-work; adult, community and informal education; and in direct care experiences;

e) Re-establish a momentum in the development of family centres, not as narrow assessment centres but as integrated, social action centres, contributing to their communities, and ecological in their perspective;

f) Consider the local authority social worker/case manager role as unavailable for the immediately post-qualified practitioner. A minimum of five years before acceptance would not be unreasonable;

g) Strive to develop the status of social work as an independent endeavour which draws much more of its legitimacy from such direct, client-in-context practice.

This distinctive practice at the cutting edge of social inclusion – evident not only in these pages but in many other instances (for example, Stones, 1994; Smith, 1996; Pithouse, Lindsell & Cheung, 1998; Batchelor, Gould, & Wright, 1999) – lends encouragement to the idea of an international forum of family centre users and practitioners. People writing and talking internationally about 'putting it all together' in centres would strengthen a rich but still fragile seam of practice.

References

Atkinson D. (2000), *Urban Renaissance – a Strategy for Urban Renewal and the Welfare Society,* Brewin Books, Studley.

Barton H. ed (2000), *Sustainable Communities – the Potential for Eco-Neighbourhoods,* Earthscan Publications Ltd., London.

Batchelor J., Gould N. & Wright J. (1999), 'Family centres: a focus for the children in need debate,' in *Child and Family Social Work,* 4, pp. 197–208.

Brookfield S. (1983), *Adult Learners, Adult Education and the Community,* OUP, Milton Keynes.

DH (2000), *Framework for the Assessment of Children in Need and their Families,* The Stationery Office, London.

Germain C. (1991), *Human Behaviour in the Social Environment,* Columbia University Press, New York.

Heifetz J. & Seppanen P. (1989), 'The most important thing we do: community educators talk about family support and education programs', in *Community Education Journal,* Spring, pp. 6-11.

Houle C. (1984), *Patterns of Learning,* Jossey-Bass, San Francisco.

Jack G. (1997), 'An ecological approach to social work with children and families', in *Child and Family Social Work,* 2, 109–120.

Jarvis P. (1987), *Adult Education in a Social Context,* Croom Helm, London and Sydney.

Lightburn A. & Kemp S. (1994), Family Support Programs: Opportunities for Community-Based Practice, in *Families and Society,* 75 (1), pp 16–26.

Lovett T. (1975), *Adult Education, Community Development and the Working Class,* Ward Lock Educational, London.

Lovett T., Clarke C. & Kilmurray A. (1983), *Adult Education and Community Action*, Croom Helm, London and Canberra.

Maluccio A., Fein E., & Olmstead K. (1986), *Permanency Planning for Children*, Tavistock, London.

Pithouse A., Lindsell S. & Cheung M. (1998), *Family Support and Family Centre Services*, Ashgate, Aldershot.

Seitz V. (1990), 'Intervention programs for impoverished children: a comparison of educational and family support models', in *Annals of Child Development*, Vol 7, 73-103.

Smith T. (1996), *Family Centres and Bringing Up Young Children*, HMSO, London.

Statham D. (1978), *Radicals in Social Work*, RKP, London.

Stones C. (1994), *Focus on Families: Family Centres in Action*, Macmillan/Barnardos, Basingstoke.

Warren C. (1997), 'Family support and the journey to empowerment', in Cannan C. & Warren C. eds. (1997), *Social Action With Children and their Families – A Community Development Approach to Child and Family Welfare*, Routledge, London.

Weiss H. (1989), 'State family support and education programs: lessons from the pioneers,' in *American Journal of Orthopsychiatry*, 59, (1), January.

Weiss H. & Halpern R. (1991), *Community-Based Family Support and Education Programs: Something Old or Something New?*, Family Resource Centre for Children in Poverty, Columbia University, New York.

Westwood S. & Thomas J. (1991), *The Politics of Adult Education*, The National Institute of Adult and Continuing Education, Leicester.

Williams F. (1998), 'Agency and structure re-visited: re-thinking poverty and social inclusion', in Barry M. & Hallett C. *Social Exclusion and Social Work – Issues of Theory, Policy and Practice*, Russell House Publishing, Lyme Regis.

Wren B. (1996), 'In defence of eclecticism,' in *Clinical Child and Adolescent Psychiatry*, Vol 1, (1), 11-18.